INDETERMINACY

Wyse Series in Social Anthropology

Editors:
James Laidlaw, William Wyse Professor of Social Anthropology, University of Cambridge, and Fellow of King's College, Cambridge
Maryon McDonald, Fellow in Social Anthropology, Robinson College, University of Cambridge
Joel Robbins, Sigrid Rausing Professor of Social Anthropology, University of Cambridge, and Fellow of Trinity College, Cambridge

Social Anthropology is a vibrant discipline of relevance to many areas – economics, politics, business, humanities, health and public policy. This series, published in association with the Cambridge William Wyse Chair in Social Anthropology, focuses on key interventions in Social Anthropology, based on innovative theory and research of relevance to contemporary social issues and debates.

INDETERMINACY

Waste, Value, and the Imagination

Edited by

Catherine Alexander and Andrew Sanchez

berghahn
NEW YORK • OXFORD
www.berghahnbooks.com

First published in 2019 by
Berghahn Books
www.berghahnbooks.com

Library of Congress Cataloging-in-Publication Data

Names: Alexander, Catherine, editor. | Sanchez, Andrew (Anthropologist),
editor.
Title: Indeterminacy : waste, value, and the imagination / edited by
Catherine Alexander and Andrew Sanchez.
Description: New York : Berghahn Books, 2019. | Series: WYSE series in social
anthropology ; 7 | Includes bibliographical references and index.
Identifiers: LCCN 2018018981 (print) | LCCN 2018038818 (ebook) | ISBN
9781789200102 (ebook) | ISBN 9781789200096 (hardback : alk. paper)
Subjects: LCSH: Social evolution. | Marginiality, Social. | Waste
products--Social aspects. | Determinism (Philosophy) | Civilization,
Modern--Social aspects.
Classification: LCC GN360 (ebook) | LCC GN360 .I52 2019 (print) | DDC
306--dc23
LC record available at https://lccn.loc.gov/2018018981

British Library Cataloguing in Publication Data

A catalogue record for this book is available from the British Library

ISBN 978-1-78920-009-6 hardback
ISBN 978-1-78920-010-2 ebook

Contents

Figures

Introduction
The Values of Indeterminacy

Catherine Alexander and Andrew Sanchez

Indeterminacy and Classification

This book explores the relationship between indeterminacy and classification, particularly the kind of classificatory order that is central to the modern bureaucratic state. At the heart of classification is the question of value and waste. What we propose here is a third term to challenge this binary: *indeterminacy*. Used here it describes that which defies classification. As Geoffrey Bowker and Susan Leigh Star point out in their pathbreaking book *Sorting Things Out*, "each category valorizes some point of view and silences another" (1999: 5). While the production of value and waste through classification has been well rehearsed (Star and Lampland 2008), here we are analyzing how value-making categories also produce waste that resists classification. It is these indeterminacies—the silenced points of view—that interest us here. Thinking of waste in relation to classification systems inevitably brings us to Mary Douglas's classic formulation in *Purity and Danger* that dirt is matter out of place (1966: 36).[1] However, as Ben Campkin notes (2013: 3), there is some inconsistency between this neat binary definition of dirt and her analysis of waste as anomalous and disruptive of the structured way through which worlds are understood. "Reflection on dirt," Douglas wrote, "involves reflection on the relation of order to disorder, being to non-being, form to formlessness" (1966: 6).

Bowker and Star have two further points that are relevant for us here. They remind us that classification is a profoundly moral process, making some places, materials, actions, and people visible, while others are "left wild, or in darkness, or even unmapped" (1999: 32); and that visibility may bring disadvantage as much as advantage (ibid.: 44). To this we add Star and Martha Lampland's comment that categories are necessarily part of a larger scheme of meaning and value that frame how knowledge is represented through classification (2008:

21): classification thus implies a totality or whole of which it is part. Whether these totalities are value systems, states, or society, they are also partly effects of the imagination (Graeber 2013).

By training our gaze on that very relation between form and formlessness that Douglas suggests, we offer a series of interventions that problematize a binary reading of waste and value and in so doing complicate such approaches to classificatory systems. We suggest that waste and value are both aspects of Douglas's "form" whereas formlessness or indeterminacy is a third modality occupying a space between waste and value.[2] Indeterminacy can also encompass these conditions, or act as an imaginary state that provides the precondition for certain value-creating interventions, or indeed operate within categories where fuzzy gradients of compliance are obscured by binary determination. Thus we highlight that classification, as a way of apprehending reality, is itself essentially indeterminate.

We show, for example, how accounting techniques can invoke, or imagine waste and value as co-constitutive, but not as opposites; how people, places, infrastructure, and materials may be in limbo, suspended spaces and times that escape ideas of either waste or value; how instances of the "anomalous" can elide different instances of category confusion with markedly different consequences; how waste as excess of meaning can threaten to explode meaning-making categories from within; and how a superabundance of legislative categories and guidance can create gaps where (for example) one legal regime does not quite mesh with the next. Indeterminacy may thus act as a third term, or challenge binary category-making from within. It is also one way in which some wastes are characterized or certain conditions of exclusion experienced.

We take forward Bowker and Star's observation that visibility (and we would add invisibility) may bring either benefit or loss to challenge analytical normativities that tend to see indeterminacy as either positive or negative. Indeed both may be different facets of the same experience. For example, in resisting gender codification people may also find themselves economically harmed, invisible as citizens, and therefore unable to claim welfare rights.

Just as bureaucratic classifications and standards appear to be abstract but are relational in their effect, so too are infrastructure's effects unevenly distributed (Star and Lampland 2008: 13; Star and Ruhleder 1996: 113). Again, introducing indeterminacy as a third term can highlight the co-constitution of advantage and disadvantage: if houses are perceived to be derelict by city officials, their inhabitants are less likely to be immediate victims of gentrification. Such housing is simultaneously rubbish and prized—to different constituencies. Recognition, whether or not explicitly referred to as such, therefore emerges as a theme throughout this volume, although the perspective twists and turns: who classifies someone or something as excessive or unknowable is a question of power. In many instances, indeterminacy is lack of recognition on someone's part, not always on everyone's part. And that is the crux of the ethnographic puzzle.

We further offer an analysis of how people who feel themselves cast out, or mourn the loss of previous status, may long for reincorporation to alternative or earlier totalities and, in contrast, consider how the fragment challenges any notion of a past or potential whole, or indeed any sense of classification or motion toward another state at all. Attention paid to the fragment signals one more engagement with indeterminacy, classification, and totalizing systems. This additional engagement puts emphasis on contingency, which includes going nowhere at all, as opposed to prior or predetermined futures.

As some of these examples might suggest, this book is largely staged through wastes as matter and metaphor embracing people, places, and materials that have been broadly classified as waste, displaced, been removed, or removed themselves from dominant systems of value. We also include two familiar waste sites (a landfill and a sorting station) to highlight both that these places can be transformative for people and materials moving from discard to value, and that indistinct remnants and wayward pollution defy containment and relation to other entities or putative wholes.

In so doing, we flag the complexity and multiplicity of relationships that waste can have with value. Depending on context and perspective, waste is (at least): the antithesis of value, that which enables value, irredeemably toxic or sterile, a resource by another name, an unrecoverable residue, not yet productive, disgusting, forgotten, or abandoned. A focus on the relationship between indeterminacy and classification also provides a means to engage with intellectual traditions that have respectively valorized, critiqued, and rejected the teleological, determining project of modernity in which indeterminacy, for good or ill, plays a central role as the dark (or joyful) other. Waste matter often appears as indeterminacy, a form that can be terrifying because it suggests dissolution and indecipherability, something that is either unknowable or uncanny in its hints at previous forms. In some cases, but not all, the seeds of value transformation can lie in that very indeterminacy.

Indeterminacy therefore appears in the following modes: lack of recognition or incorporation in a given classification system; undetermined futures or directions; and a resistance to totalizing systems.

But first, it is perhaps as well to get cognate terms out of the way before proceeding further. Here we therefore outline why our take on indeterminacy is different from or where it may include but is not synonymous with uncertainty, ambiguity, and liminality. In short, these terms are not just reducible to each other but have specific meanings and consequences.

Recent ideas on *uncertainty* fall roughly into four camps: the inability to read other people's intentions, the unknowability of the future, risk management as a response to those unknowns, and finally, the collapse or withdrawal of totalizing modernist systems. Thus, as an example of the first group of approaches, François Berthomé, Julien Bonhomme, and Gregory Delaplace (2012) approach uncertainty through linguistic anthropology and interactional sociology considering the social problem of being unable to understand the meaning of other people's intentions (see also Alan Rumsey and Joel Robbins' special issue on the opacity of other people's minds 2008). While not using these approaches, we share their assumption that uncertain conditions are common, not incidental, experiences (Berthomé, Bonhomme, and Delaplace 2012: 130). In the second group, engagements with doubt, such as Jennifer Hecht's (2003) panoramic discussion of the skeptical tradition, can be allied to uncertainty as broad questions of how we know and, more specifically, how to gauge and act on unknown futures (Pelkmans 2013a, 2013b; Carey and Pedersen 2017). These latter questions are at the heart of analyses of late capitalism since both its mechanisms and consequences are uncertainty.

Thus, in the third set of approaches are analyses of how actors in financial capitalism achieve profits by negotiating risk as a means of managing uncertainty (Appadurai 2011; Miyazaki 2013; Ortiz 2014; Riles 2013; Tuckett 2011; Zaloom 2004). One flip side of the profit to be gained from the calculability of risk, and the readiness to adapt a workforce to demand, is the erosion of labor security. This precarity is experienced in a variety of forms that rehearse Marx's insight stating capitalist profit requires a reserve army of insecurely or unemployed people. While precarity in itself is an uncertain and not an indeterminate condition, it can lead to a crumbling of previously clear identities in terms of class and gender. Further, where the worth of different kinds of work (e.g., manual labor or waste picking) is not formally recognized, this can engender a sense that distinct identities, status, and human value are being eroded. Limor Samimian-Darash and Paul Rabinow's edited book, *Modes of Uncertainty* (2015) centers on ethnographies of attempts to know the unknown and thus identify danger and mitigate risk. Their emphasis is not on uncertainty as something "out there" but on how it is deployed as a concept: a new form of governmentality via the management of risk.

The fourth topos of engagement with uncertainty is how people negotiate the political and epistemological insecurities accompanying collapses of ideology and empire. Many of these chronicle the dereliction of lives in former state socialist regimes (e.g., Alexander 2009; Rofel 1999; Verdery and Burawoy 1999; Yurchak 2005) as well as those who embrace new economic opportunities. The complex phenomenon of everyday nostalgias for socialism (e.g., Stenning 2005) finds unexpected echoes in some postsocialist state nationalist projects. As Esra Özyürek (2006) reminds us in her study of Turkey, nostalgia for the modern state in the wake of anxieties accompanying neoliberalism is not confined to the former Eastern Bloc. In part, these anxieties may be ascribed to a loss of a sense of clear direction and of one's place in the world as part of a larger whole, even if in retrospect the wholes turned out to be rather fragmented. As discussed in the third section below, the collapse of old regimes and the emergence of new ones can generate not only people who no longer fit, but also newly redundant material remains of earlier hopes and quite different regimes (Navaro-Yashin 2009; Yarrow 2017).

Uncertainty therefore chimes with our discussion of indeterminacy, but only insofar as it reflects conditions of dissolution or category loss produced by economic and political exclusion; the material infrastructure of previous times that has yet to find its place; and, finally, a sense that future pathways are rarely as determined as grand narratives suggest but emerge as a dialogue between people's attempts to plan and shape futures and contingent events beyond their control.

Ambiguity is frequently used as though it were just another term for indeterminacy. Thus ambiguity refers to the precise meaning of something being unclear or obscure; this might be seen as the recognition failure of indeterminate conditions. However, the potential confusions that arise from ambiguity are because there is a multiplicity of possible meanings at any one given time. These multiple readings may be contradictory (Widger and Russell 2018), creatively play off each other, or depend on context.[3] In other words, ambiguity is about a superfluity of possibilities, each one a legitimate reading of a meaningful category. In contrast, the condition of indeterminacy suggests the lack of such categories. There are instances, however, when the terms merge. For example, Jacques Derrida was specifically concerned with indeterminacy-as-ambiguity, multiple meaning, as in the *pharmakon* that is both poison and medicine at the same time (Rinella 2010); that is, the *pharmakon* is not either/ or but both and hence essentially indeterminate (Derrida 1981: 63–171). Precisely because it holds both these meanings at once, it also speaks to the idea of the "scapegoat" (ibid).[4] These ideas remain salient in the chapters in this book that consider the expulsion or social rejection of people.

Finally, while *liminality* may seem to mean the same as indeterminacy at times, a clear distinction between the terms is useful. In the anthropological tradition, following Arnold van Gennep ([1909] 1960) and his "recuperation" by Victor Turner (1967), liminality is not only a condition between two fixed states but, crucially, also has the characteristics of transformation and transition. These are not qualities that fit our definition of indeterminacy as something that remains between or has an undetermined future. Recently, the term has been widely adopted elsewhere in the humanities and social sciences, particularly political science, to refer to a general condition of being betwixt and between, which can be the locus of emergent political orders (e.g., Horvath, Thomassen, and Wydra 2015; Thomassen 2014). From literary studies, Arpad Szakolczai (2016) adds the oxymoronic notion of "permanent liminality." These more capacious understandings of the term partly chime with our discussions, but also attenuate the charge of the original narrower anthropological use.

These are our working definitions for the book, but are far from the last word on how these terms are understood either in everyday speech or in different disciplines. Carla Namwali Serpell, for instance, reminds us that in literary and scientific theory these terms have become heavy with particular meanings: the New Criticism has appropriated ambiguity, indeterminacy is the driving force of Derridean deconstruction, while uncertainty reflects scientific theories roughly contemporaneous with James Joyce (Serpell 2014: 308n41).

There are three more parts to this introduction. The following section provides a grounding for our chapters via a brief genealogy of how indeterminacy has been theorized in philosophy and social theory vis-à-vis questions of order, recognition, and progress, which partly hinge on whether or not the infinite variety of the world can or should be caught in categories. From this, we move in the next section to the growth of invisible, unregistered, stateless people in the contemporary world alongside tightening systems of classification and control and the material byproducts of intensified political and economic production/wasting processes: uncontainable contamination. Here we also consider four areas where social scientists have engaged recently with indeterminacy: statelessness, economic precarity, ethics, and creativity.[5] Theorizations of the former two areas typically decry indeterminacy while the latter celebrate it. In the final section, we identify our principal contributions to understanding the multiple registers of indeterminacy via our ethnographic chapters.

A Brief Genealogy of Order, Indeterminacy, and Waste in the Modern Age

Our main focus in this section is the interplay between ideas and practices of order and progress in the modern age on the one hand, and indeterminacy on the other. As we work through this genealogy, we highlight how ideas of indeterminacy, waste, excess, and ordering narratives have been woven together at different times in different ways, then how and where these ideas resonate with our volume. We begin with a sense of indeterminacy as something to move away from, toward enlightenment, order, and progress before turning to Walter Benjamin's engagements with modernity as waste, which illustrate how waste and indeterminacy have often been cast as modernity's other (Benjamin 2002; Lunn 1984). This section ends with Michel Foucault (1977, [1984] 1992) and Georges Bataille's (1985) celebratory take on indeterminacy as transgression, and Theodor Adorno, whose negative dialectics and denial of the possibility of apprehending reality have been inspirations in locating lives in all their diversity and meaning-making outside, in parallel, or in response to centrally-determined, teleological grand projects (1973).

We therefore start with Georg Wilhelm Friedrich Hegel for whom indeterminacy (*Unbestimmtheit*) and recognition (*Anerkennung*) are fundamental preconditions to the development of individuals' agency as social beings (Hegel 1977). Drawing on Johann Gottlieb Fichte, Hegel's *Phenomenology of Spirit* is important here for two reasons (Hegel 1977). First, it starts with the condition of indeterminacy as the unknown point from which logical thought moves toward determinacy. The successive moves are toward first a determinate but abstract being. Then an actualized self emerges because of the recognition by another subject of our own subjecthood: full dynamic being, in other words, is essentially relational. In this frame, we need recognition, and the relation that it implies, in other words, to become agents.

Hegel initially emphasized intersubjective encounters within social groups as linking mutual dependence to questions of recognition, solidarity, and esteem (Pippin 2000: 156) allowing (to use a different lexicon) the prosecution of life projects by a social agent. Later, in the *Philosophy of Right*, this shifted to an emphasis on the objective spirit of world history, eliding intersubjectivity, and creating a new idea of the ethical life and community where adequate recognition is achieved within an institutional system of rights (Williams 1997: 59–69): the three spheres of family, civil society, and the state. For Hegel, indeterminacy, alongside emptiness (or "loneliness," as Axel Honneth translates *Einsamkeit*), is a pathology experienced as an unhappy self-consciousness, and indeed, Honneth suggests, is characteristic of the age (2016). While our take on indeterminacy differs from the Hegelian pre-thought void, the question of who recognizes, or refuses recognition of whom and what, is a central theme of this book, allied to the moral project of classifying.

Second, *Phenomenology of Spirit* outlines the dialectical process by which history (knowledge) moves to the absolute via the two steps between abstraction and concrete appearance that gives rise to a renewed idea and so on toward an absolute totality where idea/category and reality are fused into one. Hegel's teleological vision of history is shared by many modern political projects. Thus, capitalism, socialism, and colonialism are all teleologically determined, grounded in Enlightenment concerns with development and progress, via science and technology, toward a goal of better, happier lives (see Negri 2004; Guyer 2007 for a discussion of capitalism's temporality).[6] Thus, as Vincanne Adams, Michelle Murphy, and Adele E. Clarke observe, modernist temporalities are anticipatory ones "in which the future sets the conditions of possibility for action in the present" and is able to "arrive already formed in the present" (2009: 248–49).

Drawing on Hegel's method, Karl Marx offers a dialectical framework to address questions of change and structure, also rooted in a modernist temporality of progress and finalization (Berman 2010; Huyssen 1984; Lunn 1984). At its most blunt, the final resolution of the dialectic is reified as an absolute whole, and Marxist dialectical method is reduced to a prescriptive and predictive typology (Althusser 1970; Cornforth 1961) as it most notoriously appeared in Marxist-Leninism.[7] More subtle Marxist work emphasizes the contingency of historical process and class formation (Chandavarkar 1994; E. P.Thompson 1978, 1991).

There have been critiques aplenty of this narrative of progress. What interests us here is how the ideas of surplus, ruin, excess, and waste in many forms, but particularly the indeterminate and unrecognizable, are woven through these narratives and their critiques. Thus Marx's materialist interpretation of Hegel's dialectical method located historical movement in the material conflicts inherent in each socioeconomic formation. The final stage, communism, theoretically contained no exploitative relations and was thus the end point of historical development; the social/material equivalent of Hegel's merging of idea and reality. The emergence of capitalism, as a mode of production, lay in the confluence of factors that enabled the production and appropriation of surplus for profit. Surplus labor can be interpreted in two ways, both essential for capitalism. The first is the labor that is surplus to the laborer's livelihood needs and that creates profit for the capitalist. The second is the reserve army of unemployed people hovering in the wings to meet market demand. Such people are surplus to immediate requirements, outside yet connected to formal systems of value production; simultaneously potentially valuable and wasted.

Surplus is therefore integral to the capitalist process, creating and maintaining profit, and wasting human lives. But excess, as something overflowing that cannot be accommodated, can be threatening (Alexander this volume) and must therefore be expended (wasted), to follow Bataille's reasoning (1991)[8] if it is not to become harmful. Excess also appears as the detritus of the capitalist modern age. In this spirit, Benjamin excavated modernity through the trail of waste and ephemera it left behind, his own monumental *Arcades* project, unfinished, a half-built/ruin of fragments symbolizing as well as accounting for the failed promise of modernity (2002). And yet, modernity's underlying framework of progress still seems to have a tight grip on dominant imaginaries of capitalism and socialism.

In some post-Soviet contexts, for example, revolutionary logic seemed merely to transpose "communism" with "the market" as the goal, retaining faith in determinate historical rules (Alexander 2009). Elsewhere, in the 1990s, international lending agencies as well as local governments spoke of "transition," the implication being that they knew precisely where they were heading: free market capitalism (Gaidar 1999; Lipton et al. 1992: 213; J. Sachs 1994). In the academy, the emphasis on transition moved rapidly, following Stark (1991) to languages of transformation and "path dependency," where particular pasts, rather than futures, influenced continual change.

But the modernist project of development, underscored by the same belief in progress and framed by market integration since the United States' Marshall Plan in 1948, marches on for all the steady criticism it has received over the last few decades from Andre Gunder Frank's insight that "development" was having the reverse effect (1966), and Arturo Escobar's reiteration in 1995 that development was wasting the very places it was supposed to make anew. There have been calls for postdevelopment (Dasgupta 1985), alternatives to development (Friedmann 1992), and to move after postdevelopment (Nederveen Pieterse 2000). But still, as Katy Gardner and David Lewis (2015) describe, the appeal of progress continues with, ironically, a return to a belief in technological interventions. Indeed, Wolfgang Sachs (1992: 1) described development itself as an indeterminate ruin of modernity, still with us, but pointing to a discredited future. To paraphrase Benjamin, modernity can be characterized by the wasted lands, excess materials, and people it expels to keep the project on the road. For the anthropological endeavor, to think critically about normative frameworks of progress entails a willingness to engage with ruination (Dawdy 2010), and the modern forms of life created by processes of systemic expulsion and desolation (Massey and Denton 1993; Wacquant 2010).

Waste, John Scanlan suggests, is modernity's other side (2005). We narrow this down here to indeterminate excess produced by the order of progress. Indeed, the shadows of formal rational progress appear via a scabrous version of indeterminacy as the menacing, wasted cast-offs of progress itself where the curiously contagious quality of waste leads waste workers to become as much symbolically as materially defiled by their contact with waste materials and places, the latter typically located on edges and borders just to add to their capacity for symbolic disruption. More famously, Marx's excoriation of the *lumpenproletariat* merges those who live on waste with redundancy (or "uselessness" in Scanlan's phrase 2005) in a revolutionary progressive order, and with the quality of waste itself: "the social scum, that passively rotting mass thrown off by the lowest layers in old society" (Marx 1967: 92); the dangerous class "living off the garbage of society" (ibid.).

Such language not only reappears in *The Eighteenth Brumaire*, but makes explicit the contempt and fear generated by those who are not readily classifiable: the rotting (between life and death), ruined, and indiscernible masses

> the decayed roués ... the ruined ... offshoots of the bourgeoisie ... ragpickers ... in short, the whole indefinite, disintegrated mass, thrown hither and thither, which the French call *la bohème*... This Bonaparte, who constitutes himself *chief of the lumpenproletariat*, who here alone rediscovers in mass form the interests which he ... pursues, who recognizes in this scum, offal, refuse of all classes the only class upon which he can base himself unconditionally." (Marx 1975: 148; emphasis in original)

This, Slavoj Žižek observes, is the ultimate statement of the "logic of the Party of Order" (2012: 20), where "the excremental ... non-representable excess of society" (ibid.: 21) becomes the only medium of universal representation. Western modernity, if we follow Scanlan, tends to blank out "that which doesn't fit" (2005: 80); ambiguity and confusion, he suggests, prevent meaning and lend themselves to the language of garbage (ibid.: 56).

Adorno's devastating critiques of modernity give us a way out of this binary of rigidly ordered meaning or unmeaning via an explanation and a method. First, with Max Horkheimer in *Dialectic of Enlightenment* ([1947] 2002), he locates the primal human fear of the unknown as the driver for attempts to dominate the world through technologies of knowing (see Feyerabend 1975, 2001). In such a society, unfree through fear, the other is exploited or expelled. This other, in our lexicon, is thus unknowable, unrecognizable—and rendered indeterminate. The second element we adapt from Adorno is from his *Negative Dialectics* (1973). His interpretation drew on Hegel's method but was a nondogmatic philosophical materialism, as opposed to Hegel's idealism (Jarvis 1998). Thus, for Adorno, unlike Hegel, the attempt to conjoin idea and object is negatively valued. Where unity seems to appear this is only by suppressing difference and diversity (Adorno 1973: 142–61). It is only by articulating such contradictions, and the misidentification of object and thought, that a "fragile transformative horizon" of hope appears where objects and people can flourish in their particularity.[9] We too are attempting this dialectic between theory and ethnography, outlining in the final section of this introduction how we draw on negative dialectics to frame our approach to indeterminacy.

Other critiques of modernity emphasize the repressive domination of ordering practices by celebrating transgression.[10] As William Viney suggests, accounts of people, places, and things that do not fit dominant orders are typically binary, casting matter out of place as negative (2014), the process of ejection, however, is positive (for those doing it): reaffirming system and structure (Douglas 1966). There is, however, another body of work that also counterposes waste-as-excess against rational order, but celebrates and glorifies disorder as a deconstruction of the humanist, unified modern subject. Such accounts typically draw on pre- or early modern and ethnographic accounts of alterity to challenge modernist accounts. Thus, Peter Stallybrass and Alison White's historical work (1986), Mikhail Bakhtin's on the excess of the grotesque body and carnival (2009), and Foucault's work on transgression, infinite variety, and Dionysian excess (e.g., 1977, [1984] 1992) serve to destabilize singular subjects, aligning with Bataille's invitation to consider open-ended forms of knowledge and economic exchange rooted in the productive consumption of excess (1985, 1988). This compounded excess in the modern world, its threat, and its potential is what interests us here.

The next section outlines instances of that modernist drive to domination, order, and expulsion that many of the theorists above describe—but we end by juxtaposing this with not only celebrations of open-endedness and excess, but reminders of more complex accounts of how promises of modernist order have been experienced and lamented.

Contemporary Excesses

Crisis hardens social categories, spewing people out who no longer fit. The implications of being outside the law are crucial to how political indeterminacy is experienced. The term *outlaw* is derived from Old Norse for wolf (Nyers 2006), implying a lack of distinction between human and nonhuman that can cruelly shape what it means to be outside the juridical community. Indeed, Hannah Arendt opens *The Origins of Totalitarianism* with "homelessness on an unprecedented scale, rootlessness to an unprecedented depth" caused by the chaos of war and reinforced nation-state borders (1950: vii). In this section, we consider the growth of political and economic indeterminacy as the volume of displaced people and precarious labor grows. Alongside such immediate violence (Sassen 2014), we consider the concomitant slow violence (Nixon 2011) of wasting materials and lands through ordering regimes, and how this has been theorized before turning to a different branch of engagement with indeterminacy: the realm of creative, hopeful imagination.

Thus, over the last few decades, wars, the redrawing of nation-state boundaries, and the restructuring of ethnic and citizenship categories have stranded people in temporary zones and camps that have calcified into permanence. The UNHCR estimates there are over 65.6. million forcibly displaced people worldwide, of whom approximately two-thirds are internally displaced and therefore unprotected by International Law (UNHCR 2016).[11] In the same year, UNHCR estimated there were 10 million stateless individuals (ibid.). A crisis of recognition draws attention once again to the challenge of alterity: how to unite without forcing assimilation (Povinelli 2002), how, to return to the previous section, to recognize difference and common humanity. In such contexts, indeterminacy has typically been theorized as an undesirable condition, imposed by state authority, where resistance is the positive counter move to regain or remake political subjectivities.

Michel Agier documents a further "disquieting ambiguity" of refugee camps: humanitarian interventions that appear to be linked disturbingly to penal technologies of containment, and are an exercise in "managing the undesirables" (2010). He suggests a growing and carefully maintained division between "a clean, healthy and visible world ... [and] the world's residual 'remnants,' dark, diseased and invisible" (2010: 4). Following Giorgio Agamben (1998), Agier describes states of permanent precariousness where a rhetoric of constant emergency means that refugee camps "exclude past and future" in an exceptional but enduring present (2010: 79). Nicholas De Genova (2002) and Sarah Willen (2007) similarly focus on the production of migrants' illegal statuses and spaces—and their attempts to resist ambiguity. Recently, a series of interventions have highlighted resistance, reclamation, and the forging of new political subjectivities in these atemporal, aspatial spaces (Gabiam 2016; Turner 2012) even when simple existence can be taken as resistance (Schiocchet 2010: 67). Julie Peteet notes that, for example, in Palestinian refugee camps, young men re-ascribe meaning to beatings as rites of passage that constitute forms of masculinity (2005).

Agamben shows that those who are excluded from society live exposed and threatened lives (1998: 29). Such impositions of structural indeterminacy go beyond ascriptions of criminality and move toward the negation of humanity— as in the evacuation of meaning (Thorleifsson and Eriksen this volume) of the common use of tropes for unwanted migrants as indiscernible, uncountable masses (Alexander this volume). The number of unregistered people who fall between the cracks is growing as states militarize borders, tighten population classifications, and control measures for "homeland security," and restrict welfare to those with the right kind of identification documents. In 2014, the

World Health Organization estimated that, as a consequence of such measures, two-thirds of deaths and nearly half the number of births globally are unrecorded (WHO 2017).

Alongside the indeterminate status of the world's "outlaws" and refugees, late capitalism has intensified conditions of precarity in the working lives of people in ostensibly stable political environments. Marx highlighted the reserve army of unemployed that kept nineteenth-century capitalism ticking. But now, cheaper labor can easily be found elsewhere in the world. Mechanization often replaces the need for bodies at all. Weakening labor legislation, the growth of unpaid internships, "zero hour" contracts, and corrupt or emasculated trade unions all contribute to contemporary economic precarity. Even when work is available, it may be poorly paid, unreliable, part-time, and insufficient for a livelihood. Such flexible labor has been enabled by financial deregulation and the easy global movement of capital (Harvey 1987). The essential character of formal employment has been transformed, not only rendering previous working-class identities indeterminate but as Richard-Michael Diedrich suggests for unemployed Welsh former miners, "steadily dissolving what the individual had believed to be the stable core of his ... identity" (2004: 117). The ethnographic emphasis here has been on how precariously employed persons experience their labor; studies show it is often felt as extreme vulnerability (Allison 2012; Genda 2005; Gill and Pratt 2008; Hann and Parry 2018; Millar 2014; Mole 2010; Munck 2013; Sanchez 2016; Standing 2011).

Indeterminacy has become the dominant condition of insecure work in many industries as "permanent impermanence" normalizes ostensibly temporary contracts within regular structures of production. Employment conditions and forms are thus seemingly predictable and fixed through time, yet are underpinned by profound insecurity, collapsing previously clear distinctions between regular and casual work (Sanchez 2018: 235).

In such a context of increasing political and economic indeterminacy, Hudson McFann suggests a chilling typology of how humans-as-waste (see Mbembe 2011; Yates 2011) have been produced, typically as a product of ordering regimes such as colonialism, modernity, and capitalism (McFann n.d.), which both depend on and produce surplus people, lands, and materials. Hudson McFann's typology describes the symbolic deployment of the concept of waste (following Douglas's 1966 structuralist account and Julia Kristeva's 1982 notion of the abject); the biopolitical (such as Foucault's accounts of state ordering) and the politico-economic, informed by a Marxist critique of capitalism that demands a surplus labor population and wastes human bodies (Gidwani 2013; Gidwani and Reddy 2011; Yates 2011). To this we add Zygmunt Bauman's construction of late modernity as a fluid or liquid condition that seems to counter the rigidity of an ordering regime and yet rehearses expelling unwanted bodies as just so many wasted lives (2013).

Precarity and ambiguity can also generate strategies for living beyond, or in spite of, the state, as Ida Harboe Knudsen and Martin Demant Frederiksen and their contributors (2015) trace through their notion of the "grey zone," where the informal, ephemeral, and ambiguous have become ordinary. Improvisation can intersect with forms of exclusion and regimes of governance based on legibility. The temporalities of indeterminate encounters with the state require attentiveness. It is not only in refugee camps, among asylum seekers, and on the margins of the state (Auyero 2012; Das and Poole 2004;) that suspension and waiting are ways of being and expressions of power hierarchies.[12] Akhil Gupta reminds us of the chronic suspension of many giant infrastructure projects (2015), Timothy Choy and Jerry Zee of the chemical and other pollution suspended in the atmosphere that allows/damages life (2015). Samuel Beckett, of course, identified waiting as the human condition (1956).

Just as ordering regimes waste and devalue people, so too are landscapes marked with such regimes' failures, byproducts, and cast-offs that give the lie to any notion of future-oriented improvement. The often unfulfilled promise of modernity's grand projects become inscribed upon the landscape as half-built infrastructure and ruins, which point to forgotten futures (Gordillo 2014; Gupta 2015; Hussain 2013; Ringel this volume; Stoler 2013) and shape lives transfixed in a present, waiting either for the past or the future to return, as Paul Wenzel Geissler (2010) so movingly shows through a discussion of the people who continue to live and work in an abandoned colonial field station in Kenya. Both this and Thomas Yarrow's (2017) account of Ghana's incomplete Volta Dam project, suggest a different relationship to modernity's march than suggested by the preceding pages. The failed promises of modernity can be mourned by people who live among the ruins.

Policies devised by such modernist states are typically linked to a specific mode of acting on the world to produce outcomes that are aimed at closure and containment (Hinchcliffe 2001). In the essentially limitless context of the environment and climate such aims are inherently flawed, since certitude can be misplaced and potentially damaging (see Alexander forthcoming; Wynne 1992, 1997). "Dealing with" the wastes of military and industrial extraction, consumption, and production is often only hopeful postponement, appealing to an imagined future state, when science will have caught up with its earlier incarnation and be better able to resolve the endless stream of byproducts and hybrid entities that have qualified "nature." Buried shrapnel or lurking landmines can also be a source of profound indeterminacy (Henig 2012; Kim 2014), unmapping previously known landscapes. Compared with the relative localization of such military waste, chemical (like nuclear) contamination is "amorphous and invisible" (Broto 2015: 94), exacerbated by the inability to determine the temporal and spatial reach of leaks (Topçu 2008). Pollution and contamination are thus characterized by formlessness, excessiveness, and wayward movement (Strathern 1991: 61; Tsing 2015: 28), which resist neat narratives of containment or restoration. Such accounts of remediation, however, are confronted head on by a queer ethics of hybridity, personified by the figure of Nuclia Waste, a drag queen who exuberantly foregrounds the excess and permeability of the entire environment and herself to nuclear contamination (Krupar 2012). Guy Schaffer further reminds us that queer theory is concerned with "uneven remainders, things that don't fit neatly into categories" (n.d.), that "trash" unites wastes and camp alike and that camp itself is "a mode of aestheticism devoted to excess, to failure, to ironic detachment" (ibid.), a refusal, we might say, to be integrated. Such practices align indeterminacy, unruly wastes, and queer theory, recasting indeterminacy as a mode of potentiality, resistance, escape, creativity, and improvisation (see Gonzalez-Polledo this volume; Morgensen 2016;).

In just such a light, recent scholarship in the social sciences, arts, and humanities has characterized indeterminacy as a necessary space for creativity and cultural improvisation (Hallam and Ingold 2007). Howard Becker describes artworks as fundamentally indeterminate, only existing within each moment of re-creation (2006: 23). Feminist and queer theories also invite us to consider mobility rather than stasis, processes of becoming rather than fixed categories, and the generative power of ambiguity. They also ask us to think how metaphors and performances of indeterminacy can be mobilized to resist social classification and control. Or indeed, how ritualized gender transgression, as in Gregory Bateson's (1936) account of transvestism during Naven rituals among the Iatuml of Papua New Guinea, can establish/reaffirm hierarchical, gender binary relationships, thus highlighting again the complex relationship between indeterminacy and classificatory systems. Gilbert Herdt's work on the imaginative possibilities of the "third gender" suggests another reading of Naven transvestism whereby such performances indicate the "abandonment of absolute contrast" (Herdt 1994: 41; see Halberstam 1999).

J. K. Gibson-Graham's feminist approach to political economy echoes these moves in its criticism of what is called the overdetermination of spaces, a capitalocentric, analytical tunnel vision that fails to see spaces of opportunity and alternative imaginaries (2006). Debates on imagination's preconditions again insist on the apparent freedom offered by indeterminacy (Rapport 2015; Sneath, Holbraad, and Pederson 2009). And just as imagination projects forward, so radical indeterminacy has also been described as a requirement for hope (Miyazaki 2005 following Bloch 1995) and the crucial *conditio sine qua non* for an ethical stance of openness. Roughly speaking then we are faced with analytical approaches to indeterminacy that counsel only either hope or despair.

We end this section with Felix Ringel (2014) and Stef Jansen (2016) who both highlight an emerging strand of ethnographic writing that privileges the social significance of indeterminacy. Critically engaging with Hirokazu Miyazaki and Ernst Bloch's analyses of hope, Jansen notes that recent anthropological attention to indeterminacy has allowed ethnographers to embrace global capitalism's apparent "loss of direction" and to create new methodologies that consider the significance of exclusion and the emic inability to predict change through time (Miyazaki 2010: 250; see Bloch [1959] 1986; Ringel 2012). However, both Ringel and Jansen observe that many anthropological engagements with this topic deploy a Deleuzian analytic that overly fetishizes processes of "emergence and becoming" (e.g., Anderson 2007; Biehl and Locke 2010; Pedersen 2012). Such ethnography can too easily settle for "uncovering and valorising sparks of indeterminacy" instead of interrogating how they are formed and where they lead. Like Jansen and Ringel, what concerns us are the social effects produced by these sparks, which we trace by emphasizing ethnographic rather than analytical normativities. In the final section, we describe what our ethnographies of indeterminacy reveal.

Conclusion: Ethnographies of Indeterminacy, Waste and Value

We approach indeterminacy and its relationships with the material and metaphors of waste and value through two closely related steps, both of which draw on Hegel's idea of recognition and Adorno's negative dialectics.

Our first step is to explore indeterminacy largely as an issue of classification and mis- or failed recognition of that which cannot be easily incorporated into classificatory systems. We do this by interrogating how the mechanisms of power and resistance play out in classification and indeterminacy; how people negotiate mundane knowns and unknowns and confront foreshortened futures; and how the state reads its citizens and is in turn read—or dissolves into illegibility that is resistant to encounter. And while indeterminacy can foreclose engagement with a person or institution that cannot be discerned, or can create a space for personal rule and corruption (Reeves 2015), there are instances where people may embrace ambiguity via a multiplicity of meaning, refuse categories, and find other ways of counting outside dominant classificatory modes (Alexander and Keskülä this volume). One implication of rejecting an imposed category is that the system or imagined totality that gives that category meaning is also implicitly rejected. Thus, the unhappiness of both the expatriate Russians in Eeva Keskülä's chapter and the repatriated Kazakhs in Catherine Alexander's are caught up in their repudiation not only of how they are treated, but also of the system, or the new totality, in which they find themselves. They are denied full citizenship rights but some at least, in turn, deny the state (see Simpson 2014). While the power difference scarcely needs to be spelled out in such reciprocal refusal, there are suggestions that the state also needs, in part, these recalcitrant people. The integrity of the modern nation-state and the modern human subject is challenged by, and yet requires open-endedness and mobility.

This might suggest a structuralist approach to categorization and its antinomies, returning to Douglas's classic definition of dirt as matter out of place (1966). The power of her observation is that a bewildering array of "wastes," and the visceral revulsion that may accompany them, are culturally determined. However, thinking with the third term, *indeterminacy*, which may be negatively or positively valued, or neither (suspension), or both, complicates this approach and reveals (as in Thorleifsson and Eriksen's contribution) that quite different instances are merged and lost in the category of "the anomaly." At the same time, emphasizing those or that which is expelled may reveal contestation over who and what represents order. Finally, instances where an element may fit with the dominant order, but excessively so, or simultaneously possess wanted and unwanted characteristics, can threaten to shatter categories from within (Alexander this volume).

Our second step is the familiar anthropological argument that indeterminacy, as a mode of apprehension and being, can complicate modernity's grand teleology. We focus on areas where movement, change, and transformation are not always predictable or follow more modest ambitions than state-driven narratives of an ultimate social or organizational whole to which progress is being made. But there are also instances where people neither resist nor counter teleological visions, even after the collapse of animating state regimes. Rather they may hope for the return of such projects, grieve their passing, act as though they still exist, or simply transpose the logic to a new context. Three related insights from negative dialectics follow.

The first is that state (or indeed international agency development) projects are typically based on a teleological vision of time; after all "to project" implies just such an engagement with the future. But change may be unpredictable, rarely proceeding according to a predetermined telos. This echoes interventions from Science and Technology Studies (e.g., Bijker 1995; Bijiker, Hughes, and Pinch 2012; and Latour 1996) that trace the contingency of successful technological developments, inventions, and the happy (but not inevitable) coalescence of enabling factors in the successes or failures that later come to seem predestined (see Ringel this volume for a comparable account in the case of urban infrastructure). Some ideas succeed and others fail to be taken up.

By focusing on lives outside formal scaffolds of developmental progress, we describe instances where people have been expelled from or denied full participation in mainstream societies, have embraced formlessness and open-endedness, or settled for getting by, muddling through, and attending to the job at hand. We also include those who align themselves with previous grand narratives and lost visions. It is perhaps worth noting that contemporary institutions increasingly expect employees to have their own life/career projects carefully articulated with the greater whole; those who do not subscribe to, or find themselves tangential to the latest institutional or state developmental mission or vision, are increasingly ripe for being "managed out" or cast as wasted (see Bauman, 2003).

But ethnographic attention allows us to see that a Baumanesque classification of outcasts as wasted lives is to fail to see gradation and difference, where tactics of imagination and reclamation may come into play, where value may be recovered both from rejected materials and by people whose labor is excessive for a profitable enterprise. Simply to call these wasted lives is to recapitulate analytically the expulsion into indistinction that modernity has inflicted on them. Rather, we suggest that, while regimes of modernity expel lives, materials, and places as excessive, the tension and often ambiguities of these indeterminate states can allow meaning and value to be remade, suspended, or lost. If capitalism itself is predicated on imagined futures, (Beckert 2016), then so, in theory, people can reimagine their own futures.

The next insight derived from negative dialectics is that progression to another state (whether a future condition, revaluation, or reincorporation) is not to be assumed. This is most easily seen in the complex relationships between waste and value that are imagined, practiced, experienced, and theorized. Thus waste can be matter out of place, its expulsion a restorative act of ordering. We know enough now to recognize that one person's or system's waste, might be valuable in another instance (Reno 2009). But one implication of the emphasis on structural/contextual understandings of waste (changing a waste object's context can mean it is suddenly valuable) is that it appears as though wastes invariably contain the seed of value if they can only be placed again or converted, and indeed that all valued objects and people in turn contain the potential to be wasted. The relationship between waste and value is more complex and varied than that implied by the "matter out of place" maxim. One is not necessarily the simple inversion of the other. This is where indeterminacy provides a useful third term. Wastes can be indeterminate (value never) in the sense of a forgotten or postponed limbo, unattached in terms of property rights. Or indeterminacy can simply be a state where either, neither, or both negative waste and positive value can be discerned or imagined.

Examples of such an imbrication of waste and value, or rather, the precondition of an act or representation of wasting to release value are found in Anna Tsing's *The Mushroom at the End of the World* (2015) and Sara Peña Valderrama's work on carbon sink accounting (2016). In the former, intensive industrial logging renders the land unable to support life except for one kind of fungus that thrives in such territory—and turns out to be a prized delicacy. Hope appears among capitalism's ruins.

Peña Valderrama illustrates another kind of intertwining of waste and value via a carbon sink project in Madagascar, which gathered weight and funding thanks to fallow land being constructed by project officials as both unrecoverable and potentially recoverable waste. An imagined future scenario of degradation from slash-and-burn cultivation is pictured as being "avoided" or "offset" through the project's reforestation activities. This accounting legerdemain created the fallows as essentially indeterminate, creating one kind of value via carbon credits. But this is not a hopeful story: the farmers who were literally cast out from their lands are effectively wasted. The politics of such accounting techniques are that different parties enjoy the benefits and suffer the losses.

Wastes are not simply transformed into value in these acts. Rather, the condition of indeterminacy can be seen as a mode between, or as encompassing, waste and value. In some cases, it is a threatening, negative force, sometimes translated into wastelands and waste people, sometimes a necessary imaginary to allow the economic, rehabilitive value of an alternative route to be realized, but also exists as a mode of limbo or suspension that may never be resolved, recombined, or incorporated. This in-betweeness operates temporally as well as spatially.

Engaging with emic ideas of worth uncovers contested ideas of what constitutes waste and value in a given ethnographic moment. Crucially, the moment of apparent transition from waste to value may remain unresolved or indeterminate. This is the moment that interests us. We include in this idea, as one example, lands that have been irrevocably polluted and stripped into sterility by industrial mining or the toxic chemical by-products of value production.[13] Abandonment or containment are typical responses, the latter sometimes in the hope of a future technology appearing that is able to undo toxicity. Again, people may articulate a sense of being left behind by rapid and extreme social change, for whom there is less a sense of "progress toward," than daily routines of getting by, a modest intentionality. Again, we sound a note of caution about taking such lives as intrinsically those of either resistance or oppression. Some ethnographic studies suggest marginalized people may disregard any time but the present, subverting the rather Protestant notion of the present as a site of suffering to be overcome through careful planning. In this model, marginalized people resist by performatively stating that the true domain of suffering is the future, mitigated by the impulsive act of living for the "now" (Day, Papataxiarchis, and Stewart 1999: 2). Fatalism does not always lead to present impetuosity, or a positive emic take on it.

The final inspiration we take from negative dialectics is that apparent "fragments" are not necessarily part of, nor destined to be incorporated into a whole. Many of our contributions explore tensions between imagined totalities (e.g., nation-states) and mundane experiences. Our chapters speak to an unpredictable world, partly apprehensible, where the multiple ordering regimes of modernity rely on the constant production and expulsion of putative excess. Many of the essays in this collection suggest a means of representing and of being in the world as fragments, non-unitary subjects, and things, with incomplete perspectives and understandings (Candea 2010; Strathern 1991). In what follows we outline our chapters' main contributions to understanding indeterminacy ethnographically.

The first three chapters explore open-endedness in quite different contexts, each of which reveals tensions, or surprises, between ways of knowing and managing (landfill containment, defining people, urban planning) and material or human refusals to conform to such determinate visions. Thus suspended fragments in a North American landfill generate unpredictable contamination (Reno); British trans artists' embrace of mutability in life and work inhibits access to rights through formal recognition (Gonzalez-Polledo); German postindustrial infrastructure is successively planned, redundant, and repurposed (Ringel). The following three chapters examine demographic politics from complementary angles, how internal and external others (Roma and

Travellers) are marked as indeterminate waste in Norway (Thorleifsson and Eriksen); how Russian miners who were "left behind" after the end of the Soviet Union in Estonia and Kazakhstan now find themselves unvalued (Kesküla); and how repatriated Kazakhs in Kazakhstan are simultaneously welcomed and rejected as excessive to the country's enterprise (Alexander). As many of these chapters uncover, one form of indeterminacy, whether imposed or embraced, often creates others. Our final chapter explores this explicitly through people classed as surplus labor in the Philippines, who now work as waste pickers (Schober). Despite the range of contexts, certain common themes appear, as the following sketches out.

The will to control through fixity, numbering, containment, and classifications, is typically manifested through the modern state, which expels, forcibly assimilates, or "digests" in Cathrine Thorleifsson and Thomas Hylland Eriksen's striking metaphor (see also O'Brien 2003), those who do not fit. But as Thorleifsson and Eriksen show for the Roma in Norway and Elisabeth Schober for waste pickers, one means of doing this is by imagining indeterminate wastes that migrate across domains linking wayward pollution, chaotic material wastes, and unclean people that together threaten the literal and metaphorical health of the body politic. Shifting perspective shows different responses.

Schober shows how waste pickers contest classifications of "surplus" or "wasted" labor by remaking their lives, redetermining the discards of others into a valuable resource, locating ever finer intervals in the value chain where most see only indecipherable waste. In this way, they demand formal recognition of their lives and labor. Moreover, she highlights the failure of terms such as *precarity* and *wagelessness* to capture the nuances of how people live through, off, and alongside processes of capitalism. The trans artists described by Elena Gonzalez-Polledo experience the politics of recognition and indeterminacy quite differently. Seeking in their lives and art to escape formal determinacy, they find access to rights and resources denied and may strategically move in and out of accepting "labels" and medico-legal models in order to subsist. Thus the politics of recognition and redistribution merge in the tension between wanting recognition but not codification. Ringel's description of the unanticipated ruins of industrial infrastructure, which actively inhibits future municipal development, is neatly offset by a group of residents in a rundown region who value their houses' dilapidation as a means of resisting gentrification. Ringel's point, as urban infrastructure is rendered superfluous then repurposed, is that, with each new direction, indeterminacy only appears as a retrospective point of surprise.

Both Kesküla and Alexander's ethnographies illustrate people mourning the classificatory frameworks offered by former modernist states for the social, moral, and monetary value they once conferred. In the former account, Russian miners find they are no longer a distinct category of prized worker but lumped together with other unvalued manual workers, even though the product of the miners' labor, energy, is vital for the national enterprise. Their sense of dislocation is partly expressed through constant comparison with other workers, ethnic groups, lands, and times. They fit with none of them.

Joshua O. Reno's focus on the fragment reminds us that most analytical approaches fail to account for the part that belongs to no whole nor has a trajectory other than material decay. Not all wastes are ripe for conversion to value. Such present-oriented moments reappear in Ringel's account. The landfill serves as both metaphor and case study of the indeterminacies that emerge from techniques of control. Attempts to manage unruly wastes through containment are always incomplete as leachate and gas escape. Essentially indeterminate, biogas can only be partly trapped and converted to value. For an emergent politics of indeterminate wastes, the question is not whether they can be known or not, but if they can be known enough to act upon: a matter of degree instead of binary determination.

Thus we explore what happens when binary categories or ideas as containers of meaning clash with complex lives and materials that overflow such attempts to hold them fast. Repatriated Kazakhs, for example, seem to show an excess of qualities that demarcate "Kazakhness," potentially diminishing other Kazakhs by comparison. Further, they seem to conflate distinct times, embodying the past in the present, and remind unwilling neighbors that population and labor force numbers also refer to human beings. Numbers and categories, Alexander suggests, are essentially indeterminate proxies for reality. As both Reno and Alexander show, excessive regulation can create gaps between laws that, like anomalies, are often profoundly ambiguous.

Individuals that fall between or outside categories, or find their specificity denied in generic classifications, may strive for formal recognition and attendant rights, or celebrate being outside formal schema, or move between these modes. Anomalous figures may be rejected by dominant societies (as with the Roma in Norway), or brutally made the same (as with Travellers in Norway), may lack the relations that make them a social person, but may also be symbolically potent (the miners) or, as an entrepreneur, may seize the value lurking in indeterminate spaces and times.

The figure of the entrepreneur, who appears in many of the following chapters, incarnates the need for attention to ethnographic normativities. Often an anomalous figure[14] herself, the entrepreneur can be cast as the heroic agent of innovation and capitalist value creation precisely by exploiting indeterminacy qua ignorance.[15] Alternatively, she can be morally derided for mere speculation, or reconfiguration, failing to produce any genuine added value, or indeed brokering across spheres that should legally and morally remain distinct, as in the case of rent seeking.

One last observation, before we move to our chapters. Arguably ethnography is fundamentally concerned with the mundane spaces where social rules are encountered, negotiated, modified, resisted, reincorporated, appropriated, and so on. Fenella Cannell's ethnography of power and negotiation in a Philippine community makes this explicit (1999), but this is also the indeterminate space of ethnography itself more broadly. Further, "suspension," Choy and Zee suggest, "tethers to the ethnographer" a method, or a procedure, that works to render staid common sense into an opening of possible worlds: ethnography constitutes a work of suspension, of assumptions and disbelief, one that not only describes worlds but holds them in such a way as to allow them to settle into different arrangements, possibilities." (2015: 212). Indeterminacy is at the core of ethnographic engagement.

Catherine Alexander is professor of Anthropology at Durham University, previously Goldsmiths, London. Her recent publications on indeterminacy and waste include a special issue on "Moral Economies of Housing" in *Critique of Anthropology* (2018), coedited with Insa Koch and Maja Hojer Bruun, and *Economies of Recycling* (Zed Books, 2012), coedited with Joshua Reno. She coauthored the opening chapter "What is Waste" for the UK Government's Chief Scientific Adviser's 2017 report on waste, and has written widely on wastes and third sector recycling in anthropology, environmental science, and engineering journals.

Andrew Sanchez is lecturer in Social Anthropology at the University of Cambridge. He has published widely on economy, labor, class and corruption, and is the author of *Criminal Capital: Violence, Corruption and Class in Industrial India* (Routledge, 2016). He is currently completing a project about core conceptual debates in the anthropology of value.

Acknowledgements

It is a great pleasure finally to thank publicly the three anonymous reviewers for their comments as well as the wonderfully precise and careful suggestions from Niko Besnier, Judith Bovensiepen, Matt Canfield, Alanna Cant, Michael Carrithers, Taras Fedirko, David Henig, Minh Nguyen, Felix Ringel, Stefan Schwendtner, and Diána Vonnák. Joshua Reno and Thomas Yarrow have been with this project from before its start to its end; heartfelt thanks for their intellectual generosity and patience. Ilana Gershon's keen editorial eye effected the final transformation; we owe her much. It goes without saying that remaining faults are despite their best efforts.

Notes

1. Mary Douglas was, of course, discussing dirt not waste, and the two are not always synonymous: wastes can be amorphous, unrecognizable, and hence unclassifiable; or they can be the very stuff of classificatory order, as anyone who sorts recyclates for collection knows. However, there is by now considerable literature where the equation between waste and dirt is made in a way that stays true to her overall argument (as Joshua Reno helpfully pointed out, pers. comm.)

2. Michael Thompson (2017) presented an analogous critique of Douglas's thesis by challenging the waste/value binary with a third term *rubbish*, an indeterminate but still, in his framework, a socially-constructed category.

3. Ambiguity is of course a mainstay in literary studies from William Empson's classic study onward. Note, too, in part homage Namwali Serpell's *Seven Modes of Uncertainty* (2016), which suggests that uncertainty is an essentially ethical stance, allowing freedom.

4. Thus, for example, a society that rids itself of a perceived social poison—unwanted people—is, in that act, providing the antidote or medicine to that ill.

5. There are others, of course. For example, Sarah Green's (2005) account of the Balkans that describes external discourse that insists "the region is fluidity and indeterminacy personified, right on the surface, a completely explicit fog, as it were" (2005: 12). It challenges modernist accounts of statist drives to clarity, but are also partly reproduced locally, and, as Green suggests, partly constitute lived experience. Both Green's book and Matei Candea's (2010) on Corsican identity, which also works through external and internal insistence on indeterminacy and partiality, are themselves presented as provisional, openended, and fragmentary.

6. Thus despite the fact that capitalism and state socialism have been ideologically portrayed as opposites, Susan Buck-Morss emphasized how, in the twentieth century, these two forms of organization were profoundly entwined, sharing eighteenth-century philosophical roots and a passionate belief in the emancipatory potential of industrial production for creating mass utopia (2000). Earlier, Keith Hart flagged the ideological projection of difference between capitalism and socialism during the Cold War while they had never been closer in practice (1992).

7. Note also Andrew Sanchez and Christian Strümpell (2014) for a different setting of prescriptive Marxist thought.

8. Although Bataille uses both *surplus* and *excess* in *The Accursed Share* (1991), there is a sense that it is the latter, as superabundance, which forces expenditure, or wasting-asluxury (or sacrifice and war). Excess is the accursed share.

9. See Charles Taylor's 1992 account of contemporary political demands for recognition on the grounds that recognition and identity are fundamentally linked.

10. Or highlight alternative classificatory systems and discursive formations historically (Foucault 1994) and through ethnographic comparison.

11. Article 1 of *The 1951 Convention Relating to the Status of Refugees* defines a refugee as someone who has fled his or her country "owing to well-founded fear of being persecuted for reasons of race, religion, nationality, membership of a particular social group or political opinion" and sets out the legal obligations of governments toward such people.

12. Ludwig Wittgenstein's famous paradox for rule-following encapsulates some of the experiences explored in our chapters of attempts to engage with the state and its representatives: "This was our paradox: no course of action could be determined by a rule, because every course of action can be made out to accord with the rule. The answer was: if everything can be made out to accord with the rule, then it can also be made out to conflict with it. And so there would be neither accord nor conflict here" (2001 [1953]: 69). We are grateful to Diana Vonnak for this observation.

13. Thus one might see David Harvey's concept of capitalism's spatial fix (1981) as having a second movement. If the first is to acquire more space, more territory to fuel the constant expansion inherent to capitalism, then the irrecoverable wasting of land from unsustainable resource extraction also drives the "need" to acquire more resource-rich land (see also Gidwani 2013).

14. This is taken further in Tsing's analysis of the potent imaginary of "the entrepreneur" in supply chain capitalism where sweatshop workers may hopefully imagine themselves as potentially rich entrepreneurs (2013: 159) and, in recruiting family members, further blur the fuzzy line between self- and superexploitation (2013: 167n28).

15. This, of course, as Joshua Reno points out (pers. comm.), is the fetishized ideal type of neoliberal ideology whereas (see Birch 2015), arguably, the monopoly capitalist who undergirds global capitalism is concerned with determinacy, predictability, and limiting risk where possible.

References

Adams, V., M. Murphy, and A. E. Clarke 2009. "Anticipation: Technoscience, Life, Affect, Temporality." *Subjectivity* 28: 246–65.

Adorno, T. 1973. *Negative Dialectics*, trans. E. B. Ashton. New York: Seabury Press.

Agamben, G. 1998. *Homo Sacer: Sovereign Power and Bare Life*. Stanford, CA: Stanford University Press.

Agier, M. 2008. *On the Margins of the World: The Refugee Experience Today*. Cambridge: Polity Press.

——— . 2010. *Managing the Undesirables: Refugee Camps and Humanitarian Government*. Cambridge: Polity Press.

Alexander, C. 2009. "Privatization: Jokes, Scandal and Absurdity in a Time of Rapid Change." In *Ethnographies of Moral Reasoning: Living Paradoxes of a Global Age*, ed. K. Sykes, 43–65. New York: Palgrave Macmillan.

——— . 2012. "Remont: Works in Progress." In *Economies of Recycling: The Global Transformation of Materials, Values and Social Relations*, ed. C. Alexander and J. Reno, 255–75. London: Zed Books.

——— . Forthcoming. "Cleaning Up and Moving On: Kazakhstan's 'Nuclear Renaissance.'" In *Les Chantiers du Nucléaire*, ed. R. Garcier and L. Françoise. Paris: Archives Contemporaines.

Allison, A. 2012. "Ordinary Refugees: Social Precarity and Soul in 21st Century Japan." *Anthropological Quarterly* 85(2): 345–70.

Althusser L. 1970. *Reading Capital*. New York: New Left Books.

Anderson, B. 2007. "Hope for Nanotechnology: Anticipatory Knowledge and the Governance of Affect." *Area* 39(2): 156–65.

Appadurai, A. 2011. "The Ghost in the Financial Machine." *Public Culture* 23(3): 517–39.

Arendt, H. 1950. *The Origins of Totalitarianism*. New York: Meridian Books.

Auyero, J. 2012. *Patients of the State: The Politics of Waiting in Argentina*. Durham, NC: Duke University Press.

Bakhtin, M. 2009. *Rabelais and His World*, trans. H. Iswolsky. Bloomington, IN: Indiana University Press.

Bataille, G. 1985. *Visions of Excess: Selected Writings 1927–1939*. Minneapolis, MN: University of Minnesota Press.

——— . 1988. *The Accursed Share*, vol. 1. New York: Zone Books.

Bateson, G. 1936. *Naven: A Survey of Problems Suggested by a Composite Picture of the Culture of a New Guinea Tribe Drawn from Three Points of View*. Stanford, CA: Stanford University Press.

Bauman, Z. 2004. *Wasted Lives: Modernity and Its Outcasts*. London: Polity Press.

Becker, H. S. 2006. "The Work Itself." In *Art from Start to Finish: Jazz, Painting, Writing, and Other Improvisations*, ed. H. S. Becker, R. R. Faulkner, and B. Kirshenblatt-Gimblett, 21–30. Chicago, IL and London: University of Chicago Press.

Beckert, J. 2016. *Imagined Futures: Fictional Expectations and Capitalist Dynamics*. Cambridge, MA: Harvard University Press.

Beckett, S. 1956. *Waiting for Godot*. London: Faber and Faber.

Benjamin, W. 2002. *The Arcades Project*, trans. H. Eiland and K. McLaughlin. Cambridge, MA: Harvard University Press.

Berman, M. 2010. *All That Is Solid Melts into Air: The Experience of Modernity*. New York: Verso.

Berthomé, F., J. Bonhomme, and G. Delaplace. 2012. "Preface: Cultivating Uncertainty." *HAU: Journal of Ethnographic Theory* 2(2): 129–37.

Biehl, J., and P. Locke. 2010. "Deleuze and the Anthropology of Becoming." *Current Anthropology* 51(3): 317–51.

Bijiker, W. 1995. *Of Bicycles, Bakelites, and Bulbs: Toward a Theory of Sociotechnical Change*. Cambridge, MA: MIT Press.

Bijker, W., T. P. Hughes, and T. J. Pinch 2012. *The Social Construction of Technological Systems*. Cambridge, MA: MIT Press.

Birch. K. 2015. *We Have Never Been Neoliberal: A Manifesto for a Doomed Youth*. Alresford, UK: Zero Books, John Hunt Publishing.

Bloch, E. [1959] 1986. *The Principle of Hope*. London: Blackwell.

Bowker, G., and S. Leigh Star. 1999. *Sorting Things Out: Classification and Its Consequences*. Cambridge, MA: MIT Press.

Broto, V. 2015. "Dwelling in a Pollution Landscape." In *The Anthropology of Postindustrialism: Ethnographies of Disconnection*, ed. I. Vaccaro, 91–112. London: Routledge.

Buck-Morss, S. 2000. *Dreamworld and Catastrophe: The Passing of Mass Utopia in East and West*. Cambridge, MA: MIT Press.

Campkin, B. 2013. "Placing 'Matter Out of Place': Purity and Danger as Evidence for Architecture and Urbanism." *Architectural Theory Review* 18(1): 46–61.

Candea, M. 2010. *Corsican Fragments: Difference, Knowledge, and Fieldwork*. Bloomington, IN: Indiana University Press.

Cannell, F. 1999. *Power and Intimacy in the Christian Philippines*. Cambridge: Cambridge University Press.

Carey, M., and M. A. Pedersen, eds. 2017. "Infrastructures of Certainty and Doubt." *The Cambridge Journal of Anthropology* 35(2): v–146.

Chandavarkar, R. 1994. *The Origins of Industrial Capitalism in India: Business Strategies and the Working Classes in Bombay, 1900–40*. Cambridge: Cambridge University Press.

Choy, T., and J. Zee. 2015. "Condition—Suspension." *Cultural Anthropology* 30(2): 210–223.

Cornforth, M. 1961. *Materialism and the Dialectical Method*. London: Lawrence and Wishart.

Das, V., and D. Poole, eds. 2004. *Anthropology in the Margins of the State*. Santa Fe, NM: School of American Research Press.

Dasgupta, S. 1985. *Towards a Post Development Era*. London: Mittal.

Dawdy, S. L. 2010. "Clockpunk Anthropology and the Ruins of Modernity." *Current Anthropology* 51(6): 761–93.

Day, S., E. Papataxiarchis, and M. Stewart, eds. 1999. *Lilies of the Field: Marginal People Who Live for the Moment*. Boulder, CO: Westview Press.

De Genova, N. 2002. "Migrant 'Illegality' and Deportability in Everyday Life." *Annual Review of Anthropology* 31: 419–47.

Derrida, J. 1981. "Plato's Pharmacy." In *Dissemination*, trans. B. Johnson, 61–171. Chicago, IL: University of Chicago Press.

Diedrich, R-M. 2004. "Passages to No-Man's Land: Connecting Work, Community and Masculinity in the South Wales Coalfield." In *Workers and Narratives of Survival in*

Europe: The Management of Precariousness at the end of the Twentieth Century, ed. A. Procoli, 101–20. New York: SUNY Press.

Douglas, M. 1966. *Purity and Danger: An Analysis of Concepts of Pollution and Taboo*. London: Routledge.

Empson, W. [1930] 1966. *Seven Types of Ambiguity*. London: New Directions.

Escobar, A. 1995. *Encountering Development: The Making and Unmaking of the Third World*. Princeton, NJ: Princeton University Press.

Ferguson, J. 1990. *The Anti-Politics Machine: 'Development', Depoliticisation and Bureaucratic Power in Lesotho*. Cambridge: Cambridge University Press.

Feyerabend, P. 1975. *Against Method: Outline of an Anarchist Theory of Knowledge*. London: Verso Books.

_____. 2001. *Conquest of Abundance: A Tale of Abstraction versus the Richness of Being*. Chicago, IL: Chicago University Press.

Foucault, M. 1977. "A Preface to Transgression," In *Language, Counter-memory, Practice: Selected Essays and Interviews*, ed. D. Bouchard, trans. D. Bouchard and S. Simon, 29–52. Ithaca, NY: Cornell University Press.

_____. [1984] 1992. *The Use of Pleasure: The History of Sexuality. Volume Two*, trans. R. Hurley. Harmondsworth, Middlesex: Penguin.

_____. 1994. *The Order of Things: An Archaeology of the Human Sciences*. New York: Random House USA, Inc.

Friedmann, J. 1992. *Empowerment: The Politics of Alternative Development*. Oxford: Blackwell.

Gabiam, N. 2016. *The Politics of Suffering: Syria's Palestinian Refugee Camps*. Bloomington, IN: Indiana University Press.

Gaidar, Ye T. 1999. *Days of Defeat and Victory*, trans. J. Miller. Seattle, WA: University of Washington Press.

Gardner, K., and D. Lewis. 2015. *Anthropology and Development Challenges for the Twenty-First Century*. London: Pluto Press.

Geissler, P. W. 2010. "Parasite Lost—Remembering Modern Times with Kenyan Government Medical Scientists." In *Evidence, Ethos and Experiment: The Anthropology and History of Medical Research in Africa*, ed. P. W. Geissler and C. Molyneux, 297–32. Oxford: Berghahn Books.

Genda, Y. 2005. *A Nagging Sense of Job Insecurity: The New Reality Facing Japanese Youth*. Tokyo: International House of Japan.

Gennep, A. van, [1909] 1960. *The Rites of Passage*. Chicago, IL: Chicago University Press.

Gibson-Graham, J. K. 2006. *A Postcapitalist Politics*. Minneapolis, MN: University of Minnesota Press.

Gidwani, V. 2013. "Six Theses on Waste, Value, and Commons." *Social & Cultural Geography* 14(7): 773–83.

Gidwani, V. and R. N. Reddy 2011. "The Afterlives of 'Waste': Notes from India for a Minor History of Capitalist Surplus." *Antipode* 43(5): 1625–58.

Gill, R. and A. Pratt. 2008. "In the Social Factory? Immaterial Labour, Precariousness and Cultural Work." *Theory, Culture & Society* 25(7–8): 1–30.

Giroux, H. 2012. *Twilight of the Social: Resurgent Publics in the Age of Disposability*. Boulder, CO: Paradigm.

Gordillo, G. 2014. *Rubble: The Afterlife of Destruction*. Durham, NC: Duke University Press.

Graeber, D. 2013. "It is Value that Brings Universes into Being." *Hau: Journal of Ethnographic Theory* 3(2): 219–43.

Green, S. 2005. *Notes from the Balkans: Locating Marginality and Ambiguity on the Greek-Albanian Border.* Princeton, NJ: Princeton University Press.

Gunder Frank, A. 1966. *The Development of Underdevelopment.* Monthly Review Press.

Gupta, A. 2015. "Suspension." Theorizing the Contemporary, *Cultural Anthropology*, 24 September. Retrieved 17 May 2018 from http://www.culanth.org/fieldsights/722-suspension.

Guyer, J. 2007. "Prophecy and the Near Future: Thoughts on Macroeconomic, Evangelical, and Punctuated Time." *American Ethnologist* 34(3): 409–21.

Halberstam, J. 1998. *Female Masculinity.* Durham, NC: Duke University Press.

Hallam, E., and T. Ingold, eds. 2007. *Creativity and Cultural Improvisation.* London: Bloomsbury Publishers.

Hann, C. and J. Parry, eds. 2018. *Industrial Labor on the Margins of Capitalism: Precarity, Class and the Neoliberal Subject.* Oxford: Berghahn Books.

Hart, K. 1992. "Market and State after the Cold War—The Informal Economy Reconsidered." In *Contesting Markets: Anthropology of Ideology, Discourse and Practice*, ed. R. Dilley, 214–227. Edinburgh: Edinburgh University Press.

Harvey, D. 1981. "The Spatial Fix: Hegel, Von Thunen, and Marx." *Antipode* 13(3): 1–12.

———. 1987. "Flexible Accumulation through Urbanization: Reflections on 'Post-Modernism' in the American City." *Antipode* 19(3): 260–86.

Hecht, J. 2004. *Doubt: A History—The Great Doubters and Their Legacy of Innovation from Socrates and Jesus to Thomas Jefferson and Emily Dickinson.* Sydney: HarperOne.

Hegel, G. 1977. *Phenomenology of Spirit.* Oxford: Clarendon Press.

———. 1991. *Elements of the Philosophy of Right*, ed. A. Wood. Cambridge: Cambridge University Press.

Henig, D. 2012. "Iron in the Soil: Living with Military Waste in Bosnia-Herzegovina." *Anthropology Today* 28(1): 21–23.

Herdt, G. 1994. *Third Sex, Third Gender: Beyond Sexual Dimorphism in Culture and History.* New York: Zone Books.

Hinchliffe, S. 2001. "Indeterminacy In-decisions—Science, Policy and Politics in the BSE (Bovine Spongiform Encephalopathy) Crisis." *Transactions of the Institute of British Geographers* 26(2): 182–204.

Honneth, A. 2016. *The Pathologies of Individual Freedom: Hegel's Social Theory*, trans. L. Löb. Princeton, NJ: Princeton University Press.

Horkheimer, M., and T. W. Adorno. [1947] 2002. *Dialectic of Enlightenment: Philosophical Fragments*, ed. G. S. Noerr, trans. E. Jephcott. Stanford, CA: Stanford University Press.

Horvath, A., B. Thomassen, and H. Wydra. 2015. *Breaking Boundaries: Varieties of Liminality.* Oxford: Berghahn Books.

Hussain. D. 2013. *Boundaries Undermined: The Ruins of Progress on the Bangladesh-India Border.* London: Hurst & Co. Ltd.

Huyssen, A. 1984. "Mapping the Postmodern." *New German Critique*, Modernity and Postmodernity, 33: 5–52.

Jansen, S. 2016. "For a Relational, Historical Ethnography of Hope: Indeterminacy and Determination in the Bosnian and Herzegovinian Meantime." *History and Anthropology* 27(4): 447–64.

Jarvis, S. 1998. *Adorno: A Critical Introduction.* New York: Routledge.

Kim, E. 2014. "Toward an Anthropology of Landmines: Rogue Infrastructure and Military Waste in the Korean DMZ." *Cultural Anthropology* 31(2): 162–87.

Knudsen, I. H. and M. D. Fredericksen, eds. 2015. *Ethnographies of Grey Zones in Eastern Europe: Relations, Borders and Invisibilities*. London: Anthem.

Kristeva, J. 1982. *Powers of Horror: An Essay on Abjection*, trans. L. Roudiez. New York: Columbia University Press.

Krupar, S. R. 2012. "Transnatural Ethics: Revisiting the Nuclear Cleanup of Rocky Flats, CO, through the Queer Ecology of Nuclia Waste." *Cultural Geographies* 19(3): 303–327.

Lampland, M. and S. L. Star. 2008. *Standards and Their Stories: How Quantifying, Classifying, and Formalizing Practices Shape Everyday Life*. Ithaca, NY: Cornell University Press.

Latour, B. 1996. *Aramis, or the Love of Technology*. Cambridge, MA: Harvard University Press.

Lipton, D., J. Sachs, V. Mau, and E. S. Phelps. 1992. "Prospects for Russia's Economic Reforms." *Brookings Papers on Economic Activity* 1992(2): 213–83.

Lunn, E. 1984. *Marxism and Modernism: An Historical Study of Lukács, Brecht, Benjamin, and Adorno*. Berkeley, CA: University of California Press.

Marx, K. 1967. *Capital, Volume 1: A Critique of Political Economy*. New York: International.

Marx, K., and F. Engels. 1967. *The Communist Manifesto*. Harmondsworth, UK: Penguin.

———. 1975. *Collected Works, Vol 2: The Eighteenth Brumaire of Napoleon*. Moscow: Progress Publishers.

Massey, D. S. and N. A. Denton. 1993. *American Apartheid: Segregation and the Making of the Underclass*. Cambridge, MA: Harvard University Press.

Mbembe, A. 2004. "Aesthetics of Superfluity." *Public Culture* 16(3): 373–405.

———. 2011. "Democracy as a Community of Life." *The Johannesburg Salon* 4: 5–10.

McFann, H. (n.d.). "Humans as Waste in the Discard Studies Compendium." Retrieved 17 May 2018 from https://discardstudies.com/discard-studies-compendium/.

Millar, K. 2014. "The Precarious Present: Wageless Labor and Disrupted Life in Rio de Janeiro, Brazil." *Cultural Anthropology* 29(1): 32–53.

Miyazaki, H. 2005. *The Method of Hope: Anthropology, Philosophy, and Fijian Knowledge*. Redwood City, CA: Stanford University Press.

———. 2010. "The Temporality of No Hope." In *Ethnographies of Neoliberalism*, ed. C. Greenhouse, 238–50. Berkeley, CA: University of California Press.

———. 2013. "Between Arbitrage and Speculation." In *Arbitraging Japan: Dreams of Capitalism at the End of Finance*, 43–69. Berkeley, CA: University of California Press.

Mole, N. J. 2010. "Precarious Subjects: Anticipating Neoliberalism in Northern Italy's Workplace." *American Anthropologist* 112(1): 38–53.

Morgensen, S. 2016. "Encountering Indeterminacy: Colonial Contexts and Queer Imagining." *Cultural Anthropology* 31(4): 607–16.

Munck, R. 2013. "The Precariat: A View from the South." *Third World Quarterly* 34(5): 747–62.

Namwali Serpell, C. 2014. *Seven Modes of Uncertainty*. Cambridge, MA: Harvard University Press.

Navaro-Yashin, Y. 2009. "Affective Spaces, Melancholic Objects: Ruination and the Production of Anthropological Knowledge." *JRAI* 15(1): 1–18.

Nederveen Pieterse, J. 2000. "After Post-development." *Third World Quarterly* 21(2): 175–91.

Negri, A. 2004. "The Constitution of Time." In *Time for Revolution*, 48–49. London: Continuum Books.

Nixon, R. 2011. *Slow Violence and the Environmentalism of the Poor*. Cambridge, MA: Harvard University Press.

Nyers, P. 2006 *Rethinking Refugees: Beyond State of Emergency*. London: Routledge.

O'Brien, G. 2003. "Indigestible Food, Conquering Hordes, and Waste Materials: Metaphors of Immigrants and the Early Immigration Restriction Debate in the United States." *Metaphor and Symbol* 18(1): 33–47.

Ortiz, H. 2014. "The Limits of Financial Imagination: Free Investors, Efficient Markets, and Crisis." *American Anthropologist* 116(1): 38–50.

Özyürek, E. 2006. *Nostalgia for the Modern: State Secularism and Everyday Politics in Turkey*. Durham, NC: Duke University Press.

Pedersen, M. A. 2012. "A Day in the Cadillac: The Work of Hope in Urban Mongolia." *Social Analysis* 56 (2): 136–51.

Pelkmans, M. 2013a. "Outline for an Ethnography of Doubt." In *Ethnographies of Doubt: Faith and Uncertainty in Contemporary Societies*, ed. M. Pelkmans, 1–43. London: I.B. Tauris.

———. 2013b. "Ruins of Hope in a Kyrgyz Post-industrial Wasteland." *Anthropology Today*, 29(5): 16–20.

Peña Valderrama, S. 2016. *Entangling Molecules: An Ethnography of a Carbon Offset Project in Madagascar's Eastern Rainforest*. Ph.D. dissertation. Durham, UK: Durham University.

Peteet, J. 2005. *Landscape of Hope and Despair: Palestinian Refugee Camps*. Philadelphia, PA: University of Pennsylvania Press.

Pippin, R. 2000. "What Is the Question for which Hegel's Theory of Recognition is the Answer?" *European Journal of Philosophy* 8(2): 155–72.

Povinelli, E. 2002. *The Cunning of Recognition: Indigenous Alterities and the Making of Australian Multiculturalism*. Durham, NC and London: Duke University Press.

Rapport, N. 2015. "Imagination Is in the Barest Reality: On the Universal Human Imagining of the World." In *Reflections on Imagination: Human Capacity and Ethnographic Method*, ed. M. Harris and N. Rapport, 3–22. Surrey: Ashgate Publishing Ltd.

Reeves, M. 2015. "Living from the Nerves: Deportability, Indeterminacy, and the 'Feel of Law' in Migrant Moscow." *Social Analysis* 59(4): 119–36.

Reno, J. 2009. "Your Trash Is Someone's Treasure: The Politics of Value at a Michigan Landfill." *Journal of Material Culture* 14(1): 29–46.

Riles, A. 2013. "Market Collaboration: Finance, Culture, and Ethnography after Neoliberalism." *American Anthropologist* 115(4): 555–69.

Ringel, F. 2012. "Towards Anarchist Futures? Creative Presentism, Vanguard Practices and Anthropological Hopes." *Critique of Anthropology* 32(2): 173–88.

———. 2014. "Post-industrial Times and the Unexpected: Endurance and Sustainability in Germany's Fastest-Shrinking City." *Journal of the Royal Anthropological Institute* 20(S1): 52–70.

Rinella, M. 2010. *Pharmakon: Plato, Drug Culture, and Identity in Ancient Athens*. Lanham, MD: Lexington Books.

Rofel, L. 1999. *Other Modernities: Gendered Yearnings in China after Socialism*. Berkeley, CA: University of California Press.

Rumsey, A., and J. Robbins, eds. 2008. "Anthropology and the Opacity of Other Minds." *Anthropological Quarterly* 81(2): 407–94.

Sachs, J. 1994. "Russia's Economic Prospects." *Bulletin of the American Academy of Arts and Sciences* 48(3): 45–63.

Sachs, W., ed. 1992. *The Development Dictionary: A Guide to Knowledge as Power*. London: Zed Books.

Samimian-Darash, L., and P. Rabinow, eds. 2015. *Modes of Uncertainty: Anthropological Cases*. Chicago, IL: University of Chicago Press.

Sanchez, A. 2016. *Criminal Capital: Violence, Corruption and Class in Industrial India*. Oxford: Routledge.

_____. 2018. "Relative Precarity: Decline, Hope and the Politics of Work." In *Industrial Labor on the Margins of Capitalism: Precarity, Class and the Neoliberal Subject*, ed. C. Hann, and J. P. Parry, 218–40. New York: Berghahn Books.

Sanchez, A., and C. Strümpell. 2014. "Anthropological and Historical Perspectives on India's Working Classes in Class Matters: New Ethnographic Perspectives on the Politics of Indian Labour." *Modern Asian Studies* 48(5): 1233–41.

Sassen, S. 2014. *Expulsions: Brutality and Complexity in the Global Economy*. Cambridge, MA: The Belknap Press of Harvard University Press.

Scanlan, J. 2005. *On Garbage*. London: Reaktion Books.

Schaffer, G. n.d. "Camp." *Discard Studies Compendium*. Retrieved 17 May 2018 from https://discardstudies.com/discard-studies-compendium/#Camp.

Schiocchet, L. 2010. *Refugee Lives: Ritual and Belonging in Two Palestinian Refugee Camps in Lebanon*. Ph.D. dissertation. Boston, MA: Boston University.

Simpson, A. 2014. *Mohawk Interruptus: Political Life across the Borders of Settler States*. Durham, NC: Duke University Press.

Sneath, D., M. Holbraad, and M. Pedersen. 2009. "Technologies of the Imagination." *Ethnos* 74(1): 5–30.

Stallybrass, P., and A. White. 1986. *The Politics and Poetics of Transgression*. Ithaca, NY: Cornell University Press.

Standing, G. 2011. *The Precariat: The New Dangerous Class*. London: Bloomsbury Academic.

Star, S. L., and K. Ruhleder. 1996. "Steps towards an Ecology of Infrastructure: Design and Access for Large Information Spaces." *Information Systems Research* 7(1): 111–34.

Stark, D. 1991. "Path Dependence and Privatization Strategies in East Central Europe." *East European Politics and Societies* 6(1): 17–54.

Stenning, A. 2005. "Post-socialism and the Changing Geographies of the Everyday in Poland." *Transactions of the Institute of British Geographers* 30(1): 113–27.

Stoler, Anna Laura, ed. 2013. *Imperial Debris: On Ruins and Ruination*. Durham, NC: Duke University Press.

Strathern, M. 1991. *Partial Connections*. Lanham, MD: Rowman and Littlefield.

_____. 1999. *Property, Substance and Affect*. London: Athlone Press.

Szakolczai, A. 2016. *Permanent Liminality and Modernity: Analysing the Sacrificial Carnival through Novels*. London: Routledge.

Taylor, C. 1992. *Multiculturalism and the Politics of Recognition*, ed. A. Gutman. Princeton, NJ: Princeton University Press.

Thomassen, B. 2014. *Liminality and the Modern: Living through the In-Between*. London: Routledge.

Thompson, E. P. 1978. "The Poverty of Theory: Or an Orrery of Errors." In *The Poverty of Theory & Other Essays*, ed. E. P. Thompson, 193–399. London: Merlin.

_____. 1991. *The Making of the English Working Class*. Harmondsworth, UK: Penguin.

Thompson, M. 2017. *Rubbish Theory: The Creation and Destruction of Value*. Chicago, IL: Chicago University Press.

Topçu, S. 2008. "Confronting Nuclear Risks: Counter-Expertise as Politics within the French Nuclear Energy Debate." *Nature and Culture* 3(2): 225–45.

Tsing, A. 2013. "Supply Chains and the Human Condition." *Rethinking Marxism: A Journal of Economics, Culture & Society* 21(2): 148–76.

_____ . 2015. *The Mushroom at the End of the World: On the Possibility of Life in Capitalist Ruins.* Princeton, NJ: Princeton University Press.

Tuckett, D. 2011. *Minding the Markets: An Emotional Finance View of Financial Instability.* New York: Palgrave Macmillan.

Turner, S. 2012 *Politics of Innocence: Hutu Identity, Conflict and Camp Life.* New York: Berghahn.

Turner, V. 1967. "Betwixt and Between: The Liminal Period in '*Rites de Passage*'." In *The Forest of Symbols*, 93–111. New York: Cornell University Press.

UNHCR. 2016. *UNHCR: Global Trends, Forced Displacement in 2016.* Retrieved 17 May 2018 from http://www.unhcr.org/5943e8a34.pdf.

Vaccaro, I., K. Harper, and S. Murray, eds. 2015. *The Anthropology of Postindustralism: Ethnographies of Disconnection.* London: Routledge.

Verdery, K., and M. Burawoy, eds. 1996. *Uncertain Transition: Ethnographies of Change in the Postsocialist World.* Lanham, MD: Rowman and Littlefield.

Viney, W. 2014. *Waste: A Philosophy of Things.* London: Bloomsbury.

Wacquant, L. 2010. "Urban Desolation and Symbolic Denigration in the Hyperghetto." *Social Psychology Quarterly* 73 (3): 215–19.

WHO. 2017. *World Health Statistics 2017: Monitoring Health for the SDGs.* Retrieved 17 May 2018 from http://www.who.int/gho/publications/world_health_statistics/2017/en/.

Widger, T. and A, Russell, eds. 2018. "Ambivalent Objects in Global Health", Special issue of *Journal of Material Culture* 23(4).

Willen, S. 2007. "Toward a Critical Phenomenology of 'Illegality' State, Power, Criminalization and Abjectivity among Undocumented Migrant Workers in Tel Aviv, Israel." *International Migration* 45(3): 8–38.

Williams, R. 1997. *Hegel's Ethics of Recognition*, Berkeley: California University Press.

Wittgenstein, L. 2001 [1953]. *Philosophical Investigations.* Malden, MA: Blackwell.

Wynne, B. 1992. "Uncertainty and Environmental Learning: Reconceiving Science and Policy in the Preventive Paradigm." *Global Environmental Change* 2(2): 111–27.

_____ . 1997. "Methodology and Institutions: Value as Seen from the Risk Field." In *Valuing Nature? Economics Ethics and Environment*, ed. J. Foster, 135–52. London: Routledge.

Yates, M. 2011. "The Human-as-waste, the Labor Theory of Value, and Disposability in Contemporary Capitalism." *Antipode* 43(5): 1679–95.

Yarrow, T. 2017. "Remains of the Future: Rethinking the Space and Time of Ruination through the Volta Resettlement Project, Ghana." *Cultural Anthropology* 32(4): 566–91.

Yurchak, A. 2005. *Everything Was Forever, Until It Was No More: The Last Soviet Generation.* Princeton, NJ: Princeton University Press.

Zaloom, C. 2004. "The Productive Life of Risk." *Cultural Anthropology* 19 (3): 365–91.

Žižek. S. 2012. *The Year of Dreaming Dangerously.* Oxford: Blackwell.

1

Kept in Suspense
The Unsettling Indeterminacy of US Landfills

Joshua O. Reno

Interpreters ignore the fragment. They see it as change.
—Keith Faulkner, *The Force of Time*

Discussions of waste frequently rely on the prefix *re-* from the Latin meaning a repetition or return. One recycles, reduces, and reuses waste, of course, but also rejects, redeems, revalues, restores, renovates, reclaims, and regenerates it. This suggests an underlying teleology that is at once temporal and moral. Both in the waste management and policy literature and in anthropology and beyond, waste materials are often taken to be the fragment of some pre-existing totality. Consider a discarded refrigerator. A thoughtful interpreter could take a material culture approach, recognizing that things are made meaningful by their social context, and relate that individual object back to a whole kitchen, a home, and a family, for what is a refrigerator without those associations? Our interpreter could also take a political economy approach and recognize the refrigerator as a commodity, part of a store and a brand, a factory and a labor process, a corporation, its shareholders, sales and marketing team, and capitalism, for what is the commodity without all of these associations to which it belongs? Finally, our interpreter could think through a critical ecological approach and recognize the refrigerator as an artifact made of components, mined and mixed, deracinated from their geological and environmental origins and eventually destined to break down and mix with new landscapes, biologies, and ecologies. There are more possible directions, all of them interpreting that refrigerator as a single step in an analytical journey, from the fragment it is to the role it played as part of a whole, and whatever it will be in the future.

Such analytical journeys begin with a decision that opens up some paths of inquiry and avoids others. I want to argue that describing waste objects as they travel into and out of alternative sociocultural contexts and economic spheres, or as they are extracted from nature as resources only to return as pollutants, potentially denudes waste practices of their open-endedness or indeterminacy at that moment before the fragment is something new and after it is no longer what it was (see Povinelli 2011). I will discuss this based on ethnographic consideration of a landfill in southeastern Michigan where I worked for a time as a professional "paper picker" as well as historical consideration of other infamous landfills such as the one in Love Canal, New York, together with landfill and waste regulations as they have changed in recent years in the United States in general.[1]

In this chapter, I will explain how it is that landfills suspend waste fragments from participating in totalities, be they economic, environmental, or political. This means understanding how indeterminacy can both exceed and achieve human objectives and analyses. They do so as part of a modern engineering solution to improve the human condition—landfills are meant to protect human and nonhuman beings and places from being contaminated by what the former dispose of. Suspension is a containment strategy, but that does not mean it is always effective. To the extent that landfills leak into their surroundings, they are potentially exposing a few unlucky workers and inhabitants to the concentrated wastes of many others.

Fragments and Wholes

As a paper picker, part of my job was to identify bits of rubbish on the side of the road to collect. These spilled out of the tractor-trailers that ceaselessly hauled waste loads, sometimes from very great distances, to be dumped at our site. Before paper pickers arrive on the scene to send litter to the landfill, roadside trash can be interpreted in many different ways and evoke multiple, even incommensurable values. Consider a piece of wrapper, leftover packaging, on the side of the road.

It can be a congealed source of economic value. This means it can be traced to profits, wages, inequalities, production processes, and so forth. Within recycling industries, waste can become part of altogether new forms of accounting and valuation (Alexander and Reno 2012). All of these possibilities speak to the dominant storytelling tendency of capitalism, which is to translate everything into money (see D. Pedersen 2013). But for US landfills, these stories are of no account, it is the labor of waste workers that is economically valued and, hence, carefully managed. If I did not pick paper fast enough, if I did not fill "enough" bags with roadside trash, if I were caught taking a break, my coworkers and I would be disciplined by our supervisors. Of course, this also meant that if we got away with doing any of these things, we scored a minor victory by being paid a wage for little or no labor.

One of the reasons managers would become perturbed by visible roadside trash was that county and state inspectors might stop by at any time and observe these as environmental violations. For them, the wrapper can be a risk to, or affordance for, humans and nonhumans as well. Waste on nearby road-sides is assumed to have migrated from the landfill either directly or indirectly. It might have caught on the wind, or become wedged in the wheels of an exiting vehicle. It might have tumbled out of a visiting dump truck before its load was deposited on site. The danger of such stray waste is not just that nonhuman creatures may try to consume it or dwell within it (wrappers may be found as part of a bird's nest or rodent burrow, for instance).[2] Worse, from a regulator's perspective, it may break down and release its potentially toxic materials into the water that people drink, the air they breathe, or the soil where they grow their food.

That wrapper can also be a technique or object of power/knowledge. If someone other than the paper picker feels compelled to pick it up, this might be a reaction to anti-littering campaigns and policies, which tend to target the individual environmental subject (Reno 2016: 172). These come from state initiatives, but they are also internalized. Around the landfill where I worked, for example, homeowners tend to keep clean and well-kept yards and judged others who do not. One of the most unpopular businesses on the main road to the landfill was a junkyard, which was littered with its own debris that would sometimes drift beyond the property boundaries. The junkyard owners may not have worried about how they appeared to others, or might have possessed alternative aesthetic standards. Occasionally, there would be less to pick on the roadside by paper pickers because a well-meaning neighbor picked up some litter that had fallen in their driveway or yard. Sometimes litter migrated so far into someone's yard that we worried we would be trespassing or would upset dogs if we got close to the house. A sense of environmental responsibility can also be imposed. It could issue from volunteer citizen organizations (my first

Figure 1.1. Sweet wrapper, photo by Si Griffiths. Printed with permission.

experiences of roadside picking were as a Boy Scout volunteer on the annual Environmental Cleanup Day). There is also legally mandated, paper picking community service work, typically on highways where paper pickers and locals may fear to go.

Any one of these meanings and values are plausible and each is associated with distinct analytical directions and practical decisions. Would-be ethnographers are only limited by their imagination and that of their informants.

When compared to a piece of litter on the side of the road, where possibilities abound, landfills represent an engineering solution intended to reduce possibilities, to stifle what we might otherwise imagine possible (Reno 2016). Imagine standing atop a landfill and knowing that somewhere beneath your feet lies buried a wrapper, identical to the one in the former example.

A thought often occurred to me: bits of trash I had collected as a paper picker were now encased within a mountain of waste. What had I really done but moved it from one place to another? Well, this is not such a small act. As the landfill management and environmental regulators would tell us, not all places are equivalent, and that act of transfer has real implications for the possible relations that old wrapper can participate in, including how it can (and cannot) be analyzed by anthropologists, sanitary engineers, regulatory inspectors, and activists.

Considered from an economic or accounting perspective, waste objects are external—used-up products with no or limited utility. That piece of litter may

Figure 1.2. Open face of a landfill, photo by Ashley Felton. Printed with permission.

be reclaimed by an informal recycler for cash or repurposed by an incinerator for heat, its value partly (but never completely) restored. Considered from an environmental perspective, waste is a polluting artifact of human invention—nature turned anti-nature through bodily and machine labor. This is why landfills dispatch paper pickers, so that the polluting effects of pieces of litter are mitigated, lest they rejoin and disrupt the (comparatively stable) ecologies from whence they came. Considered from a sociological or anthropological perspective, waste consists of who or what does not belong—classified as unnecessary, unholy, abject—this can be a landfill, a junkyard, their material contents, or the people who work with them (Douglas [1966] 2002; Alexander and Sanchez this volume). Whether one considers the ability of a sacrificial expenditure to link sacred and profane, or the movement of goods across regimes of value, cultural waste appears most relevant when it is re-signified (erasing its prior meaning) within a new social, linguistic, or ritual context. In each case, a moment of renewal is invested with special significance by an implicit teleology. Of interest is what becomes of waste fragments once they come to regenerate pollution, profit, or meaning.

In this sense, waste resembles money, which is also often reduced to a means and measure of exchange relations, its practical qualities lost as analysis is sped up to address the more encompassing wholes to which it gives rise (class structure, the market, capitalism, and so on). Slowing analysis down can mean, for example, taking seriously payment as a practice that can be done in many different ways fulfilling many different agendas (Maurer 2015). This is about not only the tendency to scale-up money to larger totalities beyond those of practical action, but also the ways that anthropologists have tended to imagine reciprocity as a closed circuit whose meaningful fulfillment awaits a return, regardless of its scale of operation. With waste, as with money, it can be revealing to slow down analysis, to acknowledge the suspension of repetition and return, or to delay the seemingly inevitable reintegration of the fragment within a new whole.

If waste is considered nothing more than the bad fragment of a lost whole, or as the beginning of an emergent whole, it can be difficult to appreciate the productivity of indeterminacy. This is particularly true of those moments when waste, whether of human or nonhuman origin, is suspended between totalities, sometimes for strategic purposes. In this chapter, I will consider suspension as a particular kind of work that brackets both material relations and imaginative possibilities. Suspension, in the words of Maurice Blanchot, makes manifest the violence and poetry of the fragment:

> Whoever says fragment ought not to say simply the fragmenting of an already existing reality or the moment of a whole still to come. This is hard to envisage due to the necessity of comprehension according to which the only knowledge is knowledge of the whole ... For such comprehension, the fragment supposes an implied designation of something that has previously been or will subsequently be a whole—the severed finger refers back to the hand, just as the first atom prefigures and contains in itself the

universe. Our thought is therefore caught between two limits: the imagining of the integrity of substance and the imagining of dialectical becoming. (1993: 307)[3]

Our tendency as thinkers and writers, according to Blanchot, is to think in terms of integrated wholes and, failing that, to think in terms of their inevitable reenactment. Substantive totalities (e.g., economy, society, nature, and so on) may be called upon less than they once were (Knauft 2006); yet the widespread use of more processual substitutes (e.g., economization, sociality, dwelling, and others) suggest our analytical need to perpetually reenact lost totalities in practice, as if to make up for their absence. Governing, profiting from, and critiquing waste management typically means projecting an image of a self-contained sphere of production, ecological system, or social context. Were these spheres not self-contained in some sense, arguably, it would make no sense to speak of distinct "ecologies," "economies," or "societies" in the first place (see Alexander and Reno 2012). Typically, waste is cast as a fragment lost to some totality, fated to reunite with another. Continuity does not mean harmony, however. The totality to which a waste fragment becomes newly attached may bear the scars of this separation and reunion (see Alexander this volume). This is most obvious in the case of the toxicity of slow pollution (Nixon 2011) where some form of discard rejoins ecological relations only to damage them, perhaps irreparably.

In analyses of waste, the choice is only ever which new whole a fragment will (re)join, never whether it will do so. A decontextualized fragment is thought significant only insofar as it is destined to be recontextualized in some way. This presupposes two wholes joined in a teleological series: one to be detached from and one to be reattached to. Scrapped industry waste is a fragment that can either be recovered at a profit or at a loss, but either way is re-economized as one entry among others on an accounting balance sheet. For environmental groups, waste is a fragment that may or may not be hazardous pollution, but either way is renaturalized as one additional source of harm to ecological balance, among other things. In either case, it is not a question of whether it will be profitable or costly, harmful or benign, only how the scales will tip.

Blanchot admonishes us to appreciate the emptiness of time, the nihilist insight that it lacks a perfect linear narrative. Without a teleology to count on, or account for, we appreciate fragments as they truly are, unpredictable. Keith Faulkner (2008) adds that the fragmentation of time, or its lack of substantive unity, better approximates how human engagement with indeterminate materials, and often with one another, actually feels—there are no guarantees, no sure paths. Graham Harman (2009, 2011) makes a complementary argument in his call for a non-relational metaphysics—usually glossed as an object-oriented ontology—which does not reduce objects to any parts or wholes to which they relate or might relate. This puts Harman directly at odds with many adherents of the ontological turn in anthropology who, according to Morton Axel Pedersen (2012), share a "heuristic" tendency to bracket any assumption "that the object of anthropological analysis is comprised by separate, bounded and extensive units." For Harman, in contrast, all objects are genuine fragments, as Blanchot defines them, and reducible neither to their constituents nor to whatever wholes they may (or may not) relationally compose. Not only are they separate in actuality from what they are composed of, from one another, and from any encompassing whole, but they are never encountered as whole substances themselves. Even when relating to other entities, any entity is always partly withdrawn from the relationship, the entirety of its being in some way concealed from the action. Here Harman reveals his debt to Martin Heidegger's analysis of tool-being. Describing anything in terms of "potentiality" or "virtuality" obscures being in favor of possible relations and greater totalities: "in what sense is an oak tree 'already' in an acorn?" Harman asks. "Only in the sense that the acorn contains *actual* features that get the first set of translations underway on the long and winding road to the oak. To say that something has potential is to define it in terms of the other things that it might someday affect" (2009: 128; emphasis in original).

An acorn is an apt example to demonstrate the poetry and violence of indeterminacy, in Blanchot's sense. As a vessel for one or a few seeds, any acorn can become a tree, but often they do not. Michael Marder (2013: 87–90) makes this clear in his account of seeds as exemplary of the troubling nature of vegetal life. As he points out, individual seeds are normally unproductive for the plant; they have no guarantee of teleological fulfillment in the form of a tree, nor even as nutrition for another creature. Rather than dirt, which is the most popular substantive metaphor for waste following Douglas ([1966] 2002), any waste fragment might more usefully be imagined as a seed, that is, a pluripotent, material deposit with an uncertain future (see Reno 2014). Considering waste as a fragment means slowing down analysis and contemplating that moment when the outcome is still unclear. This means not only that we are not sure which direction to go, analytically speaking, but also that there may be no totality to come, that we are guaranteed no resolution to what the fragment means or what effect it will have in the world.

Landfills in the United States consist of a vast collection of small, relatively unimportant fragments and partake of indeterminacy in telling ways. Landfills are designed to bury waste materials precisely so that they will exist in a state of permanent suspension apart from systems of economic, cultural, and ecological value. This means producing a site that is inherently unstable, one which begets unruly biosocial transformations that cannot be fully controlled or predicted (Hird 2012). Appreciating the power of fragments in suspension, she argues, helps us to understand indeterminate suspension as a strategy. It also helps make clear the powerfully felt double bind that confronts environmental justice activists. On the one hand, they cannot ignore the presence of potentially troublesome fragments of different size and significance (Gille 2013). On the other hand, it is impossible to resist them effectively without rendering them determinate. For landfills, exploring the uses of indeterminacy reveals both the limits of human comprehension and control and its simultaneous success as a political tactic.

The Suspended Animation of Waste Fragments

For something to be considered waste, "render[s] the indeterminate determinate" (Hird 2012: 454). But the indeterminacy of a form can be taken in at least two ways (Staten 1986; see also Alexander and Sanchez this volume). On the one hand, an object may be indefinite, meaning that human attempts to know what it is, what its material components are, and what it is capable of are incomplete or inexact. For example, contemporary astronomers are not sure whether the strange data retrieved from the distant star KIC 8462852 is a result of an alien superstructure, meteors, or some other unknown phenomenon. Its formlessness, therefore, has more to do with the limits of human capacities than with the actual characteristics of the thing itself. On the other hand, it may be that an actual thing is indeterminate because, even if it is more or less understood by human beings, it is inherently unpredictable. For example, if an acorn drops to the ground, there is no way to know for sure at that moment whether it will become a tree, no matter how much we know about that particular acorn or acorns in general. This kind of indeterminacy is about how things change over time and about the inherent force of time as such (Hägglund 2008). In short, the first kind of indeterminacy concerns limited capacities to know what is, and the second concerns inescapable unpredictability about what might happen.

According to Myra Hird (2012) waste management involves political and technological attempts to control indeterminacy, in both senses of the term:

> [L]andfilling, and waste management generally, introduces a resilient tension between determinacy and indeterminacy. The indeterminacy—the heterogeneous, unique mix of each landfill material intra-acting with seasons, weather, precipitation, the varying angles of the sun's rays bombarding landfill material and so on—means the management of waste ultimately fails. Fails to be contained, fails to be predictable, fails to be calculable, fails to be a technological problem (that can be eliminated), fails to be determinate. (2012: 465)

Hird associates the failure to know what waste is, to determine it, with the failure to predict what will become of it. This brings epistemology into conflict with the elusive ontology of what she terms the "inhuman"; the failure to control and manage waste, moreover, means we cannot rationally manage human society or its environmental impacts. The importance of indeterminacy, as defined by Hird, is evident at the level of bureaucratic oversight. Moreover, as I will argue below, waste generating and managing firms are typically aware of this.

Partly in response to controversies concerning earlier forms of landfills—especially the Love Canal incident, which I will discuss further below—the US Congress passed the Resource Conservation and Recovery Act (RCRA) in 1976, which has governed waste management ever since. Contemporary US landfills demonstrate the multiple kinds of indeterminacy at issue when waste fragments are examined in suspension, whether contained in a landfill or let loose in the world. Landfills specialize in keeping wastes from changing in undesirable ways, that is, in preventing them from partaking of new and forbidden totalities we might yet imagine, whether environmental, economic, or political.

In Subtitle D, RCRA attempts to limit the indefiniteness of landfilled waste by requiring the implementation of water, gas, odor, and leachate monitoring protocols. Each of these measures requires that waste management firms purchase technical equipment and hire staff with sufficient technical training to satisfy the Environmental Protection Agency's standards. And yet, the ideal design of a landfill is meant to conceal waste from being closely observed or experienced. Unlike an unregulated dump, RCRA requires that landfills use liners to prevent waste and "garbage juice" from migrating into the soil and aquifer, and also that they cover waste with enough layers of dirt to conceal its decomposition from humans who might be disturbed by its presence and non-human life forms who might be drawn to it. Landfills are designed to bury and bind waste so that creatures cannot get at it, so that people cannot see or smell it, and so that the surrounding environment does not absorb the solid waste buried within, does not take in the gas it produces, and does not soak up the liquid it leaches. In a landfill, in other words, waste is meant to become a non-relational fragment in suspension.

The act of suspension could be said to transfer the risks and dangers from others onto waste workers, precisely by combining fragments into the landfill itself, an unholy union of fragments and quasi-totality of its own (Catherine Alexander pers. comm.). But this ideal of suspension can lead to internal contradictions. This is most obvious in terms of the labor process. Substances like garbage juice or leachate do not exist apart from human beings concentrating their waste in one location and leaving it to leach material into its surroundings. What this means is not only that waste materials change, but that the people who work with them are exposed to emergent and potentially more offensive and dangerous materials and processes. My coworkers feared getting bad smells on their bodies and taking them home. But they also worried about getting sick, about catching fire, or being struck by one of the giant machines needed to stack and compact the waste into the shape of a hill.

Hird argues that as socio-technical projects, landfills are also meant to be known and, in that sense, related to, managed, and regulated. However, accounting for how their materials might unpredictably affect other beings or mingle with their natural surroundings means making their contents harder to know and experience. Consider leachate monitoring. In order to know whether a landfill is leaching garbage juice into the aquifer, monitoring wells are dug in strategic places around the site. Samples are taken periodically, often by third parties, to determine whether there are any traces of leachate at higher than acceptable levels. But to definitively determine such a calculation, one would ideally know as much as possible about the characteristics of the leachate regularly produced by the landfill, its normal state, so to speak. Otherwise, what may appear to be "normal" water may mask abnormal substances that are not being tested for. Whether one samples leachate from the landfill or channels it into separate collection areas in the open air, dealing with the indefiniteness of the landfill's products means violating the goal of containing them.

RCRA was implemented in order to stop leachate from contaminating groundwater or odors and methane from permeating the atmosphere, thereby disrupting the careful balance involved in normal hydrological and oxygenation cycles. In this sense, landfills are an artificial cage, harnessing soil cover, plastic lines, retention ponds, human and machine labor, all for the purpose of trapping waste in place and preventing it from rejoining nature or society. As material artifacts, wastes are the congealed leftovers of human labor upon nature, but now are banished to prevent a forbidden reunion. In suspended animation, they are ideally prevented from reentering local surroundings, bodies, and transformations. As the leachate example demonstrates, however, this is impossible to perfectly execute in practice. Managing a landfill involves the Sisyphean task of concealing waste fragments from engaging in forbidden socionatural relations, which paradoxically requires engaging in more labor to manipulate and know about that which ought to be concealed. This is a problem not only for private firms, but also for public regulators and the people they represent, as I will discuss further below.

In the United States, landfills are not only a product of regulatory oversight to prevent pollution, but also an economic activity pursued for the sake of profit. This suspends waste fragments in yet another way: removing salvageable goods from circulation back onto the market from whence they came. At many US landfills, since their inception in the 1930s, scavenging from the rubbish is formally forbidden, though normally tolerated so long as it does not interfere with the work of waste disposal. Ultimately, however, one cannot possibly engage in the systematic burial of so many loads of waste every day and simultaneously pause to sort through and salvage everything worth saving. This would mean burying less waste in the landfill per hour of work, which would reduce the ability of the waste firm to bury as much waste as possible in as little space and as little time as possible, and thus extract a profit from their investment in air space, workers, and machines. Therefore, even when limited scavenging is performed or allowed, landfills foreclose scavenging in a way that open air dumps do not. Waste fragments are not only formally suspended from reintegration into the environment, with uneven success, but also revaluated as primary goods in the marketplace. As with the ecological totality, furthermore, the effect is similar: prices and profits in the marketplace remain more stable due to the absence of a more robust market in secondhand goods retrieved from the waste stream.

A landfill can also take advantage of indeterminacy to promote an image of a renewable operation. This is done by controlling which fragments are re-ecologized and re-economized. Under RCRA, landfills must find a way to manage their release of methane gas, which is a powerful greenhouse gas and air contaminant. Neighbors of the landfill would routinely complain about the unpleasant odors that emanated from the site, sometimes calling regulators and getting the landfill warned or fined. Many landfills flare off gas in order to alter it before it enters the atmosphere. Another solution is to redirect gas into a power plant and generate electricity to use locally or sell on the grid. This is selective capture of what would otherwise be a regulated pollutant, for which many landfills in Europe and the United States are increasingly rewarded. So long as solid waste is kept in suspension, the reuse of selective byproducts like biogas is considered a worthy endeavor, recycling what would otherwise go to waste, and therefore constituting a "renewable" energy source. But turning some of the gas released into energy does not finally make the indeterminate determinate. This translation of gas to energy can lead to other forms of unforeseen "contamination" of human-nonhuman encounter (Tsing 2015: 28). At another, older and capped legacy landfill site in Four Corners, Michigan, the ongoing recovery of biogas would occasionally be disrupted when local cows would wander atop the slope to graze and disconnect a gas line. The successful imitation of a grassy, gassy hill, which landfill designs aim for, can unintentionally attract nonhumans intent on satisfying their own needs. As critics typically point out, the fact that the exact contents of landfills cannot be accounted for means that it is never certain what is being burned up in power plants and what additional environmental impact might result. As with leachate, without a complete and accurate depiction of what lies suspended beneath the surface, any gas that is captured will only ever represent a partial glimpse into the landfill's ceaseless productivity. Furthermore, it is inevitable that some gas will be lost to the collection system and be released into the atmosphere, given the impossibility of completely harnessing and making visible what has been so assiduously concealed.

Hird is correct: landfilling cannot hope to manage the unpredictable and inhuman possibilities of waste fragments. And yet, the reason for this is not solely due to epistemological arrogance, an assertion of knowledge over and against the natural world. It has to do with the ways in which landfills attempt to suspend waste fragments, to conceal them and thus render their destinies indeterminate, like seeds one hoards away and stockpiles, not allowing them to be planted or digested. Landfills paradoxically attempt to reduce all possibilities, but in so doing manufacture new risks and entanglements that cannot be fully known and, importantly, may never come to pass in the first place: workers may or may not get sick or catch fire, leachate may or may not migrate beyond the liner boundary and enter the drinking water.

Suspended Disbelief and Environmental Politics

By cordoning off waste, landfills attempt to avoid and harness the indeterminate environmental and economic effects that waste fragments might produce. But the waste industry accomplishes concealment of waste fragments in yet another way. There are few people who work at a landfill, and few landfills at which to work, especially as the cost of satisfying regulations requires that they grow in size to remain profitable (Thomson 2009). Moreover, these sites are located farther and farther from the people who produce the waste that is buried. Waste crosses county, state, and national borders, as landfill-laden and typically rural communities in Pennsylvania, Michigan, and Virginia accumulate the waste of many other states. There is a sense, in other words, that landfills also suspend waste fragments from being repoliticized and reproblematized by the polities and communities that produce them. In a sense, human communities are prevented from coming into being, which might otherwise form alliances, protest waste industry methods, and seek alternative ways of living, precisely because most are not affected. The environmental justice literature has made clear that exposure to the harms and nuisances of waste sites is unevenly distributed depending on race, class, and locality (Pellow 2007). For instance, the Four Corners landfill was originally planned for a whiter and wealthier community, but due to successful protests by local residents, the landfill ended up in a more rural, more impoverished, and more African-American community instead. When I worked there, most of the waste came from Canada. It was prevented from going to First Nation lands in northern Ontario and only stopped coming to Michigan when an alternative First Nation group agreed to take the waste in southern Ontario (Reno 2016). Landfills hoard seeds that are never meant to grow. But landfills do flourish in select locations, typically following the path of least resistance so that their unchecked indeterminacy does not lead to widespread political scandal. Scandal could occur just as easily as economic opportunity or environmental disruption do.

Indeterminate, meaning incomplete, knowledge may limit material interventions in the physical world, but does not thereby necessarily represent a limit to political control (Anand 2015). Shortly after the publication of Hird's argument, Zsuza Gille (2013) published a rebuttal. For one thing, Gille argued that there are many kinds of knowing, not only forms that endeavor to make waste and the environment manageable for disposal. More importantly, Gille added a warning that a scholarly embrace of waste's purported indeterminacy can render political and environmental justice critique impotent:

> Toxic wastes, nuclear wastes, and a host of industrial by-products are actually quite determinate: while they may never be fully known in some theoretical sense, we certainly know *enough* about the dangers some of them or some of their key components pose. The question is not whether they are made determinate but whether they are made determinate enough to warrant regulation. Producers of waste, however, are interested in keeping the exact composition, the exact effects, and the exact amount of these by-products unknown. (Gille 2013: 4; emphasis in original)

It may be in the interest of producers of waste to keep these details unknown so that they can avoid blame if harm is done or legal action against them is taken. For Gille, the suspension of waste from additional political or social oversight can make not knowing a political tactic. If those few who do live in proximity to waste sites wish to politicize the risks and nuisances they encounter, the careful concealment of waste and the indeterminacy this leads to may frustrate their efforts and maintain the power of large waste firms.

This is not only about flawed human representation, i.e., about indeterminacy as indefiniteness. As Hird argued in her response to Gille, not knowing waste is not only a tactic of powerful actors, but also reflects the fact that the possibilities of waste can never be fully predicted, regardless of good or bad faith on the part of industries or regulators: "While landfills and other techno-scientific ways of dealing with waste may have profound consequences for human health and the environment, these life forms are largely indifferent to our (human) political machinations concerning waste" (2013: 31). As Hird points out, not only does the unpredictability of the nonhuman environment exceed our attempts to manage waste fragments, but so too does that of human health. The indeterminacy of pollution events combines the unknowable with the unpredictable, because the growth of a human body, like the health of an environment involves probabilistic, nonlinear processes (Adam 1998; Alexander 2009, forthcoming).

Even when careful, in-depth study is undertaken to investigate the relationship between landfills and health impacts, it can be difficult to definitively prove a link. Love Canal is perhaps the most famous environmental disaster in North American history. In the 1920s, an unfinished canal between the upper and lower Niagara Rivers in western New York State, was turned into an industrial and chemical dump. Thirty years later it was covered over with soil and turned into a working-class residential community, and, by the late 1970s, toxic materials could be seen and smelled leaching into homes, schools, and the water supply. Love Canal eventually gained nationwide notoriety as the first of many Superfund sites. These are legal constructs that were introduced around the same time as RCRA so that the Environmental Protection Agency (EPA) could help clean up contaminated sites through federal oversight. Residents of Love Canal also began to notice an unusual rate of premature births, low-weight births, and birth defects. Their suspicions have been verified by repeated epidemiological studies over the ensuing decades (Austin et al. 2011; Paigen et al. 1987), and yet, these epidemiologists and anthropologists continue to warn that any results warrant extreme caution, given the few number of incidents in such cases and the difficulty establishing relationships between pollution events and health outcomes with so many intervening factors. This kind of indeterminacy was not planned by the Hooker Chemical Company, who originally sold the covered canal to the city, but Gille is right that this kind of indeterminacy is frequently used by polluting industries and inept regulators to avoid blame.

In another sense, regulations proliferate their own indeterminacies, and thus become the site of additional political contestation. As part of RCRA's Subtitle C, the EPA must define what counts as "hazardous waste" in order to regulate its proper disposal, but as recently as 2008, there were efforts to change the rule in order to make businesses more profitable and encourage more "recycling." For something to be hazardous waste, it must be classified as a solid waste, rather than a recyclate. The 2008 rule change broadened what could be excluded from the category of solid waste. In other words, what had previously been considered solid waste might no longer be. That meant it could no longer be considered hazardous waste, which meant it no longer had to be as costly or risky to eliminate or sell. Moreover, each individual state has the authority to create more restrictive rules than the EPA's; businesses can theoretically exploit, and waste regulators must negotiate, what counts as "recyclable" in interstate and international exchanges. A waste generator could satisfy regulatory goals, claiming to have made the indeterminate determinate, all while benefitting from the built-in indeterminacy at the core of government oversight.

Waste regulations thus help determine which totality waste fragments will seem destined for the domain of the economic, the domain of the ecological, or some ideal, green-capitalist hybrid. But the mutability of their rules belies any assumption of teleological inevitability. The 2008 change in the solid waste rule ultimately led to a lawsuit, filed against the EPA by the Sierra Club, to make the category of solid waste less broad and prevent "sham recycling" operations from labeling hazardous waste disposal a form of recycling. The suit was successful and in 2015 a more restrictive rule was put in place. Yet indeterminacy has not vanished at the regulatory level, it has only become more layered, as waste generators now must negotiate the indeterminacy of rule shifts.

Just as indeterminacy exists in the temporal disjuncture associated with regulatory change, it also exists in the interstices between regulatory bodies. The Department of Transportation (DOT) governs the shipment of waste loads, their proper labeling and handling, which can put them at odds with the EPA. Specifically, the DOT and EPA differ in the criteria used to determine whether a container that formerly held waste can be characterized as formally "empty." In other words, whether or not waste even exists can change depending on a shift in regulatory oversight, based on different concerns associated with what might become of waste should it exist.

Despite their unknowability and unpredictability, landfills and waste fragments are still regularly politicized, whether or not their materials leak into surrounding communities and environments (Reno 2011). The possibility that they might do so, in keeping with the dubious legacy of Love Canal, is enough to raise concerns on the part of neighboring residents. Gille's concerns become all the more relevant in these cases. There are believed to be many more Love Canals that have not yet come to light, historical and contemporary landfills whose management falls short of regulatory ideals, or regulatory oversights that have not yet been sufficiently scrutinized. Because the relationships between these landfills and the health of former and current residents living in proximity to them remain indeterminate in both senses—unknown and unknowable.

Conclusion

For Hird, environmental regulation and waste management are about the uncertain impact of waste fragments on the surrounding, inhuman environment. That there will be some environmental reckoning is not in question. For Gille, this threatens the success of efforts to politicize waste for the purposes of human social justice, that political inequality will be at issue is not in question. In both cases, concerns are amplified because of all the environmental, political, and economic transformation that waste is certainly capable of, albeit to an uncertain degree. At the little-known landfill where I worked, and infamous landfills like Love Canal, one can readily find examples that support both arguments.

Like any seed, however, though risks and possibilities abound, none may necessarily come to fruition. If it seems counterintuitive that waste fragments might fail to be economized, politicized, ecologized, it is helpful to consider why. Today the economic, the environmental, and the political in many ways appear to be irreducible totalities, in the way that the social arguably once was in a previously Durkheimian era. This may be the legacy of global capitalism, the Anthropocene, and the nation-state, that no fragment could fail to become part of an encompassing whole that bestows upon it its true and ultimate meaning. There are good reasons to see everything and everyone as fragments of these pervasive and ever-present wholes. Yet, it is worth noting, first, that these accounts will always rest on the same shaky epistemological foundations as does waste management in Hird's view. There will always be an indeterminate gap, an uncertainty, and an unpredictability that complicates any good story. When impressive totalities appear to arise—globally altered climates, globally widespread markets, national regulations—it cannot be assumed that every individual fragment relates to them at all, much less that they relate to them in the same way.

Respect for the indeterminacy, the poetry and violence, of a waste object or any fragment demands that we accept the radical possibility for things to be other than we expect. There is a decisive analytical advantage that issues from teleological certainty. It makes it easier for the analyst to claim the primacy of the direction they took as opposed to others. What should not be lost here, however, is that a direction was taken, meaning a decision was made or a set of possibilities were traced, while others were suspended from consideration. Every distinct analysis contains waste in some way, productively reduces its open-endedness, rather like a landfill. Just as every landfill may leak, no analysis is as complete as it purports to be.

Just because rubbish is encased in a landfill, ideally suspended from further relations, does not mean it has no impact on its surroundings. It only does so, however, as part of a different object, the landfill itself, which it conjoins. Consider the piece of wrapper encased in a landfill with which we began. Despite its relative stasis, trapped between many other wasted fragments, it is still part of various relationships. Its existence in the landfill has generated profits for the landfill owner (a tiny fraction of which are used to employ paper pickers). But for all intents and purposes, it is defined by being non-economic, by no longer creating value except insofar as it has been weighed and buried as abstract negative value. Its very burial has meant that there are attempts to monitor what contributions its hidden breakdown might make to the surrounding environment. But for all the exciting things it may yet do, it is in suspension for the moment and cannot be held responsible for climate change or for toxic contamination, except insofar as it loses all individuality as part of an encompassing totality: the regulated abstract risk of the landfill as a whole. Finally, its burial has had a political impact on the person who discarded it, who depends on waste removal and disposal infrastructure to live a life free of the wastes they generate. They may even feel like they have made the right decision, as a political subject, tossing a plastic wrapper in a bin instead of out the window like a common litterer. In this sense, it is indistinguishable in its individuality from everything else routinely tossed, hauled away, and landfilled, except insofar as it is part of encompassing infrastructure provisioned by public and private sources to send waste elsewhere.

Note that just because the wrapper is made a component of the landfill, its economic, environmental, and political possibilities are no more transparent or predictable, whether for the purposes of management, regulation, or political contestation. Moreover, the wrapper is no more reducible to the landfill it is added to then the landfill is to it. If, during a future landfill excavation, that wrapper is let loose and once again blows freely into the road, the whole landfill will not have changed, nor will the wrapper be decidedly different than it was encased alongside other bits of rubbish. Some materials can lie dormant in landfills for years with negligible change to their qualities: I saw pieces of newspaper emerge perfectly readable and heard about old video cassettes that were played. Even organic substances may fail to break down without sufficient microbial growth. The emergent totality of the landfill, as composite object, need not fundamentally change the fragments of which it is composed. As Harman argues:

> [T]here is no reason to think that all objects find themselves in such relations at any given moment. While it is true that a real object arises from a descending chain of countless smaller components, it does not follow that it must also enter further relations as a component of larger objects: just as an animal's long unbroken list of ancestors does not mean that it will reproduce successfully in its own right. (Harman 2011: 122)

The point is not to suggest that the waste trapped in landfills is harmless or vital materials are in actuality inert and nonrelational; it is only to suggest that distinct waste practices can radically diminish or amplify the singular destiny of fragments to various ends.

Moreover, analyses of waste, whatever direction they may take, can have a similar impact on our otherwise open-ended imaginations. Clearly wastes have political, ecological, and/or political roles to play, or stories to unfold. But this should have to be demonstrated, just as both Hird and Gille force one another to do in their exchange. The refreshing thing about their productive disagreement is precisely that it compelled them to do what otherwise is all too often left to one side: to slow down their analysis and justify the path they have chosen. They manage to show very clearly how indeterminacy can be taken in very different ways when it comes to waste: what from an ecological and inhuman perspective would seem to challenge anthropocentrism and human narcissism from an environmental justice perspective would seem to maintain inequality and incapacitate political action. In both cases, waste fragments seem capable of something unexpected. I would only add to their exchange that if we are to avoid making implicit teleological assumptions about the fate of materials, it is important to recognize that they are capable in principle of something even more unexpected: nothing at all.

Acknowledgments

Thanks to the two editors of this volume, but especially to Catherine Alexander for helpful criticism and encouragement while this chapter was being written and rewritten. Thanks also to the anonymous peer reviewers for useful suggestions to earlier versions.

Joshua O. Reno is an associate professor at Binghamton University. Most of his work focuses on various types of waste, mammalian, municipal, and, most recently, militaristic, particularly their significance for political economy and their emergent entanglement with human and nonhuman life. He coedited, with Catherine Alexander, *Economies of Recycling* (2012). His ethnography *Waste Away* is based on a large landfill in the rural outskirts of Detroit. His next book focuses on the waste of America's permanent war economy.

Notes

1. In that sense, I too am limiting my interpretive inquiry by using the national whole of "the United States," and specifically its ability to determine environmental regulations, as an endpoint for my musings about indeterminate waste objects. My point is not that attaching fragments to wholes is to be avoided, but that it should be attended to analytically and methodologically.
2. There are instances where waste might be a resource for nonhumans. But local wildlife specialists told me that they wondered if bald eagles were getting sick from eating seagulls who eat potentially toxic garbage from the landfill.
3. Blanchot's fragment might be considered the obverse of the "open wholes" that both Eduardo Kohn (2013) and David Pedersen (2013) use to characterize their respective ethnographic projects, see Reno 2015.

References

Adam, B. 1998. *Timescapes of Modernity: The Environment and Invisible Hazards*. London: Routledge.

Alexander, C. 2009. "Waste under Socialism and After: A Case Study from Almaty." In *Enduring Socialism: Explorations of Revolution & Transformation, Restoration & Continuation*, ed. H. G. West and P. Raman, 148–68. New York: Berghahn Books.

———. Forthcoming. "Cleaning Up and Moving On: Kazakhstan's 'Nuclear Renaissance.'" In *Les Chantier du Nucléaire*, ed. R. Garcier and L. Françoise. Paris: Archives Contemporaines.

Alexander, C., and J. Reno. 2012. *Economies of Recycling: The Global Transformation of Materials, Values and Social Relations* London: Zed Books.

Anand, N. 2015. "Leaky States: Water Audits, Ignorance, and the Politics of Infrastructure." *Public Culture* 27(2): 305–30.

Austin, A. A., E. F. Fitzgerald, C. I. Pantea, L. J. Gensburg, N. K. Kim, A. D. Stark, and S. A. Hwang. 2011. "Reproductive Outcomes among Former Love Canal Residents, Niagara Falls, New York." *Environmental Research* 111(5): 693–701.

Blanchot, M. 1993. *The Infinite Conversation*. Minneapolis, MN: University of Minnesota Press.

Douglas, M. [1966] 2002. *Purity and Danger: An Analysis of Concepts of Pollution and Taboo* London: Routledge.

Faulkner, K. W. 2008. *The Force of Time: An Introduction to Deleuze through Proust*. Langham, MD: University Press of America.

Gille, Z. 2013. "Is there an Emancipatory Ontology of Matter? A Response to Myra Hird." *Social Epistemology Review and Reply Collective* 2(4): 1–6. Chicago, IL: University of Chicago Press.

Hägglund, M. 2008. *Radical Atheism: Derrida and the Time of Life*. Stanford, CA: Stanford University Press.

Harman, G. 2009. *Prince of Networks: Latour and Metaphysics*. Melbourne: re.press.

———. 2011. *The Quadruple Object*. Alresford, UK: Zero Books.

Hird, M. 2012. "Knowing Waste: Towards an Inhuman Epistemology." *Social Epistemology* 26(3–4): 453–69.

———. 2013. "Is Waste Indeterminacy Useful? A Response to Zsuza Gille." *Social Epistemology Review and Reply Collective* 2(6): 28–33.

Knauft, B. 2006. "Anthropology in the Middle." *Anthropological Theory* 6(4): 407–30.

Kohn, E. 2013. *How Forests Think: Toward an Anthropology Beyond the Human*. Berkeley, CA: University of California Press.

Marder, M. 2013. *Plant-Thinking: A Philosophy of Vegetal Life*. New York: Cambridge University Press.

Maurer, B. 2015. *How Would You Like to Pay?: How Technology is Changing the Future of Money*. Durham, NC: Duke University Press.

Nixon, R. 2011. *Slow Violence and the Environmentalism of the Poor*. Cambridge, MA: Harvard University Press.

Paigen, B., L. R. Goldman, M. M. Magnant, J. H. Highland, and A. Steegmann. 1987. "Growth of Children Living Near the Hazardous Waste Site, Love Canal." *Human Biology* 59(3): 489–508.

Pedersen, D. 2013. *American Value: Migrants, Money, and Meaning in El Salvador and the United States*. Chicago, IL: University of Chicago Press.

Pedersen, M. A. 2012. "Common Nonsense: A Review of Certain Recent Reviews of the 'Ontological Turn.'" *Anthropology of This Century* 5, October. Retrieved 21 April 2018 from http://aotcpress.com/articles/common_nonsense/.

Pellow, D. 2007. *Resisting Global Toxics: Transnational Movements for Environmental Justice.* Cambridge, MA: MIT Press.

Povinelli, E. A. 2011. *Economies of Abandonment: Social Belonging and Endurance in Late Liberalism.* Durham, NC: Duke University Press.

Reno, J. 2011. "Beyond Risk: Emplacement and the Production of Environmental Evidence." *American Ethnologist* 38(3): 516–30.

———. 2014. "Toward a New Theory of Waste: From 'Matter Out of Place' to Signs of Life." *Theory, Culture & Society* 31(6): 3–27.

———. 2015. "Continuity and the Open Whole: A Comparison of Recent (Peircian) Ethnographies." *Critique of Anthropology* 35(2): 220–31.

———. 2016. *Waste Away: Working and Living with a North American Landfill.* Oakland, CA: University of California Press.

Staten, H. 1986. *Wittgenstein and Derrida.* Lincoln: University of Nebraska Press.

Thomson, V. 2009. *Garbage In, Garbage Out: Solving the Problems with Long-Distance Waste Transport.* Charlottesville, VA: University of Virginia Press.

Tsing, A. 2015. *The Mushroom at the End of the World: On the Possibility of Life in Capitalist Ruins.* Princeton, NJ and Oxford: Princeton University Press.

2

Experiments in Living
The Value of Indeterminacy in Trans Art

Elena Gonzalez-Polledo

As it is useful that while mankind are imperfect there should be different opinions, so is it that there should be different experiments of living; that free scope should be given to varieties of character, short of injury to others; and that the worth of different modes of life should be proved practically, when anyone thinks fit to try them. Where, not the person's own character, but the traditions of customs of other people are the rule of conduct, there is wanting one of the principal ingredients of human happiness, and quite the chief ingredient of individual and social progress.
—John Stuart Mill, *On Liberty*

A dictionary begins when it no longer gives the meaning of words, but their tasks. Thus formless is not only an adjective having a given meaning, but a term that serves to bring things down in the world, generally requiring that each thing have its form. What it designates has no rights in any sense and gets itself squashed everywhere, like a spider or an earthworm. In fact, for academic men to be happy, the universe would have to take shape. All of philosophy has no other goal: it is a matter of giving a frock coat to what is, a mathematical frock coat. On the other hand, affirming that the universe resembles nothing and is only formless amounts to saying that the universe is something like a spider or spit.
—Georges Bataille, *Formless*

Consider Hans Scheirl's *Dandy Dust*, a cult film produced in London during the 1990s that received wide critical acclaim. The film depicts Dandy who, in the filmmaker's synopsis, is described as "a split personality cyborg of fluid gender zooming through time to collect h-selves[1] in the fight against a genealogically obsessed family."[2] No longer capable of living on the planet of Blood & Swelling, Dandy embarks on a journey to planet 3075. Before the journey, his brain memory disc is removed. The film follows his arrival on the new planet and sees him becoming physically connected to the planet's structure.

He then proceeds to take his life into his own hands. Through a series of encounters, explorations, and plots, aspects of material and psychic reality are skillfully represented. The film ultimately shows that Dandy is unable to find wholeness in a coherent narrative. Instead, "the plot" presents, in parallel, multiple false beginnings and loose ends.[3]

Not having a narrative structure and working against conventional video grammars, Scheirl's film asks viewers to contextualize an apparently surreal nonlinear amalgamation of scenes, materials, and interactions, a collection that requires multiple potential readings often simultaneous and contradictory, to make sense of Dandy's journey. Eliza Steinbock (2013) suggests that the difficulty in establishing a coherent reading of the film invites viewers to abandon the need to make sense of the action and instead open up to its haptic interfaces and experiment, just like Dandy does, with things to make meaning. For Scheirl, the material, affective, and experiential process of art-making opens up the body to new hypothetical relations between organs, theories, affects, and living processes. As the film comes to an end, Dandy persists in refusing to condense or dehybridize his multiple identities. Making sense of the journey attunes Dandy to almost imperceptible changes, and to the complex relations between scales of embodiment, material and psychic life, the multiplicity and mutability of meaning through which his sense of transness evolves. In 2015, the British Film Institute hosted a retrospective screening of the film featuring a dialogue with many of its protagonists, which created a new appraisal of its relevance and scope. Jokes were exchanged between artists and audience about the difficulty of making sense of the film's narrative and message. A participant told Scheirl, "all these years I thought Dandy Dust was a sophisticated metaphor, now I see how you tricked us: it makes no sense at all!"

If Dandy Dust was about transgender, it aimed to deconstruct familiar ideas about transition as simply moving from one fixed point to another. As such, analyzing the film and its reception by many trans artists involved in crafting its message is a productive way of exploring deliberate engagements with indeterminacy as a perpetual condition of irresolution, an open-ended experimentation with materiality and experience. Instead of accepting taken-for-granted values of body parts, social relations, things, and technologies, Scheirl subverts such values through a haptic experiment of revaluation: body parts and waste products become equivalent in order to reframe the politics of the human form. In an earlier retrospective talk about his work, Scheirl (2004) reflected on his method as a form of psychodynamics, where the artwork disrupts conventional dichotomies, making relationships between relationships visible. Scheirl (2004) later said that Alfred Gell had inspired him to think about the person-making capacities of art, as an agent concerned with doing rather than meaning, a way of creating, not representing, worlds. For Scheirl, *trans* is primarily an adjectival method that connects multiplicity, a compositional form that undoes and rejoins materials and knowledges, producing a new form that is not predictable as a synthesis of previous forms, but is something other. From this perspective, Scheirl defines the accomplishment of the artwork as based on the indeterminacy of a method that allows him to "get away from the binaries" while bringing a critique of binary thinking to bear in critical descriptions of dynamics that frame relations between the inside and outside of the body, the interior and exterior of the artwork. In this sense, rather than completely rejecting binary distinctions, the artist engages in a process of creative deconstruction of conventions and form by reassembling textual, audiovisual, and haptic elements. Ultimately, having lost hope of making sense of the journey, Dandy has no other choice than experimenting, sensing, and "groping" (Steinbock 2013) his way into it.

Scheirl, as well as other trans artists, emphasized the creation of new possibilities via open-ended experimentation. Just as many in the trans art community rejected the medico-legal normative model of recognition, so their practice escaped determinacy by rejecting formal art genres, connecting economies and politics of representation through arts practice. Some artists, with whom I came in contact during my fieldwork (2006 to date) had been involved in the production or postproduction of *Dandy Dust*, which took several years to complete because of its complexity and insufficient funds. Those who are very familiar with the film told me about the mark it had made on London's art scene in the following decade. For my interlocutors, not only was the allegory it presented a radical metaphor of transition, concerned with exploding a coherent identity narrative, but it presented many of the complexities involved in transitioning, as well as art-making, without aiming to resolve them. This chapter explores how these frictions continued to shape trans art practice, and how, in many ways, they are still unresolved today.

I am concerned here with exploring the tensions around the recognition of trans art, people, processes, and lives. In essence, the conflicts are between recognition and codification, and highlight the difficulties between achieving visibility and being accorded value without becoming determined. Although the medical model of transition in the United Kingdom grants recognition to people transitioning from one gender to another, this model is premised on "a complete and irreversible" transformation, defined by achieving sets of physical and social standards that can ultimately reveal a person's gender and stand before expert recognition that compares individual gender embodiments to standard sexual characteristics, including voice pitch, appearance of genitalia, dressing style, and demeanor. Most people accessing health services need to perform a coherent narrative about their aim to embody the opposite gender in order to obtain healthcare. While this framework offers access to gender affirming treatment in some instances, such access is guarded by psychiatric diagnostic and treatment access requirements. This can make it very difficult for many to gain the right to healthcare, particularly if they lack the resources to go through the bureaucratic referrals process successfully or to use private health services. This model, which has been criticized by trans organizations as being discriminatory and demeaning to trans people, is currently being reviewed in the United Kingdom to make it more accessible to those who do not define their trans identities within binary forms.[4] The reforms plan to introduce a simpler administrative process for gender recognition applications instead of a process backed by medical "evidence." However, as yet, there is no state recognition of trans identities outside of the model of binary gender.

Against the pitfalls of this model of recognition, this chapter explores two instances that highlight the value of indeterminacy for trans artists looking for inclusive, alternative spaces to be visible while resisting the designation or labels of others. First, I explore the emergence and demise of a trans arts festival, which was envisaged as an alternative platform that aimed to bring together trans artists, curators, activists, and thinkers around an inclusive definition of trans art. However, community engagement with the festival made visible some of the pitfalls of representation, as feedback from those attending the festival highlighted its failure to provide an inclusive platform for the most vulnerable in the community. The critique highlighted the double edge of recognition, noted in the introduction to this volume: while it may be necessary for inclusion, at the same time it raises questions about who recognizes whom and on what basis. For some, the festival raised new questions about how visibility might relate to recognition in practice, and how negotiating visibility as a trans person might not always be possible for those whose very identity comes with a higher risk of misrecognition and permanent precarity, such as some trans women and trans people of color. Although the festival aimed to make arts practices and identities visible, the way that new definitions of trans art privileged some forms of visibility over others was ultimately seen to recapitulate the politics of recognition it set out to resist.

I then draw on my ethnographic fieldwork among artists in London to explore how they make a living from indeterminacy by imagining alternative lives and social worlds through practice and play. This argument makes connections between arts practice and emancipatory aesthetics, which are not new in relation to art practice or in relation to queer communities. Queer theorist Jack Halberstam has linked abstract art to forms of activism that stem from creative responses to failure (Halberstam 2005:103, 2011). For Halberstam, abstract art is linked to a "new vision of life, love and labour" and the practice of queer utopias; it is a possibility that lurks behind constant rejections. Queer utopias rely on manifestos, political tactics, and technologies of representation to "search for different ways of being in the world and being in relation to one another than those already prescribed for the liberal and consumer subject" (2011: 2). However, trans artists also engage subversive capacities of art-making in more subtle ways, for example, emphasizing immanence and process over determination, and carefully crafting and framing their practice by resisting formal labels and art canons, yet strategically using them to be able to access basic welfare and healthcare support.

Bringing together queer and art theory, I explore trans art practices that link politics, experimentation, and experience, seeking to create ethical living spaces through practices that blend critical engagement with visibility and

sensoriality through an "experiment in living," a creative, open-ended exploration of living through form. John Stuart Mill introduced the idea of experiments in living to defend the value of "embracing the variability of human life,"
believing that "the worth of different modes of life should be proved practically" (Mill 3003, 122: 76). Living experiments have been described across
fields from environmentalism to practices of interdisciplinary collaboration.
In these contexts, living experiments are seen to implicate both large-scale
logics and habits and sensibilities of the everyday (Hawkins 2006) in exploring
ethics and the common good without resorting to arbitrary definitions of the
good (Anderson 1991; Macbeath 1952). The trans artists I worked with made
sense of the often multiple and contradictory values of being visible, resisting,
and being refused categorization, and their engagement with arts practice
embraced indeterminacy through a speculative "infection with abstraction"
(Parisi 2013: 153) to open up utopian and ethical fields of action.

Engaging my interlocutors' interpretations of their practice, this chapter
explores conceptualism as an ethnographic proxy for life (Ssorin-Chaikov
2013; Valentine 2007). Indeed, the artists I worked with often thought of representation as a practice that did not come out of a preexisting identity, but as
transient form that reinscribed the body through a performative relation.
Trans artist and curator Gordon Hall, the indeterminacy of artworks such as
Richard Artschwager's Yes/No ball,[5] where perspective and motion determine
how the words "yes" and "no" printed on opposite sides of the sculpture come
into view, provoke engagements with the body as a virtual entity. This may
apply to abstract art more generally, because objects "do not speak in any language but that of their presence in space" (Hall 2013: 48). Since these sculp-
tures do not have an intended use, they tend to conjure up the body as an act
of imagination based on "the coexistence of yes and no, almost, in between,
not quite, both and neither" (Jerry Saltz quoted in Hall 2013: 56). In this sense,
queer art critics have described abstract art as possessing a "transgender
capacity": a potential to bring into experience "gender's dynamism, plurality
and expansiveness" (Getsy 2014: 47). These qualities derive from abstraction,
and may be located in "texts, objects, cultural forms, situations, systems and
images that support an interpretation or recognition of proliferative modes of
gender non-conformity, multiplicity and temporality" (ibid.). My ethnography
explores the difficulties of recognition in practice, and frames how meanings
of indeterminacy bring forward tensions between its positive and negative
values. Thus, by bringing anthropology into dialogue with trans studies, queer
and art theory, this chapter explores how anthropology might think through
the tensions that emerge from living indeterminacy in practice.

Against Representation

Dandy Dust was shot in London at a crucial time when medical transition
shaped trans visibility in the arts and the media. Advocacy organizations such as

Press for Change worked to create a socially acceptable image of transgender identities through media interventions and political lobbying, trans visibility permeated popular culture through photography and film.[6] This cultural and media advocacy work eventually led to the normalization of a model of civil recognition that depended on the medico-legal framework of the Gender Recognition Act (2004), a model that requires an irreversible transition to achieve social integration through binary gender embodiment.[7] While being "in the wrong body" was the mainstay of the medico-legal model of transition, and many fought to be recognized as such, the model and its exclusions were increasingly questioned in academic literature and cultural production, particularly from the late 1990s (More and Whittle 1999; Prosser 1998). For example, these tensions surrounded definitions of "transgender art." Some trans artists I met felt that art was particularly important to survive as a trans person. For some trans artists, their trans identities were the catalyst that led them to engage in artistic production, the need to explain their bodies, identities, or transitions to other trans, or non-trans audiences, and to create ways of relating outside normative gender relations. At the time of my initial fieldwork, cultural production was becoming key to a growing community of people transitioning or questioning their gender. Some of the artists I worked with performed in community venues and festivals, promoting cultural events and gaining a precarious livelihood by engaging the community in cultural production. At established bars and nightclubs, performance artists thrived in a proliferation of styles, including satire, imitation and parody, gender confessions, and disclosure of experiences of trauma.[8] At the same time, representations of transgender identities by and for non-trans people were also becoming public, "safe for consumption" versions of transgender. The push to mainstream transgender was the product of an unlikely alliance involving some trans community organizations, corporations, and political agents. As social attitudes to gender nonconformity changed, a new wave of self representation, the "transgender tipping point," meant greater acceptance for some trans identities and representations among mainstream audiences. Increasingly, however, such versions were seen not to align with trans community politics, and were oblivious to the consequences that these representations had for underprivileged members of the trans community.

A scene from my early fieldwork stayed in my memory for years, and I revisited it afresh in 2015. In 2006, a group of artists and activists put together Transfabulous, the first national festival of transgender art. The festival evolved from a fundraiser picnic in support of a local charity, to gradually become a formal event with a curated program of interventions from local and international artists, performers, community advocates, and academics. I met with one of the organizers in 2015 to ask him to recall the early days of the festival, which was based on a collective conviction that the London trans community needed cultural production. I asked my interlocutor why, being a unique offering with wide appeal, the festival was so short-lived, disappearing abruptly in 2008. A decade later, nothing like Transfabulous has emerged on the scene again. He replied that it was difficult to organize a festival of that scale without committed funding resources and that, despite efforts to be inclusive, there had not been enough public recognition of the diversity of trans experiences, nor an acknowledgement of or critical engagement with the consequences of representations. Critical audience reactions remarked that the festival provided a platform for forms of trans identity that were already more visible and culturally acceptable, contributing to perpetuating cleavages within the community, as well as creating new ones. After Transfabulous, both trans artists and audiences were invested in opening up definitions of transgender art to defy the perilous demands of state recognition, but were also seeking to find accurate representations that could speak directly to local issues and identities. Transgender artists often talk about being caught up in this "double bind," as filmmaker Jules Rosskam put it (2014): producing forward-looking work that is effective in identifying conditions other people can relate to, while becoming pedagogical objects for outsiders, "showing" something new about trans experience to non-trans audiences.

And yet, as I talked to my interlocutor about the reasons behind Transfabulous' closure, there was a wider issue about the possibility that the arts could uniquely preserve histories that would otherwise easily be lost, or else become normalized and diluted if too quickly mainstreamed. It was the age-old issue, he said, "about how a story gets to be told, who gets to tell the story, why stories always have their time and how some will never be told." The indeterminacy of the trans story, told and untold through artistic practice, hinges on relations between arts practices and the politics of their intellectual and institutional formations.

Indeed, the definition of transgender art did not exist in isolation from the festival's wider context. Transfabulous aimed to celebrate a transnational, transgenerational definition of transgender art, but the community found this generic ambition to be at odds with the complex, multiple, and unequal realities of gender, migration, employment, and privilege that limited access to art and cultural production, and restricted access to the education and resources needed to earn a livelihood in the arts. Some felt that the festival made these differences invisible while appealing to a positive, disembodied, white-by-default representation of transgender. At the time, I read the conflicts that arose around the festival also as a tension between identity and post-identity frameworks, where notions of transsexuality, as opposed to "transgender," were beginning to be seen as a step backwards. Indeed, transgender appeared as a form of utopianism, which became an area of contention for both trans and feminist scholars, in terms of identity politics, one that could just as easily become a source of death by negating others who do not make the mark, or by predicating trans visibilities on the acceptance of global power structures. Jin Haritaworn, Adi Kuntsman, and Sylvia Posocco refer to this kind of erasure as "queer necropolitics" (2014). Niko Besnier (2002) captured a similar dynamic in his description of the Miss Galaxy beauty pageant in the Kingdom of Tonga. Every year the show allowed marginalized *leiti*, a transgender identity category derived from the English word "lady," to claim a place out of hegemonic gender frameworks, acting as a universalizing force, yet also a crucial site of tension in the staging of local transgender idioms and identities.

Sian Lazar notes that cultural performances produce a sense of "experiential authenticity: the fleeting feeling of sharing the experience of a performance with others" (2008: 125), rooting participants in a shared sense of collectivity, a relation that links people, practice, and place. Trans performance traditions in London do not particularly relate to any place beyond the stage, but unite participants in the performance of cultural transgression, oral storytelling, and confessional and transition narratives. The festival itself became a key context in which arts practices became relevant without the need to be further explained. They became contexts of transformation that enabled audiences to construct their own forms of agency, and new "modes of enacting the process of reflecting on the self and the world and of acting simultaneously within and upon what one finds there" (Ortner 2006: 57). As Susan Stryker noted, it is in safe, subcultural spaces that trans identities come into being "gaff and gauntlet rather than scalpel and syringe" (1998: 150), through a recursive relation between reality and imagination.[9]

Thus, enacting tensions between identity, post-identity, and non-identity, a relation between practice and cosmology emerges as the "functional site" for trans art. These practices increasingly blur the boundaries between art and life by indexing relations and exposing an indeterminate relation between practice and meaning that reflects the negative dialectics that characterizes indeterminacy as discussed in the introduction to this volume: a state of radical potential concerned both with change and non-future-oriented ways of being, the promotion of multiple, sometimes contradictory forms of value and valuation, and a tension between holistic or categorical representations and the production of fragmented representational practices that do not add up to a coherent whole. Indeed, the tipping point in the media was surrounded by a critical turn in transgender studies that some have dubbed the "post-post-transsexual":[10] the time when transgender idioms, vocabularies, and material cultures are no longer concerned with gender, but with critiques of biopolitics, disability, political economy, pathologization, and animal studies that have moved away from identity frameworks. Examples have been received from both recognized and emergent artists,[11] from Yishay Garbasz's work on conflict zones, nuclear and postwar landscapes, to artworks and art practices that address scientific and social histories of pathologization, sometimes becoming alternative forms of gender pedagogy (McNamara and Rooke 2008; Rooke 2010). In the next section I turn to tensions between arts practice of indeterminacy and the experience of such open-ended experiments in living.

Experiments in Living

Institutional visibility was often neither easy nor unproblematic for most trans artists I worked with. Rather than fitting particular genres, it responded to challenges posed by materials. My interlocutors routinely spoke about the difficulties of inhabiting heteronormative and gender-conforming art worlds, and how their positions were routinely marginalized when it came to access to funding and exhibition spaces. However, their practices were no longer concerned with addressing the tensions of cultural politics. These artists often had precarious paid employment. In order to make a living they therefore had ceased to be occupied only with cultural politics and reimagining the conditions of the present. Rather, in their lives and their art practice alike, they "became visible" selectively and strategically, attempting to continue resisting classification. Cultural production was the bedrock of ways of living not concerned with particular futures, but with interrogating relations between practice, aesthetics, and visibility.

Consider Sidney's art practice. Her work as an experimental sound artist has featured in arts magazines, sound conferences and exhibitions, but mostly as a "feminist of color," a label with which she does not identify, but a label, nonetheless, that she sometimes claims strategically seeking for her work to be visible in some space. Her own description of her art practice is concerned with working with composition through and against interpretation to provide a sense of "spaciousness, structure, and direction," which is accomplished by playing with expectations of context, meaning, and affect. Her work begins by undoing sound structures by artificially isolating elements through recording and sampling, then through a process of listening, assembling, and altering sound sequences to generate a sense of wonder. She describes composition as a process of attunement in which mediations and transmissions take place. Sound is an enclosure that makes knowing social, spatial, and temporal: a site of transformation. In this context, Sidney says, it is useful to read transgender not as a representation but as an unstable form characterized by performative repetition and indeterminacy. Against a priori distinctions between matter and representation, working with sound brings forward material and affective linkages through which relations between material and symbolic worlds come to matter.[12]

This alternative to representationalism invites a reconceptualization of the realm of practice. Indeed, according to my interlocutors, there are reasons that this is needed: lack of access to resources particularly affects people of nonnormative genders, who are often also riddled with histories that complicate how their practice becomes visible. For example, Sidney regularly expressed concerns about how the practicalities of access to training, studio spaces, grants, and resources determined the form of her artworks more than any ideas did. Viewing arts practice through the lens of participation, anthropologists have turned to relations to take the practice of art seriously (Schneider and Wright 2005). Whether language-based, gestural, or artifactual, art practices are grounded in histories and materials that contain affordances and resistances. Indeed, as Susanne Küchler highlights, "all made things partake of intentional and systematizing thought" (2013: 25), serving as vehicles of knowledge that bind people through practice. The location and orientation of art depends less on place than it does on an assemblage delineated by a "field" of knowledge, composed of materials, agencies, places, and relations (Kwon 2002). From this perspective, the biography of Sidney's sonic objects includes the relational processes involved in their constitution: the context of their production, and the relations involved in their circulation and reception. While her tracks present indeterminate assemblages, their relational constitution and reassemblage on stage opens them to the "conditions of possibility of [the public's] association" (Kelty 2005), which depend in important ways on various degrees of public engagement, disengagement, and nonengagement (Rapport 2016). This indeterminacy of artworks, marked by contingent happenings and associations has, in other arts contexts, been considered "form as living," or indeed "living as form" (Thompson 2012), insofar as in happening, form might reconfigure social orders—through sensoriality, experimentation, and participation.

These artworks not only translate particular utopian or dystopian visions, but open up the conditions of interpretation. Sam, who earns a living as a musician and cultural producer, describes their musical practice as "knowing matter." A musician without classical training, they rely on sound medium to teach them a posteriori "the skill" of sound, and view each of their performances as a contingent process where the body must "keep up" with music and learn to remember. Sam is now an improvisational musician who sets up monthly music events. At every event, a manifesto hangs on the wall asking attendees to refrain from behaving like men or like women to let the unexpected find them as the performances unfold. Often, improvisations involving audience and musicians begin after the concert officially comes to an end, as the possibility of improvisation is opened up by unpredicted connections between invited musicians. Voices, instruments, and music take on an agential role to open up an ontological space of music (Born 2013b; Fraser 2005). One could argue that a sense of experimentation and open-endedness makes these artworks topological, in the sense of their capacity to reconfigure space (Born 2013a), but their expansive ethos also extends by resonance or contagion. In this sense, I think of these artworks as "trans-objects,"[13] open-ended explorations that may create space for the unexpected by bringing set structures to life in a context different from the one they were originally intended to inhabit, a possibility of the otherwise. Sam's life practice evolved out of a sense that the arts, and perhaps also the possibility of a social identity as an artist, opened up a way to express difference, becoming a space of survival and a "queer ecology" (Morton 2010) that invited, by association, alternative worlds into being. Their resistance to being bound by formal musical grammars and instead staging an improvisational open-ended practice that seeks to resist the telos of representation keeps the past and the future from intervening in the present. This resistance relies on practice to change the conditions of the present, working by reference to transferences between living kinds (and kinds of living) and artifacts.[14]

In this context, where does the art object end and life begin? Imagining existence at the edge of abstraction is, perhaps, the event value of the occurring arts

(Massumi 2011), but my interlocutors always returned to the value of trans experience as the real value of their art.[15] Wade, a classically-trained musician and illustrator, often talks about a tension between mainstream art and music worlds, where he learned his craft, and his experience of performing in trans spaces, which was key to his abandoning classical practice to explore improvisation. He frames his practice as a conversion between structures. His practice blurs boundaries of genres, and purposely bends these boundaries through a sense of detachment and play. Although he kept creative practices separate, working as a freelance advertiser and a classical pianist, working with color, lines, and later with texture, over time music folded into illustration. His trans experience translates a refusal to work toward fitting genres and canons. Instead, trading in "small stories" outweighs the desire to make the work suitable for larger audiences, blurring distinctions between the artwork as an object or practice and utopian spaces of transformation that are generated collectively as the artwork is received. Involving audiences and art structures in pursuit of transversality (Thompson 2015), he relies on art becoming determinate through the shared collective recognition of lived conditions. Art is, in this sense, a form of make-believe, though it may also create worlds by provoking disengagement from held belief. Wade seeks to make objects that create a systematic gap between the information received and the meaning recovered (Marchand 2010b), which remains "under-specified" and necessitates inference and context in order to derive meaning. "There may be an urge to escape and dissociate from some painful or challenging reality," he told me. "On the other hand, it's fun to dress up the subject and confuse people."

In this sense, experiments in living connect ethics, aesthetics, and life processes, by enabling an exploration of horizons of representation, a process concerned with finding other forms of life through abstract thinking, at borders between categories, genres, media, and method. Instead of staging identity-based concepts and distinctions, the trans artists I worked with understood arts practice as a way to investigate frames of experience that may lead to hyposubjectivity: a multiphasic, plural, existential condition of survival (Boyer and Morton 2016). In the context of artistic production, this condition necessitates a reevaluation of experimentality, and of relations between materials, form, and the conditions of cultural production. As such, these practices relate not to accomplishing a determined program, but to an existential project that is concerned with the possibility of becoming, to borrow Stryker's famous phrase, "something more, and something other" (Stryker 1994: 242). But, perhaps more importantly, trans abstraction thus invites us to think of arts practices as an interface that reframes physical and propositional domains as equivalent relations. These are prime sites of ontological difference, interfaces that make a difference through practice (Malafouris 2013; Marchand 2010a), which become central in both specifying and disrupting cognitive constructs (Toren 1990) that articulate relations between culture, identity, and imagination.

Conclusion: Trans-Objects and Speculative Futures

This chapter has provided a reading of arts practices as experiments in living, "excessive practices" (de la Cadena 2010), grassroots strategies that respond to the failure of politics-as-usual by deploying new logics to mobilize a political sphere. I have discussed trans art practices that deploy indeterminacy to disrupt identity politics, and remake politics of representation against institutional contexts that universalize transgender. Art practices function by obviating taken-for-granted complementarities between physical and psychosocial, material and semiotic realms, providing a basis to think through how "intrinsic" qualities—for example, aesthetic qualities or the manifest qualities of a body—might not be different from the "secondary" reactions and impressions they create, the ways through which they become known. Art practices reflect the unfinished constitution of nature, subjectivity, and materiality, which are not only known through, but are themselves relations. This exploration of the material and epistemic frames of experience and transition posits new questions about how anthropology can learn with bodies, their capacities and indeterminacies, to reimagine the method of ethnography. As such, as Caroline Gatt and Timothy Ingold suggest, these experiments and practices can become a critical research tool of an anthropology that "seeks to correspond with, rather than to describe, the lives it follows" (2013: 144), opening up frictions in categorical thinking to reflect the value of indeterminacy as a way of knowing.

Somewhere between practice and object, the trans-objects I have described are based on a structural search of perceptual concretion, as everyday practices which "tak[e] on a generative role as a phenomenological, experiential entity" (Small 2016: 163), shuttling "between viewer and maker just as they move between the categories of work of art and ready-made thing" (ibid.: 175). They are, in this sense, both happening and events of the imagination, exaptations "whereby structures that may have evolved for one purpose are co-opted for quite different functions for which they happen to come in handy" (Ingold quoted in Sneath, Holbraad, and Pedersen 2009: 21). It could be argued, following Deidre Wilson and Daniel Sperber (2012), that these experiments may lead to differentiation not only at the individual level but also at the social level. Performing translations between materials and psychic experiences, across and beyond forms and feeling, through texture and sensation, art adopts a transmaterial form: it queers materiality to travel across multiple worlds of meaning. This is resonant of some art, including Scheirl's, that may apparently focus on transgender while in fact also addressing trans-culture, trans-media, and trans-class (Erharter et al. 2015: 31n3). Thus, trans art practices are in many ways "technologies of existence" (Massumi 2011) through which people understand backwards and live forwards, as the way that objects are "inter-given" as their potential for transforming experience is relayed from one experience to another. Experimenting with understandings of transition and trans life leads both artists and participants to a "hypothetical twin world" (Jones 2014), where life and the social become newly remembered. Such practices are, most importantly, social ways to make things happen, implicating practice, methods, and publics in the making of worlds. This assemblage recalibrates retrospectively the value of indeterminacy, producing a posteriori the conditions it presupposes.[16] While escaping formal norms, indeterminacy allows artists make other worlds, and while this condition predicates possibility, it can also make everyday survival more difficult. As such, art practices are exemplar sites where indeterminacy is reclaimed as a capacity for difference, yet becomes a key site of friction between the idea and everyday practice of difference.

Acknowledgements

I extend thanks to the anonymous participants who shared their ways with artistic practice for the purposes of this research. I am deeply grateful to Catherine Alexander for her generous editorial engagement with this piece, which allowed me to develop the argument in its present form. Errors remain my own.

Elena Gonzalez-Polledo is currently a lecturer in Anthropology at Goldsmiths, University of London, having held academic positions at the London School of Economics and the University of Sheffield. Publications include *Transitioning: Matter, Gender, Thought* (Rowman and Littlefield International, 2017) and the edited collections *Painscapes: Communicating Pain* (Palgrave Macmillan, 2017) and *Queering Knowledge: Analytics, Devices and Investments after Marilyn Strathern* (Routledge, 2018).

Notes

1. H-selves is an abbreviation of his- or her- selves.
2. The film's original synopsis, written by the artist, is accessible online. Retrieved 18 May 2018 from http://bak.spc.org/couch/interviews/hansinfo01.htm#top.
3. For example, Dandy says to Aunt Theodora: "I am Dandy Dust." "Oh, that makes sense," comes the reply. "Do me a favor and stay that way for a while."
4. See the UK Government's Transgender Action Plan, accessible online. Retrieved 15 September 2017 from https://www.gov.uk/government/publications/transgender-action-plan.
5. See images online. Retrieved 15 September 2017 from https://mcachicago.org/Collection/Items/Richard-Artschwager-Yes-No-Ball-1974.
6. First, long traditions of photographic representation captured gender variance in ways that words never could (Cameron 1996; Volcano 2001), becoming grammars of possibility that inspired people to transition and to imagine their bodies and their lives, beyond the prejudice of mainstream media representations.
7. The Gender Recognition Act (GRA), currently under revision after a 2010 investigation led by the Equalities and Human Rights Commission, grants access to a modified birth certificate to those who applied on the basis of recognized standards of medical

transition, including having undergone periods of hormonal treatment and/or surgery. The law is premised on binary gender recognition and on transitioning in one direction only once in a lifetime. See Gonzalez-Polledo's (2017) ethnographic analysis of how the process of transitioning in the United Kingdom is also thought and lived beyond this model.

8. See also examples elsewhere, including Christiane Erharter et al. (2015) and Ochoa (2008).

9. Cultural production frames the conditions in which transgender becomes visible, asking viewers to reveal the gaze that frames cultural identity and difference. For Prosser, this question contains others: "how do you relate to an image and to the (transgender) other? where are you looking from?" (Prosser in Volcano 2001: 7). Prosser reflects Michel Foucault's ([1970] 2001) description of painting and perspective.

10. According to Susan Stryker and Paisley Currah (2014), this is the time of the post-post-transsexual, when the "post-transsexual" critique of an assumed homogeneity of trans-sexual identities is extending beyond transgender as a form of cultural critique concerned with social justice. "Post-transsexual" was first described by Sandy Stone (2008) in her critique of Janice Raymond's *The Transsexual Empire*, thus paving the way for a definition of transgender. Stryker and Currah coined this term to suggest a shift.

11. Such as Juliana Huxtable, Tobaron Waxman, Heather Cassils, among many others.

12. A process that counters the representationalist project, which works through representational homologies. While representationalism is premised on an inherent distinction between matter and representation, Barad highlights how the intra-agential constitution of "things" is determined by the measurement practices that produce their value (See Barad 2007: 71–94; see also Bal 2002).

13. The term trans-object relates to the work of the visual artist Helio Oiticica (how/why?), and has been described by Ramirez (2007) and Irene Small (2016). The artist Helio Oiticica coined the name *trans-ojeto* (Ramirez and Olea 2004; Schneider and Wright 2013) in search of *parangolés*: structures designed to bring alive the practice of painting, for example by setting in motion wearable color fabrics designed to be inhabited and danced in space, those composing a living picture.

14. These transferences, according to Maurice Bloch, are not unique to arts processes, permeate cultural cognition and are premised on the availability of material symbols that can "make the jump," based on a recognition of the unity of living kinds (1998: 62). My argument is that arts practice in these contexts works as the interface where transferences between living kinds and objects happen.

15. My use of the term "semblance" is inspired by Susanne Langer (1953) and Brian Massumi (2011), but Silvia Posocco (2015) uses Ludwig Josef Johann Wittgenstein's notion of "family resemblances" similarly to think through the relation between material remains and knowledge.

16. Arjun Appadurai has shown that relations between a model or meaning and its counterpart activity are not necessarily symmetrical, since models may recalibrate reality retrospectively as well as prospectively, producing the conditions that they also presuppose. Appadurai illustrates this double performativity describing how derivatives contract, as ritualized performances, and produce retrodictively the conditions of their own felicity: "this retro-creativity of certain performatives ... exposes the fact that the entire ritual is an exercise in enacting uncertainty in such a form as to increase the likelihood of resolving it" (2016: 125), which determines "the terms in which uncertainty is understood" (Appadurai 2016: 138).

References

Anderson, E. S. 1991. "John Stuart Mill and Experiments in Living." *Ethics* 102: 4–26.

Appadurai, A. 2016. *Banking on Words: The Failure of Language in the Age of Derivative Finance.* Chicago, IL: The University of Chicago Press.

Bal, M. 2002. *Travelling Concepts in the Humanities: A Rough Guide.* Toronto: University of Toronto Press.

Barad, K. M. 2007. *Meeting the Universe Halfway: Quantum Physics and the Entanglement of Matter and Meaning.* Durham, NC: Duke University Press.

Bataille, G. 1985. "Formless." In *Vision of Excess: Selected Writings, 1927–1939,* ed. and trans. A. Stoekl with C. Lovitt and D. Leslie, Jr., 31. Minneapolis, MN: University of Minnesota Press.

Besnier, N. 2002. "Transgenderism, Locality, and the Miss Galaxy Beauty Pageant in Tonga." *American Ethnologist* 29: 534–66.

Bloch, M. 1998. *How We Think They Think: Anthropological Approaches to Cognition, Memory and Literacy.* Oxford: Westview Press.

Born, G. 2013a. "Introduction—Music, Sound and Space: Transformations of Public and Private Experience." In *Music, Sound and Space: Transformations of Public and Private Experience,* ed. G. Born, 1–71. Cambridge: Cambridge University Press.

———. 2013b. "Music: Ontology, Agency, Creativity." In *Distributed Objects: Meaning and Mattering after Alfred Gell,* ed. L. Chua and M. Elliot, 130–154. Oxford: Berghahn Books.

Boyer, D., and T. Morton. 2016. "Hyposubjects." *Cultural Anthropology,* 21 January. Retrieved 18 May 2018 from http://www.culanth.org/fieldsights/798-hyposubjects.

Cameron, L. 1996. *Body Alchemy: Transsexual Portraits.* Pittsburgh, PA: Cleis Press.

Carter, J. B., D. Getsy, and T. Salah. 2014. "Introduction." *TSQ: Transgender Studies Quarterly* 1: 469–81.

Cotten, T. 2012. *Transgender Migrations: The Bodies, Borders, and Politics of Transition.* London: Routledge.

Crawford, L. 2015. *Transgender Architectonics: The Shape of Change in Modernist Space.* Farnham, UK: Ashgate Publishing.

de la Cadena M. 2010. "Indigenous Cosmopolitics in the Andes: Conceptual Reflections beyond 'Politics.'" *Cultural Anthropology* 25: 334–70.

Erharter, C., D. Schwärzler, R. Sircar, H. Scheirl. 2015. *Pink Labour on Golden Streets: Queer Art Practices.* Berlin: Sternberg Press.

Foucault, M. [1970] 2001. *The Order of Things: An Archaeology of the Human Sciences.* London: Routledge.

Franklin, S. 2006. "The Cyborg Embryo: Our Path to Transbiology." *Theory, Culture & Society* 23: 167–87.

Fraser, M. 2005. "Making Music Matter." *Theory, Culture & Society* 22(1): 173–89. doi:10.1177/0263276405048440.

Gatt, C., and T. Ingold. 2013. "From Description to Correspondence: Anthropology in Real Time." In *Design Anthropology: Theory and Practice,* ed. W. Gunn, T. Otto, and C. Smith, 139–158. London: Bloomsbury.

Gell, A. 1998. *Art and Agency: An Anthropological Theory,* Oxford: Clarendon.

Getsy, D. 2014. "Capacity." *Postposttranssexual: Key Concepts for Twenty-First Century Transgender Studies.* S. Stryker and P. Currah. Special issue of *Transgender Studies Quarterly* 1(1–2): 47–49.

———. 2015. *Abstract Bodies: Sixties Sculpture in the Expanded Field of Gender.* New Haven, CT: Yale University Press.

Gonzalez-Polledo, E. 2017. *Transitioning: Matter, Gender, Thought.* London: Rowman and Littlefield International.

Halberstam, J. 2005. *In a Queer Time and Place: Transgender Bodies, Subcultural Lives.* New York: New York University Press.

_____. 2011. *The Queer Art of Failure.* Durham, NC: Duke University Press.

Hall, G. 2013. "Object Lessons: Thinking Gender Variance through Minimalist Sculpture." *Art Journal* 72(4): 46–57.

Haritaworn, J., A. Kuntsman, and S. Posocco. 2014. *Queer Necropolitics.* Abingdon, UK: Routledge, Taylor & Francis Group, a GlassHouse Book.

Hawkins, G. 2006. *The Ethics of Waste: How We Relate to Rubbish.* Lanham, MD: Rowman & Littlefield.

Johnson, D. 2014. "Voice, Performance, and Border Crossings: An Interview with Tobaron Waxman." *Transgender Studies Quarterly* 1: 614–19.

_____. 2015. *The Art of Living: An Oral History of Performance Art.* London: Palgrave Macmillan.

Jones, S. 2014. "Pretty, Dead: Sociosexuality, Rationality and the Transition into Zom Being." In *Zombies and Sexuality: Essays on Desire and the Living Dead,* ed. S. McGlotten and S. Jones, 180–198. Jefferson, NC: McFarland & Company.

Kelty, C. 2005. "Geeks, Social Imaginaries, and Recursive Publics." *Cultural Anthropology* 20: 185–214.

Küchler, S. 2013. "Threads of Thought: Reflections on Art and Agency." In *Distributed Objects: Meaning and Mattering after Alfred Gell,* ed. L. Chua and M. Elliot, 25–39, Oxford: Berghahn Books.

Kwon, M. 2002. *One Place after Another: Site-Specific Art and Locational Identity.* Cambridge, MA: MIT Press.

Langer, S. K. 1953. *Feeling and Form: A Theory of Art Developed from Philosophy in a New Key.* London: Routledge & Kegan Paul.

Lazar, S. 2008. *El Alto, Rebel City: Self and Citizenship In Andean Bolivia.* Durham, NC: Duke University Press.

Macbeath, A. 1952. *Experiments in Living.* London: Macmillan.

Malafouris, L. 2013. *How Things Shape the Mind: A Theory of Material Engagement.* Cambridge, MA: MIT Press.

Marchand, T. H. J. 2010a. "Making Knowledge: Explorations of the Indissoluble Relation between Minds, Bodies, and Environment." *Journal of the Royal Anthropological Institute* 16: S1–S21.

_____. 2010b. "Embodied Cognition and Communication: Studies with British Fine Woodworkers." *Journal of the Royal Anthropological Institute* 16: S100–S120.

Marres, N. 2012. "Experiment: The Experiment in Living." In *Inventive Methods: The Happening of the Social,* ed. C. Lury and N. Wakeford, 76–95. London: Routledge.

Massumi, B. 2011. *Semblance and Event: Activist Philosophy and the Occurrent Arts.* Cambridge, MA: MIT Press.

McNamara, C., and A. Rooke. 2008. "The Pedagogy and Performance of Sci:Dentities." In *Creative Encounters,* ed. R. Levinson, H. Nicholson, and S. Parry, 174–93. London: The Wellcome Trust.

Meltzer, E. 2013. *Systems We Have Loved: Conceptual Art, Affect, and the Antihumanist Turn.* Chicago, IL: University of Chicago Press.

Mill, J. S. 2003. *On Liberty,* ed. David Bromwich and George Kateb. New Haven, CT and London: Yale University Press.

More, K., and S. Whittle. 1999. *Reclaiming Genders: Transsexual Grammars at the Fin De Siecle.* London: Cassell.

Morton, T. 2010. *The Ecological Thought.* Cambridge, MA: Harvard University Press.

Namaste, V. K. 2005. *Sex Change, Social Change: Reflections on Identity, Institutions and Imperialism.* Toronto: Women's Press.

Ochoa, M. 2008. "Perverse Citizenship: Divas, Marginality, and Participation in 'Loca-Lization'." *WSQ: Women's Studies Quarterly,* 36(3): 146–169.

Parisi, L. 2013. *Contagious Architecture: Computation, Aesthetics, and Space.* Cambridge, MA: MIT Press.

Posocco, S. 2015. "Substance, Sign, and Trace: Performative Analogies and Technologies of Enfleshment in the Transnational Adoption Archives in Guatemala." *Social & Cultural Geography,* 16(5): 567–84. doi:10.1080/14649365.2015.1009855.

Povinelli, E. A. 1993. "'Might Be Something': The Language of Indeterminacy in Australian Aboriginal Land Use." *Man* 28(4): 679–704. doi:10.2307/2803992.

———. 2002. *The Cunning of Recognition: Indigenous Alterities and the Making of Australian Multiculturalism.* Durham, NC: Duke University Press.

Prosser, J. 1998. *Second Skins: The Body Narratives of Transsexuality,* New York: Columbia University Press.

Ramirez, M. C. 2007. *Hélio Oiticica: The Body of Colour.* London: Tate Publishing in association with The Museum of Fine Arts, Houston.

Ramirez, M. C., and H. Olea. 2004. *Inverted Utopias: Avant-Garde Art in Latin America.* New Haven, CT: Yale University Press.

Rapport, N. 2016. *Distortion and Love: An Anthropological Reading of the Art and Life of Stanley Spencer.* Farnham, UK: Ashgate Publishing.

Raymond, J. G. 1979. *The Transsexual Empire: The Making of the She-male.* Boston, MA: Beacon Press.

Rooke, A. 2010. "Trans Youth, Science and Art: Creating (Trans) Gendered Space." *Gender, Place and Culture* 17: 655–72.

Rosskam, J. 2014. "Porous Cels." *Transgender Studies Quarterly* 1: 586–89.

Sansi, R. 2015. *Art, Anthropology and the Gift.* London: Bloomsbury Academic.

Scheirl, H. 2004. "The Earth Is Pregnant with Art: A Trans- ... World." *The Repolitization of Sexual Space in Contemporary Artistic Practices.* San Sebastian, Spain: Arteleku.

Schilt, K. 2010. *Just One of the Guys?: Transgender Men and the Persistence of Gender Inequality.* Chicago, IL: University of Chicago Press.

Schneider, A., and C. Wright. 2013. "Ways of Working." In *Anthropology and Art Practice,* ed. A. Schneider and C. Wright, 1–24. London: Bloomsbury Academic.

Small, I. 2016. *Hélio Oiticica: Folding the Frame.* Chicago, IL: University of Chicago Press.

Sneath, D., M. Holbraad, and M.A. Pedersen. 2009. "Technologies of the Imagination: An Introduction." *Ethnos* 74: 5–30.

Ssorin-Chaikov, N. 2013. "Ethnographic Conceptualism: An Introduction." *Laboratorium* 2. Retrieved 18 May 2018 from http://www.soclabo.org/index.php/laboratorium/article/view/336/864.

Steinbock, E. 2013. "Groping Theory: Haptic Cinema and Trans-Curiosity in Hans Scheirl's Dandy Dust." In *The Transgender Studies Reader 2,* ed. S. Stryker and A. Z. Aizura, 101–118. London: Routledge.

Stone, S. [1992] 2008. "The Empire Strikes Back: A Post-Transsexual Manifesto." In *Body Guards: Cultural Politics of Gender Ambiguity,* ed. J. Epstein and K Straub, 280–304. London: Routledge.

Stryker, S. 1994. "My Words to Victor Frankenstein above the Village of Chamounix: Performing Transgender Rage." *A Journal of Lesbian and Gay Studies* 1: 237–54.

———. 1998. "The Transgender Issue." *A Journal of Lesbian and Gay Studies* 4: 145–58.

Stryker, S., and A. Z. Aizura. 2013. *The Transgender Studies Reader 2*. London: Routledge.

Stryker, S., and P. Currah. 2014. "Introduction." *Transgender Studies Quarterly* 1: 1–18.

Thompson, N. 2012. *Living as Form: Socially Engaged Art from 1991–2011*. Cambridge, MA: MIT Press.

──────. 2015. *Seeing Power: Art and Activism in the Age of Culture Production*. New York: Melville House.

Toren, C. 1990. *Making Sense of Hierarchy: Cognition as Social Process in Fiji*. London: Athlone Press

Turner, V. W. 1969. *The Ritual Process: Structure and Anti-Structure*. London: Routledge & K. Paul.

Vaccaro, J. 2010. "Transbiological Bodies: Mine, Yours, Ours." *Women & Performance: A Journal of Feminist Theory* 20: 221–24.

Valentine, D. 2007. *Imagining Transgender: An Ethnography of a Category*, Durham, NC: Duke University Press.

Volcano, D. L. 2001. *Sublime Mutations*, Berlin: Konkursbuchverlag.

Wilson, D., and D. Sperber. 2012. *Meaning and Relevance*. Cambridge: Cambridge University Press.

3

The Production of Indeterminacy
On the Unforeseeable Futures of Postindustrial Excess

Felix Ringel

I start this chapter with an anecdote from my fieldwork in Bremerhaven, a typical postindustrial harbor city in northern Germany, where I carried out fieldwork intermittently from 2014 until 2017. Many a night during fieldwork I wearily cycled back to the southern part of the city where I was staying at the time. Usually my route would take me over the intersection of two streets, Pestalozzistrasse and Kistnerstrasse. Pestalozzistrasse is a fairly wide street that leads from the city center to the northern half of the harbor, which once provided thousands of jobs for the city's inhabitants. Several decades ago, I presume, it must have been a very busy street, day and night; however, whenever I cycled along it, there were hardly any cars, cyclists, or pedestrians. The remaining modernized harbor businesses needed fewer workers than their predecessors, so the streets did not serve the functions for which they had been initially designed. Nonetheless, the intersection remained regulated by a traffic light, and I repeatedly debated with myself whether or not I should stop and wait for the green light when the roads were so evidently empty. Irritated by the city's failure to adapt its infrastructure more quickly to its current use, I wondered whether urban planners were leaving the roads as they were in case of another unexpected change in the city's fortunes. If so, they were showing remarkable foresight: in these postindustrial times, they might have been keeping this infrastructural excess as a hidden reserve despite its indeterminacy, for a different future yet to come. For that, however, its existence had to be rendered indeterminate first, in order to maintain its openness for a different future in the present.

The refugee crisis in 2015, for instance, was such an unexpected future; it caused an unforeseen rise in local population and prompted the sudden revaluation of the city's postindustrial infrastructural and material excess in myriad ways. The municipal government had to reconsider the value of houses readied for demolition; many citizens retrieved household items they had stored for years in basements; planners reconsidered the city's superfluous traffic lights and roads, which might be put to good use again since the city's population was once more on the rise. Such practices of revaluation helped to reconsider the temporal properties of postindustrial excess, whose future had until recently been avoided, forgotten, or forfeited. The changing temporal properties of postindustrial excess are the main subject of this chapter. For their analysis, I scrutinize the idea of indeterminacy. On a metaphysical level, I understand indeterminacy not as the given, all-determining context of human life and material objects. Rather, I propose that indeterminacy is a product of the social negotiation and revaluation of people's expectations. In the ethnographic material I present below, it is a value often only momentarily attached to postindustrial infrastructures, objects and people. In most cases, this is done in a moment that both my informants and I describe as a moment of surprise. I want to draw attention to such moments, when we are forced to reconsider the present and future of these objects of thought and adjust our expectations anew. The future we reconsider, I propose, is not per se open or indeterminate. In the moment of surprise we do not reveal this openness—but we produce it.

I thus follow the overall claim of this volume that we should look at the social life of indeterminacy, rather than take it for granted. In Bremerhaven, it is not the existence of all houses, streets, or traffic lights that is subject to the production of indeterminacy. Instead, only the existence of very specific houses, streets, and traffic lights is rendered problematic. These specific objects have been expelled from the current postindustrial order but, through their unexpected revaluation, they have once again become the object of human agency, scrutiny, and practice (Howe et al. 2016: 552). In the context of socialist-industrial modernity's infrastructural excess in postsocialist Vietnam, Christina Schwenkel (2013: 273) defines the temporal quality of such ruins as an "ambiguous duality" of "permanence and instability, hope and despair." This ambiguity describes what Catherine Alexander and Andrew Sanchez in this volume's introduction refer to as the "condition of indeterminacy," which I take as being constituted in a moment of revaluation: when hope is added to postindustrial despair, and a future is given to something that did not previously have a future. In postindustrial times, however, this ambiguity can also be sustained for other purposes. A lesson learned from the experiences of surprise and indeterminacy is that we will have to live with this ambiguity because there might be yet other surprises ahead: any futures can be lost again, and any hope can be disappointed.

I approach the idea of indeterminacy as a presentist. For a presentist, metaphysically, it is only the present that exists: the past and the future do not exist, except as representations in the present (see Adam 1990; Ringel 2016a). For a presentist, then, indeterminacy is not a transhistorical condition or force.

Rather, it describes a certain temporal quality of an anthropological object of analysis in a specific present, irrespective of this present's pasts and indeterminacy's viability in the future. This means that these objects' existence (in the present) neither is, nor has been, nor will ever be fully determinate, fixed, or predefined, not even by indeterminacy. Because its existence was not predetermined with regard to its past, its present is also not predetermined with regard to its future (see Nielsen 2014). This object only exists in the present. This present is only in hindsight created as a state of ambiguity and potential surprise, when this object's existence is rendered problematic, i.e., indeterminate. For example, that the traffic lights from the introductory vignette above would become superfluous was not predetermined. At any point, history could have taken a different turn; that it has not done so, does not change this fact. However, each present can be evaluated as more or less determinate with regard to their futures regardless of how this future actually turns out to be.

The same argument can be made in relation to the roads in the above example. Their current redundant existence was neither determinate nor foreseeable; the recent mismatch between their width and the actual traffic flows, a typical phenomenon of the postindustrial era, rather constitutes them as objects out of sync with their current present as much as with the expectations that were initially invested in them. However, they are not simply ruins of industrial modernity's anticipations or the physical residue of other devalued past expectations (see Dawdy 2010; Hell and Schönle 2010; Schwenkel 2013; also Ferguson 1999). They are objects of debate and consideration in the present. Moreover, they will also not necessarily remain ruins of recent postindustrial expectations (see Gupta 2013; Nielsen 2014). Even as ruins, these roads might regain value at any point in the future, as Mathijs Pelkmans (2003, 2013) shows in the case of postsocialist ruins in Georgia and Kyrgyzstan or Catherine Fennel for postindustrial Chicago (2012). But this potential change would not be a sign of indeterminacy-as-context, but it would indicate that indeterminacy first has to be produced. This chapter therefore offers a fresh take on the analysis of modernity's ruins via a consideration of how the "condition of indeterminacy" can inform their presents and futures.

In Bremerhaven's postindustrial present, indeterminacy became a recurrent issue (see Jalas, Rinkinen, and Silvast 2016), and the postindustrial future of Kistnerstrasse, Pestalozzistrasse, and their traffic lights remains open-ended: they could be demolished or replaced tomorrow or remain unchanged and work to no purpose for decades to come; or perhaps if the city's fate takes yet another turn, they might return in full glory to their past's function in the future. There is hope and despair, as Schwenkel would have it, in such a presentist conceptualization of indeterminacy. However, human beings are intimately entangled in the production of indeterminacy, often exhibiting something I have elsewhere defined as temporal agency (Ringel 2016b). They very flexibly navigate (Vigh 2006) between different and competing expectations, persistently create new values and quickly overcome their own surprises at different turns. The social production, maintenance, and contestation of relations to the future are often not threatened, but enhanced by indeterminacy. In this sense, indeterminacy creates a pause that allows for temporal agency to act upon the present and its relations to the future: the surprise of the unexpected compels a response. Gisa Weszkalnys (2015: 632), in her article on the indeterminacy of first oil in São Tomé and Príncipe, refers to this undetermined moment as a "sustained pause." I take her point: this pause "is not a bad place to start" (ibid.: 633) our analysis.

My argument falls into three parts: first, by reflecting upon the unforeseen futures of industrial infrastructure in postindustrial times, particularly the city's main street Columbusstrasse, I operationalize the temporal aspects of the anthropology of infrastructure in order to consider the production of both determinacy and indeterminacy. Second, by thinking through current issues in the anthropology of time in relation to questions of agency, I focus on the production of determinacy. For this, I explore Bremerhaven's immediate responses to what has been termed the "refugee crisis," documenting my informants' attempts to produce determinacy and secure new futures for refugees and their livelihoods as well as for their own city. Finally, in the third part, I turn to the numerous local houses, known in Bremerhaven as "scrap houses" (*Schrotthäuser*). These houses are so dilapidated that they are formally deemed too unsafe to live in. For very good reasons, maintenance work is not done to them by their inhabitants. With the help of this last ethnographic example, I advance the idea of the production (and maintenance) of indeterminacy as a mode of being in the postindustrial era. Indeterminacy allows me to attend to the work in, and on, the postindustrial present, acknowledging the production of indeterminacy (and determinacy) as complex and contested socio-political processes that, rather than being charged with "lacking" a relationship to the future, offer a new and complex relationship to the present. Despite the unforeseen dimensions of precarity and uncertainty in our times, the indeterminacy of the postindustrial present effectively incites and encourages human agency rather than suppresses it (see Muehlebach and Shoshan 2012). Before I develop this argument fully, I further introduce my postindustrial field site, and expand on the question of postindustrial excess in the anthropology of infrastructure in the next section.

Excess Urban Infrastructure and Indeterminacy

Bremerhaven was founded in 1827 as the harbor of Bremen, 60 km north of the old Hansa city. The rich city of Bremen feared for its trade capacities because the river connecting it to the North Sea, and thereby to the world at large, was increasingly silting up. Bremen thus bought a piece of land from the Kingdom of Hanover and built a new harbor from scratch. Since its foundation, this harbor city has seen many changes, from its initial growth and the widespread devastation during World War II to the city's rebirth during the German *Wirtschaftswunder* (economic miracle) in the 1950s and the subsequent drastic postindustrial decline that started in the 1970s. Fissures in its economic history, however, are most clearly illustrated by the history of its harbor(s).

The Old Harbor marks the center of Bremerhaven. It was here that everything began. Later, in the nineteenth century, this harbor was extended toward both the north and south of the city's coastline, facilitating the movement of people and things to and from ever more shipping vessels. Currently, millions of containers are unloaded each year in the northern part of the harbor. Toward the south, the Fishing Harbor, once the home of West Germany's national high-sea fishing fleet, now showcases several firms producing offshore windfarm equipment such as rotor blades and gondolas. Plans for the future add a further industrial zone for the Green Economy and an entirely new Offshore Terminal.

During the constant transformation of the harbor due to very different structural changes, parts of the harbor have at times lost their socioeconomic value. The dilapidated Old Harbor, for instance, for a very long time only served as a giant parking lot, accommodating neither ships nor other economic activities. The same holds for the New Harbor, which lay as barren as its predecessor, particularly in the early postindustrial era of the 1970s. Only now, after a huge postindustrial makeover that started in 2004, are most inhabitants of Bremerhaven once again proud of these long-term brownfield sites. Even the most critical skeptics of these developments are impressed by the many touristic attractions, stylish marina, and several high-end apartment blocks with their sought-after views over the river delta. However, Bremerhaven's spatio-material layout and existence has been subjected to many unpredictable revaluations. The notion of surprise and cautious hopes dominates my informants' accounts in the postindustrial era.

One example clearly demonstrates the social production and use of indeterminacy in this context: the controversial construction of the new offshore terminal. This future project is supported by the municipal senator responsible for the city's harbor and economy, but at the same time, most people expect that there will not be a need for another terminal because of the current (and clearly unexpected) crisis of the local offshore wind industry.[1] However, as the young and dynamic senator never tires of pointing out when arguing for the construction: more than a hundred years earlier, Bremerhaven's famous Emperor's Lock (*Kaiserschleuse*), still one of the biggest of its kind, was also built against then contemporary expectations, during a time when only four ships in the whole world needed its colossal dimensions. But these expectations turned out to be wrong. Against all critical predictions, the *Kaiserschleuse* went on to serve the city well for a hundred years because its size had unexpectedly proven to become necessary for global trade. That this ambitious plan did actually work, despite many skeptical predictions, must have taken even its most fervent advocates by surprise, underlining the potential elusiveness of all planning practices (see Abram and Weszkalnys 2013). Although serving a political purpose, the senator's hopeful statement retrospectively invokes a past condition of indeterminacy in order to allow for the valence of a current infrastructural project's still unlikely promise of success. In a hundred years or so, the senator might, indeed, turn out to be right with his predictions of the future of the offshore terminal.

However, such revaluations of postindustrial infrastructure in the present pose a more general problem to the still growing academic interest in the topic of infrastructure (Harvey et al. 2017; Howe et al. 2016; Larkin 2013). As Dominic Boyer (2017: 174) notes, "one associates the term 'infrastructure' with massive, durable works of material artifice ... their scale and ubiquity suggest a temporality of perdurance." However, as many scholars convincingly point out, infrastructure's success and durability, materially as well as socially, depends on, among other things, human agency and practice (e.g., Mains 2012; von Schnitzler 2013). This means, ontologically, infrastructures are not per se durable: their existence in time is shaped by factors other than their material make-up. As we have become aware of in postindustrial times, their determinacy has to be continually produced through similarly enduring practices of maintenance and care (see Graham and Thrift 2007; Jansen 2013; Ringel 2014; also Crapanzano 2007; Graeber 2012).

Infrastructures initially caught the attention of anthropologists and other social scientists because of their material hugeness, their invisibility as *infra*structures (Star and Ruhleder 1996) or their symbolic value (Larkin 2013; Pelkmans 2003). However, with the retreat of the modernist welfare state, infrastructures often became a problem. Many scholars came to realize that they had taken them for granted throughout industrial modernity, including the fact that these infrastructures work and that there will be more of them (see Howe et al. 2016: 550). The spectacular failure of industrial infrastructures' longevity and robustness, and the acknowledgement of the previously unnoticed necessary maintenance work to uphold them, has already added temporal dimensions to the study of infrastructure (e.g., Graham and Thrift 2007). Postindustrial times and spaces have underlined the rather precarious and fragile existence in time of infrastructures, even the most robust steel-and-concrete structures, iron railways, or undersea fiber cables. After initial disbelief, their existence and futures have been rendered indeterminate in the postindustrial present.

As I discuss elsewhere (Ringel 2018), this is also the case for whole cities and their entire infrastructure. For example, the shrinking East German city of Hoyerswerda was suddenly made redundant following the decline of state-socialism and German reunification. More than a third of Hoyerswerda's socialist New City has subsequently been demolished, including eleven-story apartment houses, streets, schools, kindergartens, supermarkets, and major parts of the subterranean infrastructure—sewage systems, electrical wires, etc.[2] As this extreme example shows, it is therefore hard to discern even a normal building's existence in time (Ringel 2014). Whether in times of growth or decline, infrastructure also seems to be constantly lagging behind sociopolitical changes due to its presumed robustness and perdurability. As recent history has shown, however, it can nonetheless become fragile at any point.

In Bremerhaven, in contrast, the devaluation of industrial infrastructure happened over a much longer period of time. Let me unpack the moment of (temporal) revaluation of only one particular postindustrial infrastructure in more detail, the city's main street: Columbusstrasse. Although subject to slow decay through wind, rain, snow, use, and more, this built object has not changed its material composition or physical and chemical qualities. Rather, what changed completely was the context in which this street found itself affected by the drastic socioeconomic changes suffered in Bremerhaven.

Throughout its existence, many different expectations have already been invested in the future of Columbusstrasse. Conventional party politics seem to be infused with the clashes of such expectations. Debates usually entail different political factions and their respective representations of the future. However, the same people and factions often find themselves in the awkward position of having to revalue their own previous predictions. This can be embarrassing. Local politicians, for instance, were for a long time very proud of the six-lane motorway that cuts right through the elongated city all the way from the north to the south.

I was told that, in the 1970s, predictions of a further population increase to 250,000 (from then approximately 130,000) inhabitants were part of the ruling Labor Party's argument for the construction of this arterial street and the

Figure 3.1. Columbusstrasse, Bremerhaven City Center, photo by the author.

widening and full replacement of Columbusstrasse's smaller predecessors. Only forty years later (and with an unpredicted population of 115,000 people), Columbusstrasse has not turned out to cater to a city with 250,000 inhabitants since Bremerhaven never reached this population level.

Rather, for years, Bremerhaven was West Germany's fastest shrinking city: its shipyards and high-sea fishing industry had already closed by the late 1970s; after German reunification, it also lost its role as the US army's port of embarkation, forfeiting several thousand inhabitants more or less overnight. For the last decade or so, it has tried to reinvent itself as a "Climate City," which, under the recent Labor Party and Green Party coalition, involved progressive policies on public transport, the expansion of the city's cycle path network and public support for e-bikes and other alternative forms of individual transport. Now, the mismatch between the local population (quantitatively and in relation to its traffic behavior) and the size and quality of the urban infrastructure forces the city's authorities to reconsider the main traffic route's future. In hindsight, the promises of the infrastructure plans from the 1970s turned out to be misleading.

The city's elaborate road infrastructure of the late industrial era, however, has currently not just partly lost its value; with shifts on very different scales and beyond the city's control, it is suddenly seen to constitute a material obstacle to the city's future. This transforms Columbusstrasse, which had been a well-functioning street for decades, into not only a ruin of past planning and expectation—and plans, indeed, do often fail in very unexpected ways (see for example, Alexander 2007)—but also into a ruin of much more recent anticipation. The present problematization of Columbusstrasse renders its existence indeterminate, referring its contemporary existence to the past while excluding its present from the future. Columbusstrasse's condition of indeterminacy is a product of recent times, an outcome of a sociopolitical process of renegotiation.

One aspect of Bremerhaven's recent reinvention was to invest a large portion of federal funds into tourist infrastructures in order to fight the city's postindustrial crisis. As a result, the old harbor area currently houses several supraregional tourist attractions: the older German Shipping Museum (opened in the 1970s) is now flanked by the German Migration Museum, the Climate Center (an experience-based science center), a brand-new shopping mall called Mediterraneo, a high-end marina, and a four-star hotel and convention center. Unfortunately, these newly built Harbor Worlds (*Havenwelten*), located directly on the seafront and the city's main dykes, are cut off from the older city center and its shopping mall, theaters, art museum, and restaurants by the six-lane inner-city motorway. Two pedestrian bridges cross Columbusstrasse, one of which is itself a tourist attraction with its sophisticated glass-design jacket, linking the new sights of the Old Harbor with the city's main shopping mall. However, although adjacent, these two parts of the city are still not actually connected in the sense of being organically interwoven. Columbusstrasse is thus not merely excessive and redundant in postindustrial Bremerhaven, but actively wasteful of the city center's capacity to reinvent itself.

In January 2014, the city administration presented the expert report of a consultant planning office, which had been asked to develop ideas for new connections between the new *Havenwelten* and the city center. They included reducing the number of lanes of Columbusstrasse, constructing pedestrian and cycle paths, and planting rows of trees to improve the areas' attractiveness. This was intended to transform the former transport axis into something like a promenade. Furthermore, several transverse links would guide the streams of visitors across it, for which particular visual devices (special lights and floor coverings) were to be installed. Bremerhaven's Lord Mayor described the report's outcome as a handbook of ideas, "on the basis of which we can gain a totally new perception of the possibilities in our city"—another straightforward political use of indeterminacy. Indeed, these ideas, he underlined, "will finally synchronize different phases of our city's development." In 2016, the city reorganized its annual city festival with the same intentions in mind, and thereby tested this possible future in practice. With much effort, visitors and locals alike were guided between the area around the Old Harbor (with its many fairground booths) and the central market square (the venue for the temporary street food festival), all in order to overcome the burden of Columbusstrasse. In its original dimensions, it seems, this street faces a rather unsecure future. In its newly planned dimensions, it might potentially rest more comfortably in future presents. The times have changed and with them this street's existence. Whereas its future has not been questioned for several decades, it is now the very concrete subject of much thought and planning. As we see, before its future could be, at least, momentarily determinate again, its existence in time had first persistently to be rendered indeterminate.

However, despite the overall surprisingly indeterminate social life of robust urban infrastructures, many of my informants found Columbusstrasse's unexpected indeterminacy in the form of unexpected potential futures only surprising for a moment. They quickly adjusted to its new prospects. As Alexei Yurchak has it in his felicitous phrasing (2004), old Columbusstrasse was to "last forever," until it suddenly "was no more." However, as in Yurchak's example of the last Soviet generation, this sudden change was noted but did not constitute a problem for long. With regard to the future of Columbusstrasse some still worried it might take them longer to get around the city, and some members of the Conservative Party showed some remorse about the road's reduction. Others, in turn, jokingly suggested that the city might never actually find the funding to carry out this revitalization. And since the future remained hard to predict, the street's present continued to be (made) indeterminate.

The short-lived nature of surprise by my informants indicates that they might have different metaphysics in mind with regard to Boyer's idea of infrastructure's "temporality of perdurance." In fact, although they had not previously considered the road's transformation, they quickly seemed to be busy with its new futures, discussing and doubting potential benefits and problems in further attempts to determine this new future. They used this sustained moment of indeterminacy to go ahead, or to keep the present open for other futures. Particularly the local shop-owners invested the new plans—and the street's newly indeterminate present—with much hope for more sales and clientele.

As we have seen in this section, the existence of Bremerhaven's industrial urban infrastructure in time can be rendered indeterminate despite its robustness. This underlines its surprising fragility and adaptability. Most ethnographies of infrastructure emphasize that infrastructure is always embedded in its specific and always changing sociocultural context. But in such accounts, the infrastructure usually stays the same whereas the sociocultural context changes. However, ontologically both infrastructure and its social context are subject to change, and their indeterminacy, as much as their determinacy, has to be produced. For several decades, the existence of Columbusstrasse was unproblematic. Only the recent changes have made its position in the present awkward, and thereafter sparked intense discussions and thought in an attempt to determine its new futures. This moment of indeterminacy should not draw attention away from the many times and periods in which determinacy was successfully produced and upheld, and during which the temporal existence of these infrastructures remained unproblematic. The next section links the production of determinacy more thoroughly to recent debates in the anthropology of time and agency. This time, other forms of excess in Bremerhaven sustain my argument.

Excess People/Things /Futures? The Production of Determinacy during the European "Refugee Crisis"

Reyhane suddenly appeared at a meeting of the Working Committee for Migration and Refugees (Arbeitskreis Migration und Flüchtlinge), one of the many initiatives that organized support for the refugees who arrived in the city since 2014. Fourteen-year-old Mohammad, her only son, had accompanied her to the One World Center where the meeting took place, but did not dare to enter. His mother was pregnant back then, and had left her two daughters and her husband behind in Athens in order to find Mohammad, who, in a group of seven other minors, had attempted successfully to reach Germany overland by foot, crossing almost half the continent in permanent fear of being caught by some state's police force or custom officers. At that point, the whole family had been refugees for more than seven years. Once reunited in Germany, Reyhane and Mohammad were "allocated" to Bremerhaven, where they were given a temporary flat in an overcrowded *Auffanglager* (reception center). Reyhane is usually a strong and determined woman, but the worries about the imminent birth and her family's situation in Greece made her ask for help at this Working Committee's meeting, which she had heard about from other refugees. Tears were running down her cheeks as she told her story to Kerstin, a local activist and friend, and me, the two most confident English speakers of the group. Before the baby's birth, she wanted her family to be together again, to have a safe place to stay, and enough to eat, but at that very moment she did not know what to do. Kerstin and I decided to help her and became the family's *Paten* (godparents).

Two days later, I visited them in their new flat, to which they had moved from the overcrowded reception center across the street just after our first meeting. The houses in Hansastrasse, as Kerstin told me later, had initially been erected just after the end of World War II to house other refugees: German nationals from previously German areas in Eastern Europe. That is how Kerstin's mother had arrived in Bremerhaven, a story she usually referred to when explaining her motivation to care for refugees: "My family came as refugees, too!" Interestingly, the whole of Hansastrasse, with its remaining 1950s apartment blocks, had already been readied for destruction before the refugee crisis, which is why they were empty in the wake of the crisis and were available for a different future. Excess housing for excess people provided an unexpected fit. Excess urban infrastructure from the times of the industrial, postwar era, built for refugees who came to Bremerhaven in order to find work in the harbor, had first lost its function in the postindustrial times of population shrinkage, then became an obstacle and a liability rather than something useful, and suddenly, to everybody's surprise, the formerly useless infrastructure was of great value again. It soon sheltered more than two hundred people, mostly families and young single men from different parts of the world.

This move to Hansastrasse was timely indeed. The city (as well as the whole German state) was, in the eyes of many local activists, too slow in adjusting to

Figure 3.2. Hansastrasse, Bremerhaven, photo by the author.

the arrival of what turned out to be almost a million refugees in 2015 alone, particularly from Syria and Afghanistan. The time it takes to develop new infrastructures was given as the main reason for the delay, but for many it was more a matter of thoughtfully using what was already there. For such critics, the state apparatus needed too long to adjust. The refugee crisis, one could say, found the state initially empty-handed. Since the state was seen failing to manage the crisis, volunteers did what they had expected the state to do: provide the refugees with the means of livelihood—non-bureaucratically, if need be.

To be fair, the city's administration managed to supply Reyhane and Mohammad with many good quality basics in their slowly furbished flat. On my first visit, I noted their two new beds, two mattresses, two duvets, one fridge, one table (but no chairs), one sink, and one oven. Much later a washing machine arrived, too. In addition, they owned one knife, two spoons, two forks, some crockery, and one cooking pot. I was taken aback, however, by the absence of linen, pillows, and pillowcases. Kerstin and I immediately organized these for the two as well as more kitchen utensils. When asked about what they needed most, Reyhane, to our surprise, put carpets and a television at the top of the list. Kerstin was a genius in finding things for Reyhane and Mohammad. Even a wonderfully old-fashioned four-piece sofa set soon adorned their living room. Kerstin and I were surprised by how many things we and our friends suddenly discovered at home, which had been hidden, in limbo, and out of sight, stored in attics or in basements. Faced with people who did not own

Figure 3.3. Donated Items at the Headquarters of the Equal Rights Club, Hansastrasse, Bremerhaven, photo by the author.

much more than the clothes they were wearing, these objects were reconsidered as surplus to their owner's need. This instant revaluation made the donors' material excess evident.

My experiences and Kerstin's prompted us a few months later to unite a few of the helper organizations to develop and implement our own guerrilla strategy against the city administration's too slow response to the crisis. In cooperation with the local newspaper, the Working Committee for Migration and Refugees had asked Bremerhaven's inhabitants to donate what they could spare and what was in good condition. We tried to specify, but, frankly, since most of the refugees arrived at the most with a plastic bag full of the most necessary things, everything was needed: mainly clothes and kitchen utensils, but also bicycles, toys for the children, footballs, and also linen and duvet covers. The results were impressive. Over a whole week, people came to the Kurdish-Turkish Verein für gleiche Rechte (Equal Rights Club), whose headquarters were also located in Hansastrasse, and brought mountains of clothing, bedding, kitchen pots, and even two dozen bikes.

The volunteers were overwhelmed and soon too exhausted to sort through and order the heaps of donated items. The refugees living across the street would come in and take the goods they needed. There were some distribution issues (people competing for the same items, for instance), and a few things could not find a new owner, but most of the donated items were put to full use again. The social life of these items, indeed, suddenly had a new future—as many donors commented: they had not used these things for ages and had in many cases even forgotten that they owned them. Reyhane, by the way, was both extremely grateful and careful about which items to choose for her family. Not all donated goods had the right value for her (see Alexander 2009): some looked too old-fashioned, others were deemed unnecessary.

These ethnographic examples of the sudden production of a new present and future for refugees and their new material goods exemplify the quotidian production of determinacy in times of crisis. Such practices, I claim, showcase temporal agency (Ringel 2016b) because they act upon the present and future of these "excess" people and items. These "items" are of a different type than the huge and robust ones discussed in the previous section. Linen and six-lane urban motorways, as much as this postindustrial city overall, can be given a new future. However, this particular form of temporal agency caters to a hope for change that does not wait for something new to emerge, but deals creatively with what is already there. In such cases, the indeterminacy of excess (newly found in the evaluation of these things as a hidden reserve) is immediately transformed into a new determinate state: the refugees are to stay in Bremerhaven, and the things shall help them there. Although this is creating a new future for these people and goods, it is, I claim, to be seen as a work in and on the present. This present had to be opened first by being rendered indeterminate after these items' past of non-acknowledgement, and before they can be given an at least preliminarily determinate future.

The revaluation of the existence in time of the refugees in Bremerhaven and the goods that were given to them upon their arrival, as much as the revaluation of the urban infrastructures from the previous section, entail the production of moments of indeterminacy and prospects of determinacy. Such acts of the revaluation of the future create a new present in which people, things, and infrastructures have suddenly become newly aligned. By giving each a different future, new relations in the present were established. On the basis of this observation, I will try to develop further my presentist perspective on indeterminacy in the next section. Both determinacy and indeterminacy can be easily constructed; the former usually prospectively (as a value in, as well as a relation to, the future), the latter usually retrospectively (in contrast and relation to past evaluations and expectations). Considering the present beyond a moment of indeterminacy, marked by surprise, might enhance our understanding of indeterminacy as a condition of the postindustrial present that is not just momentary, but can be sustained over time—in each consecutive present anew—for specific purposes.

The Maintenance of Indeterminacy

The last section uses yet another ethnographic example for this chapter's theoretical argument. This time, it is concerned with Bremerhaven's poorest, but also most beautiful neighborhood, the Goetheviertel (Goethe district), named after its central street dedicated to Germany's most famous poet. This is the only nineteenth-century Wilhelminian district to have fully survived the World War II bombings of Bremerhaven; its houses are often quite elaborately adorned with a variety of historicist symbols, statues, and designs. Nonetheless, this still is the poorest district in Germany's poorest city: it features some of the country's highest unemployment, poverty, and crime rates. It also came to house many refugees, including Reyhane and her family, despite the fact that some of the houses in Goetheviertel were filled with trash and their stairways barely usable. Others were even closed down by German building law, officially declared to be a *Schrotthaus*, a scrap house.

In the German language, *Schrott* is different from trash, waste, or excess, as it is usually too solid to be waste of a disposable kind. It is rather defined by its loss of function. Hence, in German something is quickly referred to as *Schrott* when it is broken or does not function anymore. However, these *Schrott*-houses are still somebody's property, and only a few years ago, the city had initiated a federal law on scrap houses to be more easily *rekommunalisiert*, i.e., to be lawfully reappropriated by the city. Once the property problems are solved, the city might want to demolish these *Schrotthäuser* in neighborhoods like the Goethe district in order to start a process of gentrification.

The futures of these houses and their inhabitants are therefore the subject of many official and voluntary attempts at reviving the Goethe district.

Nonetheless, visitors from Bremen, Hamburg, or Berlin are surprised that these attempts seem to fail and that gentrification had not done its wonders here yet. At first sight, the houses look impressive, and many people think that this should be an up-and-coming district in no time at all. With a second look, however, one quickly notices that they are empty, full of mold, and rapidly decaying. Despite that, however, some of their flats are still rented out illegally and only temporarily occupied.

Figure 3.4. Schrotthaus, Goetheviertel, Bremerhaven, photo by the author.

The broken-down character of these buildings was produced by the deliberate lack of maintenance. Several of my informants date the beginning of their district's decline back to the 1980s, when the city transformed the whole district into an investment area, facilitating the sale of the houses to investors from all over the world. These foreign investors saw the potential for good revenues, but when these revenues failed to appear due to a collapsed housing market, the investors stopped maintaining their properties for many decades. Now, because of the often shocking and fragile material state of the houses, the municipality has often deemed them unfit for either renovation or new investment.

As another kind of excess, a material one too stubborn to be properly expelled from the present, however, the scrap houses unexpectedly depict a kind of postindustrial agency: they allow the district's current inhabitants to stay. This time, these houses' material and legal indeterminacy creates hope for those living in and around these investment ruins. The scrap houses, due to their complicated legal status and awkward material conditions, help the local residents resist gentrification and prevent them from being excess inhabitants in their own district. This has been the case for some time now. But the improvement of the Goethe district is looming and, for some, in the end, it will be inevitable. Everybody expects it to happen, and at the same time, there continue to be delays, or, as Nikolai Ssorin-Chaikov has it in the case of Siberian

Figure 3.5. Schrotthaus, detail, Goetheviertel, Bremerhaven, photo by the author.

state-led modernization, people continue to "defer" (2003) this improvement. This allows the maintenance of indeterminacy of the overall Goethe district, renegotiated in every moment anew, with a variety of actors, including the houses. Resident groups have raised their voices; social clubs have opened their doors to the local poor; several cultural festivities take place in the district every year. In hindsight, these constant renegotiations of the district's present and future are attempts at sustaining the district's indeterminacy, to prevent the looming inevitability of a gentrified future and hold the present open for other futures.

Brigitte Hawelka, a cultural anthropologist by training, is the district's newly appointed *Quartiersmeisterin* (district manager). She sees speedy gentrification and people's expulsion as the biggest dangers for the district's future. However, her work falls into a context of very different, controversial expectations. Although the city administration wants her to initiate gentrification, many such attempts failed before Brigitte took over. The district's inhabitants, in turn, have heard many promises for making their district a better and safer place, but also continued living there despite the non-fulfillment of these promises. In this sense, I presume, it would be a bigger surprise for everybody involved if the wished-for prosperous future suddenly appeared. Meanwhile, most actors maintain the moment of indeterminacy with their differing hopes, fears, and expectations: the houses could still be rescued or demolished and times could still become better or worse. The inhabitants of the Goethe district in particular thereby maintain their district's present indeterminacy as a potential against all odds and promises. The city, too, keeps the idea of the district's potential alive in order to convince potential investors to stay tuned for a better future.

In this vague, but contested context, Brigitte's work focuses on making life in the district better in the present for those living here, while at the same time being able to sell these efforts to her employers as promoting the district's further development. Not incidentally, her first campaign included the production of a flyer on waste separation and garbage collection in several different languages, catering to the district's heterogeneous population and most inhabitants' curiously most urgent problem: waste. In Brigitte's mind, the goal should not be to make the district look cleaner and thereby more attractive to new investors; the goal should be to create a district in which its inhabitants can feel more at home. Again, this is only possible because the robust indeterminacy of the scrap houses still holds the present open for other futures than the expected gentrified ones.

With the contradictory effect and agency of the scrap houses in mind, this cultivated reconsideration of the present and the future of the Goethe district appears to point to a different "condition" of indeterminacy. Again, rather than being the general condition of life in the district, and of the urban infrastructure it consists of, the houses' material and legal limbo assists the continuous (re)production and maintenance of the district's indeterminacy. It thereby keeps the future of the district's current inhabitants and houses as tentatively open as possible. Most importantly, this maintenance work continuously proves to be adaptable to new concerns, demands, and expectations of ever-novel presents and their respective futures.

Conclusion

The city's postindustrial present is shaped by many forms of excess, mostly infrastructural and material excess in the form of modern institutions and objects that have lost their value with their industrial past, but also human and demographic excess, who face similar futures of redundancy and obsolescence. Recent geopolitical conflicts that resulted in the European refugee crisis have, in the eyes of many skeptical commentators, increased this postindustrial crisis in the West, pushing European welfare states, it is widely predicted, to their limits. More hopeful commentators claim that the refugees might actually help to overcome the postindustrial crisis of the European welfare state by balancing out the apparent mismatch between public infrastructures and population sizes in many shrinking socioeconomic settings. The current and ongoing revaluations of postindustrial excess add further stories to the social life and existence of infrastructures, things, and people in our times. They also help to reconsider indeterminacy as the presumed context to which social life is subjected.

By thinking through moments of revaluation in Germany's poorest city, I have drawn attention to the local production of the determinacy and indeterminacy of local infrastructures, material goods, and the city's population. Although the concept of indeterminacy has often been seen as a hopeful resource for much wanted and awaited change (because it necessarily disrupts operations of power; see, e.g., Biehl and Locke 2010), it is also recurrently depicted by many scholars and commentators as an existential obstacle to human agency (because it counteracts attempts at producing security). Instead of seeing it as a general condition of human existence and the material world, I here approached it as a product of human practice that targets the temporal existence of very specific things and people. As my ethnographic material has shown, in this postindustrial context, indeterminacy is produced, used, and maintained, as much as overcome, depending on one's plans, wishes, and expectations, in order to maintain a present in which a different future actually is or simply remains to be possible.

By focusing on the production of indeterminacy, I claimed that human agency is very well equipped to adjust present concerns to changing expectations of the future. The constant and simultaneous attempts at the production of the determinacy and indeterminacy of particular objects and people assist this adjustment. Rather than context, indeterminacy is a product of human practice and socio-political negotiations. Industrial urban infrastructures such as harbors or roads thereby cautiously find their place, function, and existence in postindustrial times, as do people and things in the wake and solution of the refugee crisis.

The new and more determinate futures of Columbusstrasse, Reyhane and her family, someone's old bedclothes, and the Goethe district are, if cautiously, emerging. These attempts at creating a new future for what is already there might fail again, but after this potential failure, these ideas of the future might be replaced by other expectations yet again. At any point in time, the same or different people might have different ideas of the future. This is the ongoing production of indeterminacy, which provides the title for this article and guided my presentist take on the topic. However, to ground local hopes for a better future in the usually short-lived moment of indeterminacy and surprise is not to be understood as a structural explanation for change. Rather, it is meant as an incentive for the continuation of temporal agency and for more anthropological and ethnographic attention to the work that is invested into people's presents and futures. The outcome of the many present conflicts about the future will remain indeterminate, but this indeterminacy, as this chapter has shown, is not the context in which the value of these excess infrastructures, things, and people is assessed. Rather, indeterminacy only marks the epistemic space, or pause, remaining between a whole variety of sometimes failing, sometimes more successful expectations. These ideas of the future already roam the present, as do the conflicts and revaluations that occur over their viability.

Acknowledgements

I am grateful to the anonymous reviewers for their insightful comments on earlier drafts of this chapter. In addition, I owe special thanks to Catherine Alexander for her helpful feedback and careful editorial work.

Felix Ringel is a COFUND International Research Fellow in the Anthropology Department at Durham University. His work on time, the future, and urban regeneration has been published in leading anthropological journals such as *The Journal of the Royal Anthropological Institute*, *Critique of Anthropology* and *Anthropological Theory*. He is the author of *Back to the Postindustrial Future: An Ethnography of Germany's Fastest-Shrinking City* and the coeditor of *The Cambridge Journal of Anthropology*'s special issue on *Time-Tricking: Reconsidering Temporal Agency in Troubled Times*.

Notes

1. With a halt in Germany's federal renewable energy policy (*Energiewende*), investments into the offshore windfarm industry decreased in recent years. As a result, several companies in Bremerhaven went bankrupt and had to close down. In 2017, two further companies announced their closure to the dismay of my informants. Several hundred employees will lose their jobs.
2. The sudden mismatch between actual population and the size of the urban infrastructure led to new problems and some rather counterintuitive solutions: many of the sewage

canals in Hoyerswerda stopped working because there was not enough water to move excrement through the pipes; in order for the pipes to continuously function, the people in charge of them had to shrink the diameter of the pipes, adjusting them to the similarly shrunken number of inhabitants.

References

Abram, S., and G. Weszkalnys. eds. 2013. *Elusive Promises: Planning in the Contemporary World*. New York: Berghahn Books.

Adam, B. 1990. *Time and Social Theory*. Cambridge: Polity Press.

Alexander, C. 2007. "Soviet and Post-Soviet Planning in Almaty, Kazakhstan." *Critique of Anthropology* 27(2): 165–81.

———. 2009. "Illusions of Freedom: Polanyi and the Third Sector." In *Market and Society: The Great Transformation Today*, ed. C. Hann and K. Hart, 221–39. Cambridge: Cambridge University Press.

Biehl, J., and P. Locke. 2010. "Deleuze and the Anthropology of Becoming." *Current Anthropology* 51(3): 317–51.

Boyer, D. 2017. "Revolutionary Infrastructure." In *Infrastructures and Social Complexity: A Companion,* ed. P. Harvey, C. B. Jensen, and A. Morita, 174–86. New York: Routledge.

Crapanzano, V. 2007. "Co-futures (Commentary)." *American Ethnologist* 34(39): 422–25.

Dawdy, S. L. 2010. "Clockpunk Anthropology and the Ruins of Modernity." *Current Anthropology* 51(6): 761–93.

Fennell, C. 2012. "The Museum of Resilience: Raising a Sympathetic Public in Post-Welfare Chicago." *Cultural Anthropology* 27(4): 641–66.

Ferguson, J. 1999. *Expectations of Modernity: Myths and Meanings of Urban Life on the Zambian Copperbelt*. Berkeley, CA: University of California Press.

Graeber, D. 2012. "Afterword." In *Economies of Recycling: The Global Transformation of Materials, Values and Social Relations,* ed. C. Alexander and J. Reno, 277–90. London: Zed Books.

Graham, S., and N. Thrift. 2007. "Out of Order: Understanding Repair and Maintenance." *Theory, Culture & Society* 24(3): 1–25.

Gupta, A. 2013. "Ruins of the Future." AAA annual meeting, Chicago, IL.

Harvey, P., C. B. Jensen, and A. Morita, eds. 2017. *Infrastructures and Social Complexity: A Companion*. New York: Routledge.

Hell, J., and A. Schönle, eds. 2010. *Ruins of Modernity*. Durham, NC: Duke University Press.

Howe, C., J. Lockrem, H. Appel, E. Hackett, D. Boyer, R. Hall, M. Schneider-Mayerson, A. Pope, A. Gupta, E. Rodwell, A. Ballestero, T. Durbin, F. el-Dahdah, E. Long, and C. Mody. 2016. "Paradoxical Infrastructures: Ruins, Retrofit, and Risk." *Science, Technology, & Human Values* 41(3): 547–65.

Jalas, M., J. Rinkinen, and A. Silvast. 2016. "The Rhythms of Infrastructure." *Anthropology Today* 32(4): 17–20.

Jansen, S. 2013. "Hope For/Against the State: Gridding in a besieged Sarajevo Suburb." *Ethnos* 79(2): 1–23.

Larkin, B. 2013. "The Politics and Poetics of Infrastructure." *Annual Review of Anthropology* 42: 327–43.

Mains, D. 2012. "Blackouts and Progress: Privatization, Infrastructure, and a Developmentalist State in Jimma, Ethiopia." *Cultural Anthropology* 27(1): 3–27.

Muehlebach, A., and N. Shoshan. 2012. "Introduction." Special issue on Post-Fordist Affect, *Anthropological Quarterly* 85(2): 317–44.

Nielsen, M. 2014. "A Wedge of Time: Futures in the Present and Presents without Futures in Maputo, Mozambique." *Journal of the Royal Anthropological Institute (N.S.)* 20(S1): 166–82.

Pelkmans, M. 2003. "The Social Life of Empty Buildings: Imaging the Transition in Post-Soviet Ajaria." *Focaal* 41:121–35.

_____ . 2013. "Ruins of Hope in a Kyrgyz Post-Industrial Wasteland." *Anthropology Today* 29(5): 17–21.

Rabinow, P. 2003. *Anthropos Today: Reflections on Modern Equipment.* Princeton, NJ: Princeton University Press.

_____ . 2008. *Marking Time: On the Anthropology of the Contemporary.* Princeton, NJ: Princeton University Press.

Ringel, F. 2014. "Post-Industrial Times and the Unexpected: Endurance and Sustainability in Germany's Fastest Shrinking City." *Journal of the Royal Anthropological Institute (N.S.)* 20(S1): 52–70.

_____ . 2016a. "Beyond Temporality: Notes on the Anthropology of Time from a Shrinking Fieldsite." *Anthropological Theory* 16(4): 390–412.

_____ . 2016b. "Can Time be Tricked?: On the Future of Temporal Agency." *The Cambridge Journal of Anthropology* 34(1): 22–31.

_____ . 2018. *Back to the Postindustrial Future: An Ethnography of Germany's Fastest-Shrinking City.* New York: Berghahn Books.

Schwenkel, C. 2013. "Post/Socialist Affect: Ruination and Reconstruction of the Nation in Urban Vietnam." *Cultural Anthropology* 28(2): 252–77.

Von Schnitzler, A. 2013. "Traveling Technologies: Infrastructures, Ethical Regimes, and the Materiality of Politics in South Africa." *Cultural Anthropology* 28(4): 670–93.

Ssorin-Chaikov, N. 2003. *The Social Life of the State in Subarctic Siberia.* Stanford, CA: Stanford University Press.

Star, S. L., and K. Ruhleder. 1996. "Steps toward an Ecology of Infrastructure: Borderlands of Design and Access for Large Information Spaces." *Information Systems Research* 7(1): 111–34.

Vigh, H. 2008. "Crisis and Chronicity: Anthropological Perspectives on Continuous Conflict and Decline." *Ethnos* 73(1): 5–24.

Weszkalnys, G. 2015. "Geology, Potentiality, Speculation: On the Indeterminacy of First Oil." *Cultural Anthropology* 30(4): 611–39.

Yurchak, A. 2004. *Everything Was Forever Until It Was No More: The Last Soviet Generation.* Princeton, NJ: Princeton University Press.

4

Human Waste in the Land of Abundance
Two Kinds of Gypsy Indeterminacy in Norway

Cathrine Moe Thorleifsson and Thomas Hylland Eriksen

Human Waste in an Overheated Continent

The amount of waste produced in Norway grew by 58 percent between 1995 and 2013 (Statistics Norway 2015). In the same period, the gross domestic product (GDP) almost trebled (from NOK 221,000 to NOK 604,000 per capita) while the immigrant population quadrupled, from about 200,000 to about 800,000 between 1990 and 2015. In other words, the tendency is for the economy and the minority population to grow faster than net waste production.

Of course, these numbers are incommensurable. However, since both human mobility and rubbish challenge boundaries, they can be related to each other. In Norway, like in many European countries, landfills have been closed down since the 1990s to be relaunched as "recycling centers" where household and industrial waste is sorted into as many as thirty categories and recycled or incinerated for energy use. The ultimate aim is to abolish the very category of material waste. A popular slogan from Oslo's renovation agency thus reads "Rubbish doesn't exist, only resources gone astray." Reviewing Thomas Hylland Eriksen's book about waste for a general readership (T. H. Eriksen 2011), the intellectual historian Trond Berg Eriksen (2011, no relation) concluded by asking what kind of waste would be produced by a society where material excess had been transformed into value. Implicitly drawing on Mary Douglas's structuralism, Berg Eriksen assumed that a category of waste was cognitively necessary for human beings in order to maintain the boundaries around the social order, suggesting that perhaps certain categories of people would then be considered forms of waste, in place of literal, stinking waste material.

While a pertinent metaphor, it echoes Zygmunt Bauman's (2004) reflections in *Wasted Lives*, which describes ways in which modernity not only produces material waste, but human waste. Wasted humans are the excessively overflowing, superfluous, or redundant individuals considered of little use or value to modern society. The human waste of a globalized era with enhanced mobility may consist of refugees, asylum seekers, migrants, and not least *sans papiers*, undocumented migrants. Presumably, having nothing to offer, there is no cure for being considered human waste by nation-states and little chance of recycling (Bauman 2004: 56). In a similar vein, following Mary Douglas's famous analysis on dirt ([1966] 2002), "dirtiness" can be seen more generally as an aberration of the system, the categories of people that are not considered to belong fully to society. Douglas's notions can be superimposed on the categorization of human waste as "dirty" posing an anomaly to the quest for utopian unity and order as designed by modern nation-states. From a state perspective, the freedom to travel across borders can be a threat when it is demanded by marginal categories of people.

While the concept of "human waste" is powerful, it reveals less about the various ways in which people are made into waste. Bodies marked or imagined as indeterminate operate along racial, gender, and economic lines. Humans are not a priori human waste. They become expendable and disposable by concepts and state practices of dehumanization (Butler and Athanasiou 2013). The local context will necessarily inform how marginalized and minoritized populations are perceived and interpreted by states, societies, and individuals as unwanted human waste, or as potential value that can be recycled and incorporated into a new social body.

This chapter compares two marginal groups in contemporary Norway: itinerant Roma and *tatere* or Travellers. In Norway, itinerant Roma, with no intention or realistic prospect of being assimilated into their land of temporary stay, embody ambivalence. In recent years, conflict has repeatedly erupted between itinerant Roma and settled Norwegians over the use of space, livelihoods, and rights. Itinerant Roma are provisionally included and ascribed value by nongovernmental organizations and concerned individuals. At the same time, they are fiercely excluded from any imagined community. In contrast, the other group—known as *tatere* or *reisende* (Travellers)—is indeterminate in a different sense. Defining themselves as "mixed," their way of life combines Gypsy and Norwegian elements in such a way that their membership in the national population becomes ambiguous and contested, but not impossible. Moreover, the two groups have also chosen diverging strategies in dealing with their structural and symbolic exclusion.

In mainstream Norwegian society, including the state, as we will show, itinerant Roma are widely perceived simply as "matter out of place," whereas *tatere* are better viewed as an anomaly challenging categorical boundaries. While these forms of exclusion may be familiar from other European societies, we argue that Norway differs in the centrality accorded to nature in its national mythology and identity. As the findings of the case studies will show, Gypsies are conceived by the state and ordinary Norwegians as threats to the established social order, but even more so to the purity of the Norwegian nature, which symbolically mirrors the integrity of the Norwegian nation. In contrast to other European contexts, such as postsocialist Hungary, we find that prejudice toward itinerant Roma in Norway is more linked to ideas about social purity than grounded in perceptions of threat to the wealth and welfare of the majority population.

For centuries, Gypsies occupied specialized economic niches in Norway as elsewhere in Europe, and were associated with metalwork, handicrafts, trade, and musicianship. The progressive loss of these niches since the nineteenth century has turned the groups, always marginally and patchily incorporated into greater society, into stigmatized outsiders. Modern state society was less flexible in the domains of provisioning and trade, more regulated, governed, and regimented, and the kind of informality typically engaged in by Gypsies was increasingly deemed unacceptable.

Confirming a basic idea from the theory of nationalism (e.g., Gellner 1983), this chapter shows that the state's boundary-making has progressively rendered indeterminate social positions difficult to maintain. Moreover, we show that straddling the boundary is a different exercise in comparison to eschewing boundaries altogether. Elaborating on Douglas's basic structuralism, we intend to distinguish between two kinds of waste: the abject and unequivocally filthy and the anomalous and indeterminate. Modes of exclusion practiced by the state and majorities differ markedly in the two cases, as we will also show. Being indeterminate, like Douglas's anomalous pig and pangolin, can in some cases be empowering: seen through the perspective of Barth's (1963) methodological individualism, the anomaly mutates into an entrepreneur capable of exploiting indeterminacy and turning it into an advantage. Recent anthropological research has shown how Gypsies used their indeterminacy to negotiate their belonging as well as new creative, economic strategies (Brazzabeni, Cunha, and Fotta 2016).

Our data shows that even populations rendered "human waste" by the state can themselves claim or be ascribed value and agency by various actors. This insight challenges Douglas's tendency to overlook the many in-between states and how judgements of humans as "waste" or value, even within the context of structural state exclusion, can vary across time and place. The other kind of exclusion considered below, that of Roma Gypsies, differs in that the Roma are not so much considered "matter out of place" as "matter with no rightful place." They cannot, to borrow a metaphor from Catherine Alexander (2009), be "recycled" within the parameters of the modern state. In the following we present some of the methods through which Roma and Travellers have been dehumanized and excluded to identify historical (dis)continuities in techniques and tropes of antiziganism. The two cases demonstrate how the status of indeterminacy can both function as a zone of domination and control as well as resistance and creative transgression.

Roma and Travellers

For centuries, Roma Gypsies, Europe's largest ethnic minority, have been categorized as "socially dangerous." Deployed as the internal Other of Europe, the Roma have been subjected to deportation and statelessness, forced assimilation as well as incarceration and massacre. In Nazi-dominated Europe, itinerant Gypsies were, like the Jews, persecuted and targeted for annihilation on racial grounds. An estimated 258,000 were murdered in the Romani Holocaust *Samudaripen* (Weiss-Wendt 2013).

More than half a century after the Nazi genocide on Roma, antiziganism—discrimination and dehumanization of Roma—is thriving in a Europe hit by economic downturns, migration pressures, and a marked swing to the right politically. In addition, the Roma lack much of the symbolic protection offered to Jews after the Holocaust.

Both itinerant and settled Roma face discrimination in education, housing, and access to government services. There has been a measurable increase in hate crimes against the Roma, and the use of xenophobic discourse on Roma is integral to populist politics in a number of countries (Farkas 2014; Hancock 2007; Okely 1983; Stewart 2012). In postsocialist Hungary, the right-wing party Jobbik ("The movement for a better Hungary"), with an explicit anti-Roma platform, is currently (2018) the third-largest party in parliament. The existence of an alleged "Roma problem" has since the onset of the the the so-called refugee crisis been exploited by the Hungarian right-wing government to justify the exclusion of migrants from Muslim-majority lands. Practices of populist securitization mark minoritized figures such as the migrant, the Muslim, or the Roma as the defining Other, warning against the internal or external strangers that are "invading" or threatening their national culture and security (Holmes 2000).

Underpinning these processes of externalization is a popular emphasis on ideas about bio-social purity, culture, and "roots" in a particular land (Gullestad in Banks and Gingrich 2006). Douglas Holmes (2000) calls these territorially based essentializing ideas "integralism." The examination of integralist ideas promoted by the state and majority population reveals some of the ways in which nationhood is being renarrated (Bhabha 1990), reimagined (Anderson 1991), and reinvented (Hobsbawm and Ranger 1992 in relation to populations who find themselves minoritized by the demographic majority (Das and Poole 2004).

The contemporary state externalization of itinerant Roma as undesirable "human waste" or "exception populations" (Agamben 2005) that must be controlled follows surprisingly similar patterns across European contexts. From the United Kingdom to Hungary, popular resistance toward (itinerant) Roma is grounded in fears of economic and cultural dislocation. Xenophobic views and practices are at their most virulent and widespread at the precarious edges of proper society, among globalization's losers, who are especially receptive to the simple answers to complex questions typically offered by right-wing politicians and ideologues. During fieldwork in Hungary and England in 2015 among supporters of the populist, radical right, Thorleifsson's informants in two postindustrial towns expressed anxiety over being made redundant in a precarious labor market. While xenophobia was grounded in structural factors and economic grievances, their expression was often cast in cultural terms, blaming differentiated Others of posing a threat to "our" cultural heritage and way of life (Thorleifsson 2017).

While antiziganism is a well-documented phenomenon (Stewart 2012), less academic attention has been accorded its character and dynamics in Norway (but see Engebrigtsen 2012). Our findings from the Norwegian context indicate that prejudice toward itinerant Roma is more linked to ideas about protecting sociocultural purity, than perceived economic competition and fear of being outcompeted in the labor market. We show that the widespread association of itinerant Roma with disorder and waste is a key feature of contemporary antiziganism. In discourse and practice, Roma have been marked as a threat to the ordered and disciplined Norwegian body, indirectly helping to reinvent the boundaries of Norwegianess. Attitudes and exclusion processes toward itinerant Roma in Oslo can be instructive not only for understanding social exclusion in the welfare state and its boundaries, but it also reveals some of the dominant categories of Norwegian self-identity, the culture/nature divide and cultural notions of the abject.

The other Gypsy group to be discussed presently, the *tatere* or Travellers, have a different history, identity, and relationship to greater society. First described in the sixteenth century, there has been disagreement as to whether they should be considered Gypsies at all. Their origins have been variously attributed to Gypsy immigration and the domestic underclass. In all likelihood, the truth is somewhere in between. Many Travellers describe themselves as "a mixed people." Their language, known in Norway as *Romani* (as opposed to the *Romanés* spoken by Roma), is classified as a Gypsy language, but it contains many Scandinavian words. Today, around five thousand persons identify as Travellers, but at the most, only a few hundred speak the language well. There are also Swedish and Finnish Travellers who consider themselves members of the same group as the Norwegian ones.

Travellers have historically engaged in many of the same economic activities as Roma, but they also took seasonal work at farms, and were known for having a good hand with horses. Following decades of persecution, to be described below, Travellers are today mostly settled, but many travel extensively in the summer months. They have several organizations, to some extent competing and mutually exclusive ones, negotiating with the Norwegian government for reparations and funding. Both Roma and Travellers are recognized under Norwegian law as "national minorities," along with the Jews, the Kven (a northern ethnic group of proto-Finnish origin), and the forest Finns of the eastern borderlands with Sweden.

We now move to describing, analyzing, and comparing the boundary work engaged in by the Norwegian majority population in relating to Roma and

Travellers, thereby identifying two modes of exclusion and two forms of social indeterminacy and also revealing some central categories of Norwegian boundary-making. In the first case, we show how the indeterminacy of external others, the itinerant Roma, generate ambivalent and hostile societal responses as well as creative attempts by individuals to bypass the ordering logic of the state through acts of compassion. The indeterminacy of traveling bodies have lead to state securitization, criminalization, and practices of ethnic profiling and suspicion. Although the Norwegian Travellers, the internal Others of the nation-state, also have been subjected to discourses and practices of antiziganism, their indeterminancy has simultaneously been used as a site of transgression, resilience, and creative resistance.

Roma as Disturbance

According to unofficial estimates, the number of itinerant Roma in Oslo on a three-month tourist visa is between five hundred and a thousand, a rather small number when compared to other European cities.[1] Still, their survival strategies make itinerant Roma highly visible in public spaces in the larger cities. Many have appropriated parks, woods, and abandoned buildings to create temporary homes. Facing enormous difficulty in gaining access to standard forms of employment, itinerant Roma survive by engaging in various kinds of street activities, such as begging or informal work.[2] In Oslo, the relationship between itinerant Roma and Norwegians is first and foremost defined through the very visible contrast between material abundance and economic deprivation. Poverty is low in Oslo compared to other European countries, and the itinerant Roma are significantly poor according to Norwegian standards.

While anti-racist values and principles of tolerance have been an integral part of public education in Norway for more than half a century, the reception of the foreign Roma has been ambivalent and largely negative from the state as well as the citizenry. As non-citizens, they are not entitled to any financial support from the state,[3] so religious non-governmental organizations have established relief services for Roma offering housing, clothes and food distribution, and advice on how to behave and beg "the Norwegian way."

Compassionate individuals have opened their homes and provided employment (Bråthen 2014). At the same time, public discourse and practice toward itinerant Roma have been hostile. The right-wing populist Progress party in the ruling government coalition has increasingly advocated the criminalization of begging as a significant electoral device, a law that would, in practice, remove the dominant source of income for itinerant Roma. Roma beggars have experienced people kicking their cups used for collecting money and been rejected when trying to deposit bottles at stores, and provisional Roma settlements have been removed by force without prior warning (Antirasistisk senter 2012; Djuve et al. 2015). Discussions in social media have been particularly heated, with certain participants referring to itinerant Roma in genocidal rhetoric, comparing them to the invasive Iberian slug, in other words a pest which should be removed.[4] Such blatant animalistic dehumanization renders the very humanity of Roma questionable, signaling Otherness in a way that can serve to justify discrimination and violence. Like other forms of exclusion, antiziganism can be justified through the ostensibly apolitical deployment of the language and symbolism of nation and culture. The settled Norwegians we interviewed[5] saw itinerant Roma as a threat to the public order and the security of citizens. Some judged the itinerant Roma bluntly as perpetrators of crime, describing them simply as thieves and cheats. A twenty-three-year-old man from the suburbs of Oslo, whom we met in a café at the Oslo central station, said:

> I do not understand how one can pity Roma. They have chosen to come here. Personally, I do not give a damn about beggars in general. They are just ordinary people who do not bother to work for money. Not all beggars are organized, but most of them are organized criminals or work for organized criminals. So if you give money to the Roma beggars, you are directly or indirectly sponsoring crime.

His friend, a twenty-six-year-old man, shared his view. "This has nothing to do with social deprivation. It is silly to defend organized crime. There are many naïve fools here in this country who let gypsies take advantage of them. So no wonder why the streets are full of rabble." Although several of our informants expressed aversion to Roma, they claimed that the issue was not racism, but fear of filth and crime. All themes show continuity in centuries-old stereotypes about Roma as lazy, dirty, and immoral. Moreover, alleging criminal behavior to entire categories of people is indeed a central feature of contemporary forms of racism.

Although Roma migrating from EU member-states can freely travel to Norway under the Schengen Agreement, it is clear that some migrating bodies are more desirable than others. Migrants who are like the imagined Norwegian "us"—white, cultured, skilled, productive, healthy, and wealthy—are deemed worthy of inclusion into a new social body by the state and majority population. Those who are like "them"—the ones seen as uncivilized, unskilled, the poor, the unclean, and the unproductive—are the socially undesirable migrants, deemed threatening to societal order and the integrity and security of dominant society.[6]

Polarized Views

In February 2015, Cathrine Moe Thorleifsson met Natalia, a twenty-three-year-old Roma from Târgu Jiu in Romania. Natalia used to work in agriculture, but like other Roma, she was excluded from the unskilled labor market when domestic unemployment rates rose following the onset of the European economic crisis in 2007. In broken English, she explains: "Things are so bad in

Romania. I want to work and make money and help my family." In Oslo, she generates income by selling the street magazine *Folk er Folk* (People are People), a relative of the British *The Big Issue*.[7] She spends the cold winter nights in a church run by the Church City Mission. With her, she carries a photo of her three-year old daughter who she had left with relatives. She lifts the end of her skirt to reveal worn-out shoes. During the coming weeks, she calls Cathrine several times, sometimes crying. The winter in Oslo is cold, and she is looking for a woolen blanket. Another day, she is still coping, we walk her daily route. In Byporten ("The City Gate"), an upscale shopping center attached to the Oslo Central Station, she purchases hot water from a friendly Swedish waitress, pours noodles into a paper cup, and stirs the concoction with sticks intended for coffee that sells for ten times the price. They sit down at a bench for a while. In the midst of our conversation, a private security guard passes by. Natalia freezes for a moment while turning her back against him. He approaches the pair, looking suspiciously at Natalia while asking if Cathrine is all right. Upon her confirmation, he nods firmly then moves away. Natalia quickly takes a few more bites of the sandwich before she utters with a sigh, clearly upset. "They don't like that I am here. The man says go, go. I don't know why. What have I done? I am not a thief."[8]

Natalia's story demonstrates many of the features of liquid life in a globalized Europe characterized by the freedom of movement and labor. She has planned in conditions of uncertainty, estimating both the burden and benefits of leaving Romania. She has to adapt to a precarious and unfamiliar situation and is dependent on the host society and networks for basic needs like shelter and food. Then there is the dark side of liquid life. Itinerant Roma, with no intention or realistic prospect of being assimilated in their land of temporary stay, signify everything that Norwegians are not: they are unsettled, transnational, uneducated, and without legitimate sources of income.

The Norwegian ambivalence toward itinerant Roma was inscribed in the spatial design of the Evangelical Contact Centre, a foundation under the Pentecostal charismatic movement. The contact center was initially established in 2012 as a low threshold service for drug addicts and homeless people in Oslo. While the center holds no official registration records, the leader, Stian Ludvigsen, estimates that more than half of the users are itinerant Roma and Travellers. Every Tuesday and Thursday, between four hundred and six hundred people are served a hot meal, a figure which indicates that the police estimate of a grand total of five hundred to a thousand traveling Roma in Norway must be too low.

It is a cold Tuesday in February and the line outside the center is long. Surrounding us and the manager Stian Ludvigsen, in the middle of a large room, are some veteran drug users. A middle-aged man is sleeping with his forehead touching the table. A young man dressed in worn clothes gratefully receives the meal of the day: white rice with minced meat and a piece of chocolate. "He is our hero," says Maria, a Roma woman, touching Stian's shoulder, proud to know him. Many eat in silence, quickly finishing the meal. Others are chatting over coffee, not in a hurry.

The room is around sixty square meters, separated in two by a dividing wall. The inner space is reserved for Norwegian citizens, the majority of whom are drug users. The space closest to the entrance is reserved for poor non-Norwegians, most of whom are itinerant Roma. For the Norwegian users, their drug addiction is considered only a temporary ailment for which the cure is salvation and guidance into better ways. They have a place in the nation-state, thus their stigma as outsiders can be healed, removed, or cured into social inclusion. In the view of the Protestants who run the center, they can be recycled. In a lead that we are unable to follow further here, the parallel between salvation and recycling is mentioned by Catherine Alexander and Joshua Reno (2012), who end their introduction to *Economies of Recycling* by observing that "the language of recycling for materials and labourers alike is often tinged with connotations of Protestant redemption" (Alexander and Reno 2012: 26).

The front room of the center seats bodies of indeterminacy. The itinerant Roma and other non-Norwegian poor are being shown the same human compassion and warmth, receiving the hot meal of the day and a bag of food past its use-by date. However, their seating indicates their imposed status as human waste, unwanted bodies not eligible for human recycling schemes, receivers of charity but not of redemption. Even practices grounded in solidarity and compassion mark Roma as human waste. Not fitting into the orders of designed togetherness, the itinerant Roma are excluded from any imagined national community.

Providing emergency relief to itinerant Roma comes with a price. When the Roma first started to approach the Evangelical Centre in 2012, the leader noticed strong opposition among the contact center's financial sponsors, the vast majority of whom are members of the Pentecostal movement. "They wanted to give coffee and sausages to Norwegians only." Torn between his personal conviction and the unwelcoming attitudes of the congregation, Stian turned to guidance and support in religion. "I met the poor people standing at our doorstep. Those who line up for hours because they can't afford a hot dog at Narvesen [nationwide newsagent chain]. Those who eat from rubbish bins. I was frustrated. I took the Bible in my hands. I closed my eyes and let the pages part. The Bible fell open at Matthew 2:35–40."

He cites the verse: "For I was hungry and you gave me something to eat, I was thirsty and you gave me something to drink, I was a stranger and you invited me in, I needed clothes and you clothed me, I was sick and you looked after me, I was in prison and you came to visit me." He adds: "I knew what God wanted."

Based on his epiphany, Stian decided to implement an open-door policy, welcoming everyone in need. His decision to include Roma in the center's user group generated negative responses from the financial donors, the traditional user group, and the local community. Tensions between Norwegian drug addicts and itinerant Roma were initially considerable. An unknown neighbor demonstrated opposition by pouring super glue in the door lock on a nightly basis, resulting in the installation of a surveillance camera. Another person residing in the neighboring building had on several occasions targeted the Roma lining up for meals with a water hose. Ludvigsen noted that harassment and discrimination of itinerant Roma users occurred on a regular basis and became worse during heightened negative media coverage.

Excess and Expulsion

The desire for modern urban order has resulted in an increased emphasis on a clean local environment. Norwegian waste management and recycling schemes are deemed successful by the state when it comes to removing waste. The value and communal obligation of producing a clean city is taught in schools from an early age. Since 1976, Rusken, a governmental organization, engages up to two hundred thousand people every year in volunteering activities to create a "cleaner and more beautiful Oslo." Adult volunteers and schoolchildren are given plastic bags, dressed up in fluorescent yellow vests, and sent out to remove litter from the local environment.

For decades, Rusken has been seen as the established authority of public cleanliness. Rusken is also partly responsible for collecting the waste from the abandoned or forcefully removed temporary Roma settlements in Oslo. From a waste management perspective, Rusken has repeatedly presented Roma survival strategies as scandals of pollution. On 5 October 2011, one could read in the online city guide, *dittOslo.no*, under the headline: "Barbecue dogs, and poop in the bushes," that "garbage, old clothing, musty food, excrement and rat bones are tossed around. The smell of this mixture lies as a whiff over the area. Ducks and dogs have also been on the menu."[9]

The Rusken chief Jan Hauger expressed concerns about public health: "The Roma defecate outdoors, often without cleaning themselves. Then they beg for money with which they later pay in the shop," implying that the Roma are likely to spread disease.

Covering the same story, the liberal-conservative newspaper *Aftenposten* published an article with the headline "This Seagull Was Meant to Be Eaten." According to the article, Rusken volunteers entered a vacated house at Grünerløkka, owned by the municipality, but occupied by Roma. "When they arrived there were eight, ten or twelve Roma there. On the wall hangs a skinned dog, ready for grilling. The head on the floor. The [volunteering] cleaners were totally shocked." Rusken chief Hauger emphasized that this was the only case where they had seen domestic animals being killed. However, he said that during the summer, Roma had begun to catch and consume rats, seagulls, and pigeons, barbecuing them near the Akerselva River. Needless to say, all three species are considered unclean among Norwegians. Nurturing moral panics by connecting particular categories of people to the consumption of unclean food is a central feature of intersecting racisms across European contexts. For instance, the British tabloid *Daily Mail* once claimed that Eastern European immigrants were eating swans (Malone 2010). In the bureaucratic logic of cleanliness promoted by Rusken, shared by the vast majority of ethnic Norwegians, human feces outdoors are seen as a matter out of place. "Human waste" making waste visible disturbs the ideal of a clean city and the flow of municipal waste management. The article attributes disease and dirtiness to itinerant Roma accused of posing a threat to public health. Rather than discussing the cultural and structural conditions leading to their practice or defecation outdoors, the newspaper produced an unequivocally negative portrayal of Roma as dirty waste-producers and consumers of unclean animals.[10]

Whether the practice of eating rats and dogs actually took place is doubtful, owing to the strict purity rules for food that most Roma adhere to and that would not allow them to consume these animals, which are considered polluting. Although the statements and allegations to Rusken chief Hauger were partly refuted, such postings may nevertheless fuel prejudice.

In particular, the presence of Roma who have set up makeshift camps around Lake Sognsvann just outside the city has been a heated topic in public discourse. Located on the western outskirts of the city, the area is used extensively for recreational purposes. The disproportional attention given to Sognsvann in comparison to urban spaces where Roma have set up camps might be due to the valorization of nature, forming a central aspect of dominant ideas of Norwegianness.

Due to its close proximity to the city proper and easy access by public transport, Sognsvann can credibly be regarded as a space transgressing established norms for the ideal social use of nature in Norwegian identity. For around two decades, it has been used as meeting place for people, mainly gay men, who solicit anonymous sex.[11] The newspaper headline "You Can't Go Anywhere without Stepping on Condoms" reflects the problem of litter allegedly caused by gay sexual activity. While this practice might create a similar sense of scandal of pollution to the Roma untidiness, it does not challenge Norwegian national identity to the same degree because Norwegian sexual minorities are included in the imagined nation. Mobile bodies deemed indeterminate by the majority population that allegedly disturbs nature with waste and their presence is considered far more threatening to national landscapes, norms, and identity than the presence and litter caused by Norwegian sexual minorities. A white, thirty-five-year-old Norwegian man working in the financial sector from the western part of Oslo shared his sentiment during an interview.

> I like running in the woods, but for a long time now I have avoided Sognsvann. The Roma settlements there are disgusting, with feces all over the place. It would be nice if they actually bothered to buy toilet paper, at least if they could find a dustbin. It is absolutely terrible. I just wonder why one must spoil the surroundings just because one is poor and homeless ... Why can't one keep it a little neat, just to keep some sense of integrity? I think it is quite natural that Roma are looked down on when

they behave in such a way that they are bothering the rest of society. Had they at least showed some willingness or ability to adapt, I don't think they would have faced as many troubles as they do today.

In his view, the Roma coping strategies, which include setting up makeshift camps in the forest, disrupt his weekly routine of recreation in the forest. He judges them as being undisciplined and dirty campers, tying neatness and cleanliness to moral values and integrity. Blaming the outsiders for their behavior, he effectively establishes himself as a "clean" and righteous citizen versus the "dirty" outsiders who "are bothering society." In general, camping in the forest or mountains is seen as a quintessential Norwegian activity strengthening the central value of nature's purity in the national identity. Leaving rubbish behind after a camping trip is frowned upon. The Roma thus pollute not only nature, but they also pervert the sacred Norwegian relationship to nature. The strong emphasis placed on pollution and degradation of parks and wilderness areas, often eclipsing accusations of theft and criminality, reveals the centrality of nature to the predominant Norwegian self-understanding (T. H. Eriksen 1993; Gullestad 1992). The pollution of valorized landscapes by categories of people occupying an ambivalent position in the nation-state, thus contribute to their further classification as undesirable "human waste."

The widely held negative views of the presence of itinerant Roma in culturally valued nature has also prompted legal disputes. In June 2013, Statsbygg, the main organization advising the Norwegian government in construction and property affairs, proposed the enforced removal of Roma camps around Sognsvann, stating that they caused pollution in "Norwegian nature" and posed a threat to public health. The call for eviction followed a visit by Oslo municipality on 10 October 2012, when an infection control doctor stated that drainage of surface water from the camps could contaminate the water in the southwestern part of Lake Sognsvann and thus pose a public health threat. Initially, the district court [*Oslo Byfogdembete*] declined the claim noting that the "pollution aspect was fairly modest in light of the submitted photos" and could not be characterized as "substantial damage or inconvenience."[12]

Statsbygg appealed to the district court. In September 2013, the district court deemed the camps illegal according to the Outdoor Recreation Act, which states that "camping or another form of residence is not permitted for more than two days at a time without the permission of the owner or user."[13] Around forty Roma migrants were given forty-eight hours to leave the camp, which was deemed illegal. The camp was dismantled at nine thirty in the morning, and within a few hours the makeshift tents were reduce to wreckage, carried away in rubbish vans.

The case shows how the arguments first triggering political action against itinerant Roma was based on speculation about potential health hazards and pollution in Norwegian nature. While the court deemed the actual waste produced by Roma was not a sufficient cause for forced eviction, waste in presumably unspoiled nature was judged misplaced in the moral sense of inappropriateness. Attributing disease and dirtiness to the Roma settlement became a central means to demarcate the boundaries of the ordered Norwegian social environment.

The rubbish vans sent by the municipality efficiently removed human waste, fulfilling its modernist promise. The clean-up operations at Sognsvann can be analyzed as purifying events aimed at reinstalling the order of Norwegian landscapes. By removing the daily reminders of disruptive Otherness, settled Norwegians are allowed physical and moral escape from (human) waste, the dark and shameful secret of modernity. In the dominant Norwegian understanding, nature is clean, fresh, and genuine, as opposed to the seductive falsehoods of culture. Their transgression of the culture/nature boundary, along with their unsettledness, negligible contribution to the Norwegian economy and lack of something "meaningful to do" shows in no uncertain terms why Roma are imagined and viewed as dangerous, superfluous people who visit without asking or being asked, leaving a trail of rubbish and human excrement behind.

Imperfect Norwegians

Between five hundred and seven hundred Roma have Norwegian citizenship. Although their relationship with greater society is tense, they have not been targeted by the animosities of recent years. They know their way around Norwegian society and have actively dissociated themselves from the recent arrivals. They also do not consider themselves part of the same group as the *tatere* or Travellers, to whom we now turn.

Perhaps owing to the nature of their group as self-professed "mixed"—there are no strict rules—it is impossible to assess the number of Travellers in the country. Estimates vary between four thousand and ten thousand (NOU 2015: 18). Physically indistinguishable from Norwegians, Travellers may distinguish themselves through dress (leather vests and moustaches common among men, long, flowery skirts among women), or they may choose to undercommunicate their ethnic identity. It thus came as a big surprise to the general public in 2008 when Åge Aleksandersen, one of the country's most popular singer-songwriters, revealed that he had Traveller origins of which he himself had been unaware until he was an adult. Especially in the twentieth century, following assimilationist policies from an ever stronger and more active state, Traveller identity tended to become a secret identity, often known only to the insiders.

Travellers engaged in a series of traditional pursuits, including seasonal farm work. They would then typically be lodged in barns, sleeping on haystacks near the farm animals. Many produced objects such as candlesticks and embroidery work, selling them at markets or door-to-door, and they had a reputation for being skilled repairmen. The wealthier dealt in horses as well. These niches gradually vanished with the modernization of society, and the Travellers were pushed into increasingly marginal modes of sustenance while beginning to exploit new niches. Their skills with horses, for example, have been transformed to mechanical skills, and many Travellers work in the second-hand car trade or as mechanics. The pressures of schooling, sedentarism, and wage work turned the Traveller way of life into a social problem to be dealt with by the authorities since the growth of the bureaucratic state in the mid to late nineteenth century.

According to a recent White Paper on the situation of the Travellers, "the *tatere* or Romani people are a group with an attachment to Norway since the sixteenth century, a distinctive language and way of life, and their own culture" (NOU 2015: 39). The very comprehensive White Paper, which also includes a detailed supplement written by two historians (Brandal and Plesner 2015), thus explicitly delineates the Travellers as a cultural minority indicating that they should be endowed with rights along with the other recognized national minorities.

This perspective on the Travellers is comparatively new. For centuries, they were mainly considered imperfect Norwegians, unlike the Roma who are indisputably a separate ethnic group; and assimilationist policies were comprehensive and strong from the mid-nineteenth century to the late twentieth century. Their history in Norway is longer than that of Roma, who mainly came to the country from the late nineteenth century, migrating from east and southeast Europe. There are similar minorities in other European countries, but, as noted by Kent Hallman (n.d.), there have been few attempts to relate these groups to one another. Hallman writes:

> Ragnhild Schlüter (1993) wrote briefly on socio-cultural similarities between Norwegian Romani/Travellers and non-Romani Traveller populations in Europe, such as "Irish Travellers" on the British Isles, and the "Jenische" in Germany. These populations, however, do not have Romani vernaculars nor do they identify as Romani by ethnicity, and there is no indication of extensive interaction between these communities and Norwegian Travellers. (n.d.: 3)

Scholarly interest in the Travellers has been limited, although two of Norway's most famous social scientists both took an interest in them. Eilert Sundt (1852), a pioneering sociologist and the founder of Norwegian ethnology, wrote an empirical study of the Travellers in the mid-nineteenth century, with a view to including and assimilating them into the incipient Norwegian nation-state. Fredrik Barth (1952) did a short stint of fieldwork among Travellers as a student in the early 1950s, revealing an attraction to the nomadic way of life that he would later exploit more fully in his mature work. It is worth noting here that self-ascription and that of others, not purity of genetic descent, are the main criteria for inclusion into the Traveller category. This insight, favoring social dynamics over descent, would later be developed in a highly influential way in Barth's edited *Ethnic Groups and Boundaries* (Barth 1969).

However, the social science interest in the Travellers has been scarce, perhaps for precisely the same reasons that they are interesting as a case of social and cultural indeterminacy. According to the White Paper, they have "their own language," but Scando-Romani is today a language of limited usage. Although many Travellers know expressions and perhaps songs in Romani, it is not a living vernacular. In early modern Norwegian literature, Travellers involved in criminal activities sometimes exchange a few words in their "secret language," which was also described as *røversprāk* (criminal language). The emphasis on their having "their own culture" is also clearly an attempt to remove stigma and define them on a par with other cultural minorities. Until recently, Travellers were described as vagrants and part of the criminal classes, not as a cultural minority.

Enforced Assimilation

Throughout their five-hundred-year history in Norway, the Travellers have been subjected to social exclusion, hierarchical subordination, and later assimilationist policies, including enforced work and sedentarism. The state forcibly removed children from their parents in a manner reminiscent of Australia's "stolen generations," who were usually children of mixed European-Aboriginal race (see Read 1982). This Australian practice ended around 1970, two decades before the end of active assimilationism directed at Travellers in Norway.

When the Norwegian parliament passed a new and stricter law on vagrancy in 1900, making it de facto illegal not to have a fixed abode, a major argument was that vagrancy was detrimental to society and could lead to social unrest (NOU 2015: 45). This law entailed a de facto criminalization of the traditional livelihoods of Gypsy groups, and remained in force, at least partly, until 1995. In 1907, a law restricting peddling was passed, further criminalizing the mobile and flexible way of life defining the Travellers as a group. These laws and their enforcement show the emerging biopolitical ambitions of the bureaucratic state (Foucault 2008), that is its desire, and ability, to legislate over human bodies. They also served to create boundaries between "real" Norwegians and transgressors.

Since the late nineteenth century, Traveller children had regularly been taken from their parents and placed in institutions or foster homes, the objective being to obliterate the group. The parallel to the Australian scheme whereby "half-caste" children were brought into institutions in the hope that breeding with whites would "wash the blackness out of them" is striking. The similarity with Australian policy is strengthened further if we look at the sterilization practices from the 1930s onward. Although it was aimed to weed out individuals marked as inferior by the state, sterilization of people with unwanted characteristics affected the Travellers disproportionately. The program began in earnest in 1934, a time when eugenics was popular in many European countries independent of the rise of Nazism. However, sterilization of Travellers is known to have happened as late as the 1960s. Travellers who were coerced into being sterilized have more recently (since the 1990s) demanded reparations from the government.

In 1935, a proposed law against the use of horses in trading was defeated, but a similar law was passed in 1951. While the stated rationale of the law was a concern with animal welfare, its effect was to considerably reduce the Travellers' chances of reproducing their traditional way of life. Today, elderly Travellers may speak of this law as "the last nail in the coffin" for their autonomy.

However, as we have shown, their social autonomy was already severely reduced by 1951. The most sustained and systematic effort to incorporate Travellers into mainstream society, however, was carried out by a church foundation, Norsk Misjon blant hjemløse (The Norwegian mission among the homeless), generally known as Misjonen. Founded in 1897, it was dissolved only in the late 1980s. Misjonen engaged in a range of activities aimed at assimilation (and salvation, compare the earlier remark about recycling and salvation), the most infamous being its work colony, Svanviken Arbeidskoloni, which opened in 1908 and was closed only in 1989. It had as its exclusive objective to turn Travellers into settled, Christian Norwegians. Travellers went there to avoid prison (if nothing else, they had violated the law on vagrancy), and many stayed on for fear of losing their children. At Svanviken, the Sunday church service was mandatory. Moustaches—a symbol of Traveller manhood—were banned. The Scando-Romani language was also periodically forbidden in the work colony until the 1960s (Brandal and Plesner 2015: 207). The aim was clear and confirms an underlying cultural logic valorizing certain practices and rejecting others, favoring clear and unambiguous boundaries rather than tolerating fuzziness and indeterminacy.

All the significant laws aimed to weaken the Traveller way of life were biopolitical laws restricting mobility: the laws on vagrancy, the ban on horses, the restrictions on peddling, and the placing of Traveller families in Svanviken work colony. Other practices—sterilization, the removal of children—instead aimed to obliterate Traveller identity as such. While the increasingly brutal treatment of Travellers indicate the growth of state power and its accompanying boundary-making, there is also something generic about the fraught relationship between Travellers and settled populations, which is also reflected in our earlier example of wandering Roma, namely the widespread, if not universal, tension between farmers and nomads. To nomads, the land has worth at particular moments when they extract food and shelter; to farmers, it is their main capital income-generating source. Those who do not constantly maintain the land, therefore, are perceived as irresponsible and dangerous from a sedentarist point of view. Travellers, typically associated with ramshackle houses and untidy yards littered with rusty vehicles (almost like the Roma at Sognsvann), thus challenge the social order by rejecting the established physical order. Significantly, those "untidy yards" may often be recycling centers, as many Travellers have been—and are—involved in scrap metal trade and other forms of recycling.

Travellers Today

By the twenty-first century, following a century of systematic attempts to destroy them as an identifiable group, Travellers lick their wounds and regroup in several, admittedly competing organizations claiming reparation payments and financial support from the state. Since the rise of the indigenous movement in the 1980s, in which the circumpolar Scandinavian Sami played an important part, minority policy has shifted, and the state now supports various forms of salvage work, provided it is compatible with mainstream society. In Elverum, near the Swedish border in the vast, forested area stretching hundreds of miles north from Oslo, a permanent exhibition at the museum, Latjo Drom, serves as a mnemotechnical device both for Travellers in search of their roots and for majority Norwegians. Some groups and individuals can get state support for cultural activities, and children who were institutionalized before 1985 may now (since 2005) file for reparations. However, in spite of this seeming sea change in the public attitude toward this anomalous group, structural dilemmas persist.

Many Travellers today engage in occupations that signal continuity with their past adaptations. Some are tinsmiths, roofers, car mechanics, housepainters, or carpenters. Many continue to engage in trade, sometimes as a side-pursuit, and sell goods at markets or door-to-door. Some even retain their interest in horses, now in the realm of horseracing. The ideology of independence remains strong, and all other things being equal, Travellers prefer not to work for others.

Problems remain. In the White Paper and its accompanying supplement (NOU 2015; Brandal and Plesner 2015), many Travellers point out that their weak formal schooling presents a range of challenges in a country where official forms and accounts are ever more important. Accounting for their economic activities in spreadsheets and submitting bimonthly VAT accounts is a major problem for many. The lack of formal training in their crafts is also an increasing problem, especially in the older generation (NOU 2015: 98–99). Moreover, the fast replacement of the cash economy with cybermoney is also widely perceived as alienating and troubling.

Finally, although Norway ratified the International Charter of Minority Languages in 1993, which secures protection for Scando-Romani, this is little known, and there are no public facilities available for learning Scando-Romani nor do regular publications appear in the language.

Skirmishes and frictions with the majority continue to occur. Nik Brandal and Ingvill Thorson Plesner have interviewed a campsite owner who is nonplussed by the rowdiness and expansive behavior he sees in Travellers who spend summers at the site, claiming that this leads to difficulties with his regular visitors, be they from Norway, Germany, or the Netherlands (2015: 200). There are also many cases of people who have been denied employment when it became known that they were Travellers, including a much-publicized story about a woman who was sacked as a taxi driver when her ethnic identity became known.

While the Roma case easily lends itself to highlighting the nature/culture boundary and Norwegian perceptions of dirt as visibly polluted nature, the conflicts involving Travellers are mainly about sedentarism, wagework, and education, three pillars of the modern state; but Travellers are also problematic insofar as they are neither fully outside nor fully inside. We now conclude by way of a comparison between these two forms of indeterminacy, indicating what they can tell us about Norway, the boundaries created by the modern state, and indeterminacy as such.

Two Kinds of Human Excess

The assumption of universal sedentarism characteristic of the nation-state contradicts assumed features of liquid life in a globalized Europe characterized by increased cross-border mobility and ease of travel. As a result of EU freedom of labor and movement rules, notably the Schengen agreement (of which Norway is part, although it is not a full member of the EU), Oslo has—like other European cities—become a site of new encounters between people who were formerly separated. Viewed generally, antiziganism can be seen as a feature of the re-nationalization processes militating against the parallel processes toward European and global integration, which are seen in the rise of (far) right parties and movements across the continent. Norway, until recently insulated from economic downturns because of its oil and gas wealth, has been dominated by culturalist accounts of difference rather than discourses of economic uncertainty. In Oslo, the presence of "human waste" in the form of homeless, begging Roma, the embodied daily reminders of European precarity, has produced hostile discourses, the acts of compassion described above being the exception and not the rule. As we have shown, discourses on cleanliness, order and security have veiled and legitimized racist antiziganism. Framed either as oppressed victims (of human trafficking) or profit-seeking strangers, the Roma are first and foremost associated with physical dirt and disorder, second with dysfunctional and humiliating ways of life. In particular, the association of itinerant Roma with scandals of waste and unsavory disturbances of natural purity has contributed to their dehumanization. They are quintessentially "matter out of place."

Initially, their indeterminacy lies in the paradoxical fact that they can travel to the country legitimately, in spite of the fact that the right-wing Progress Party, a coalition partner in the center-right government, has an openly and unequivocally negative stance on the Roma presence. In addition, however, Roma do not fit into the dominant self-understanding of Norwegians as hard-working, nature-loving Protestants who jealously guard the boundaries between nature and culture. Their failure to conform to central norms has resulted in the kind of dehumanizing language that we have exemplified, justifying practices of exclusion. They are not a surplus population, but a disposable one.

The Travellers are indeterminate in a different way. Nobody challenges their right to be in the country—they have "always been here"—but their right to difference is continuously being addressed in a critical way. Within the Traveller category, there is considerable mistrust in government and authorities, and there remains stigma in the sense that many conceal their ethnic identity outside intimate circles. There is, for example, internal disagreement about whether to place their children in kindergartens; as opposed to the proverbially high levels of trust in shared institutions characterizing Scandinavia, thus, the Travellers see themselves as not fully respected, and return this lack of respect to its addressee. While government has sought to evict (discard) Roma, it tries to assimilate (swallow) Travellers. While Roma transgress the boundary between culture and nature, Travellers challenge the internal boundaries of the modern state. Whereas the Roma reject the values and practices of majority society, the Travellers challenge the boundaries themselves, being a hybrid group, simultaneously inside and outside the Norwegian mainstream. Both show, in different but comparable ways, how modernity rejects those who use it without reproducing its boundaries, turning them into sand in the machinery, to be swallowed and digested or unceremoniously discarded. Conversely, there are Travellers who self-consciously defy the categories of mainstream society through, as the editors of this volume put it in their introduction, "critiques of modernity emphasize the repressive domination of ordering practices by celebrating transgression." The case of Norwegian Travellers shows that indeterminacy, while often the outcome of processes of state, domination, and control, can simultaneously function as a site of resilience and even creative resistance. While the indeterminacy of Norwegian Travellers has led to new creative forms of economic activities and subjectivities, the indeterminacy of migrating Roma is a site of less potentiality for struggle. The presence of itinerant Roma is legal according to EU law, but is contested by various national actors. The status of Roma is considered indeterminate, both in relation to the nation-state as well as to the culture/nature boundary inherent in Norwegian nationalism. The space for revalorization is thus narrower. The two different cases explored in this chapter show that the potential for transgression tied to indeterminacy changes over time and place. Indeterminacy and the (im)possibilities for transgression thus need to be explored and unpacked in place, in the historical, political, and social context in which they occur.

Acknowledgments

We would like to thank the editors of this volume for excellent comments on the first draft. The research on which this article is based was funded by ERC AdvGr no. 295843, "Overheating: The Three Crises of Globalization."

Cathrine Moe Thorleifsson is a researcher at the Centre for Research on Extremism at the University of Oslo. Thorleifsson earned her doctorate in Anthropology from the London School of Economics and Political Science in 2012. Her chief research interests are nationalism, migration, borders, belonging, and intersecting racisms. She is the author of *Nationalism and the Politics of Fear in Israel: Race and Identity on the Border with Lebanon* (I.B Tauris 2015) and the forthcoming *Nationalist Responses to the Crises in Europe: Old and New Hatreds* (Routledge 2018).

Thomas Hylland Eriksen is professor of Social Anthropology at the University of Oslo. His research has mainly focused on globalization and identity politics, and he is the author of many books in English and Norwegian, including textbooks, monographs, and critical essays. His most recent books in English are *Fredrik Barth: An Intellectual Biography* (Pluto 2015), *Overheating: An Anthropology of Accelerated Change* (Pluto 2016), *Identities Destabilised* (coedited with E. Schober, Pluto 2016), *An Overheated World* (ed., Routledge 2018), and *Boomtown: Runaway Globalisation on the Queensland Coast* (Pluto 2018).

Notes

1. The number of migrating Roma in Norway changes according to the season and other factors, such as access to the unskilled labor market in their home country or other European countries. The majority of Romanian citizens in Norway self-identify as Roma or Tiani Romanian. They often speak Romanian besides their mother tongue (Engebrigtsen 2012).
2. Begging on average generates a daily income between 100 to 200 Norwegian kroner (approximately US$12 to $25), sometimes more. This is a substantial amount of money when compared to the income level in Romania, where the daily salary of a teacher is around 50 NOK ($6). The surplus is sent as remittances to the family and relatives, aimed at covering expenses such as food, health care, schooling, and housing.
3. The established Roma, who arrived in Norway from Romania in the late nineteenth century, are entitled to state support because they are citizens.
4. https://www.facebook.com/groups/229190177223730/?fref=ts.
5. Fieldwork on Norwegian–Roma relations was carried out in Oslo by Cathrine Moe Thorleifsson from January to April 2015.
6. Islamophobia is also on the rise in Norway, but will not be dealt with in this context.
7. The NGO *Folk er Folk* (People Are People) was established in March 2012 to advocate for Roma rights, fight prejudice, and provide employment below the tax line of 4000 NOK. In June 2012, the street magazine *Folk er Folk* was launched. It was modeled after =Oslo (a magazine sold by Norwegian drug addicts) to provide an alternative to begging. The organization has been criticized by expert in labor law Sverre Langfeldt for not taking formal responsibility for labor by itinerant Roma commissioned by private individuals or companies.
8. Thorleifsson tried several times to get an interview with the private security firm Nokas, but no one wanted to go on the record.
9. All translations are our own unless otherwise stated.
10. While defecation outdoors at Sognsvann in this particular context was caused out of necessity, in other situations it can be consistent with the itinerant Roma distinction

between inside and outside. Historically, traveling gypsies with caravans regularly rejected internal toilets and defecated at the actual or perceived boundary of a site as a way of demarcating symbolic boundaries against the dirty *gaje* (non-Roma) population. Itinerant Roma may also prefer the outdoors to other facilities considered to be polluted (Weyrauch 2001).

11. According to the organization for the promotion of gay and lesbian health, around a thousand condoms are distributed monthly around the Sognsvann area.

12. http://www.domstol.no/globalassets/upload/obyf/internett/aktuelt/kjennelser/18_kjennelsemidlertidigforfoyningikketatttilfolge_33224066.pdf.

13. https://www.regjeringen.no/en/dokumenter/outdoor-recreation-act/id172932/.

References

Agamben, G. 2005. *State of Exception*. Chicago, IL: The University of Chicago Press.

Alexander, C. 2009. "Illusions of Freedom: Polanyi and the Third Sector." In *Market and Society: The Great Transformation Today*, ed. C. Hann and K. Hart, 221–39. Cambridge: Cambridge University Press.

Alexander, C., and J. Reno. 2012. "Introduction." In *Economies of Recycling: The Global Transformation of Materials, Values and Social Relations*, 1–32. London: Zed Books.

Anderson, B. 1991. *Imagined Communities*, 2nd ed. London: Verso.

Antirasistisk senter. 2012. *Tilreisende rom i Oslo* [Itinerant Roma in Oslo]. Oslo: Antirasistisk senter.

Barth, F. 1952. "The Social Organization of a Pariah Group in Norway." *Norveg* 5: 125–44.

Barth, F. 1963. "Introduction." In *The Role of the Entrepreneur in Social Change in Northern Norway*, ed. F. Barth, 5–18. Bergen: Universitetsforlaget.

Barth, F., ed. 1969. *Ethnic Groups and Boundaries: The Social Organization of Culture Difference*. Oslo: Universitetsforlaget.

Bauman, Z. 2004. *Wasted Lives: Modernity and its Outcasts*. London: Polity Press.

Bhabha, H. ed. 1990. *Nation and Narration*. London: Routledge.

Brandal, N., and I. T. Plesner. 2015. *Vedlegg til NOU 2015:7: Assimilering og motstand* [Appendix to NOU 2015:7: Assimilation and resistance]. Oslo: Government of Norway.

Brazzabeni, Micol, Manuela Ivone Cunha, and Martin Fotta. 2016. *Gypsy Economy: Romani Livelihoods and Notions of Worth in the 21st Century*. New York: Berghahn Books.

Bråthen, M. 2014. "Jeg har lært dem å kjenne som fine, ærlige mennesker" [I have learned to know them as fine, honest people]. NRK, Retrieved 28 March 2015 from https://www.nrk.no/ostlandssendingen/xl/mama-inger-hjelper-romfolk-1.11782144.

Butler, J., and A. Athanasious. 2013. *Dispossession: The Performative in the Political*. Cambridge: Polity Press.

Das, V., and D. Poole, eds. 2004. *Anthropology in the Margins of the State*. Santa Fe, NM: School of American Research Press.

Djuve, A. B., J. Horgen Friberg, G. Tyldum, and H. Zhang. 2015. *When Poverty Meets Affluence: Migrants from Romania on the Streets of the Scandinavian Capitals*. Oslo: FAFO.

Douglas, M. [1966] 2002. *Purity and Danger: An Analysis of Concept of Pollution and Taboo*. New York: Routledge.

Engebrigtsen, A. 2007. *Exploring Gypsiness: Power, Exchange and Interdependence in a Transylvanian Village.* Oxford: Berghahn Books.
———. 2012. *Tiggerbander og kriminelle bakmenn, eller fattige EU-borgere?* NOVA notat 2/2012.
Eriksen, T. H. 1993. "Being Norwegian in a Shrinking World: In Continuity and Change." In *Aspects of Modern Norway,* ed. Anne Cohen Kiel, 5–39. Oslo: Scandinavian University Press.
———. 2011. *Søppel: Avfall i en verden av bivirkninger* [Waste: Excess in a world of side-effects]. Oslo: Aschehoug.
Eriksen, Trond Berg. 2011. "Lukten av søppel" [The smell of rubbish]. *Morgenbladet,* 1 April 2011.
Farkas, L. 2014. *Report on Discrimination of Roma Children in Education.* Brussels: European Commission.
Foucault, M. 2008. *The Birth of Biopolitics: Lectures at the Collège de France, 1978–1979.* Basingstoke: Palgrave Macmillan.
Gellner, E. 1983. *Nations and Nationalism.* Oxford: Blackwell.
Gotaas, T. 2007 *Taterne: livskampen og eventyret* [Travellers: The struggle for life and the adventure]. Oslo: Andresen & Butenschøn.
Gullestad, M. 2006. "Imagined Kiship: The Role of Descent in the Rearticulation of Norwegian Ethno-nationalism." In *Neo-nationalism in Europe and Beyond: Perspectives from Social Anthropology,* ed. A. Gingrich and M. Banks, 69–91. New York: Berghahn Books.
Gullestad, M. 1992. *The Art of Social Relations.* Oslo: Scandinavian University Press.
Hallman, Kent. n.d. "Norwegian Travelers ('Tatere') and the Making of Romani Diaspora: Ethnic Renewal Sparked by International Travel and Global Communication." Unpublished manuscript.
Hancock, I. 2007. *We Are the Romani People.* Hertfordshire: University of Hertfordshire Press.
Hawkins, G. 2003. "Down the Drain: Shit and the Politics of Disturbance." In *Culture and Waste: The Creation and Destruction of Value,* ed. G. Hawkins and S. Muecke, 39–52. Lanham, MD: Rowman and Littlefield.
Hobsbawm, E. J. and T. Ranger. 1992. *The Invention of Tradition.* Cambridge: Cambridge University Press. Holmes, D. 2000. *Integral Europe: Fast-Capitalism, Multiculturalism, Neofascism.* Princeton, NJ: Princeton University Press.
Keene, E. ed. 1988. *Natural Language.* Cambridge: University of Cambridge Press.
Malone, A., 2010. "Slaughter of the Swans." *Daily Mail,* Retrieved 31 January 2018 from http://www.dailymail.co.uk/news/article-1261044/Slaughter-swans-As-carcasses-pile-crude-camps-built-river-banks-residents-frightened-visit-park-Peterborough.html.
Midtbøen, A., and H. Lidén. 2015. *Diskriminering av samer, nasjonale minoriteter og innvandrere i Norge: En kunnskapsgjennomgang* [Discrimination of Sami, national minorities and immigrants in Norway: An overview of extant knowledge]. Report 2015:01. Oslo: Institutt for samfunnsforskning.
Mudde, C. 2007. *Populist Radical Right Parties in Europe.* Cambridge: Cambridge University Press.
NOU (Norges offentlige utredninger). 2015 *Assimilering og motstand: Norsk politikk overfor taterne/romanifolket fra 1850 til i dag* [Assimilation and resistance: Norwegian politics toward the Tater/Romani people from 1850 until today]. Oslo: Government of Norway.
Okely, J. 1983. *The Traveller-Gypsies.* Cambridge: Cambridge University Press.

Oslo Byfogdembete (Oslo District Court). 2013. Kjennelse (Court order). Retrieved 3 September 2015 from https://www.domstol.no/globalassets/upload/obyf/internett/ aktuelt/kjennelser/18_kjennelsemidlertidigforfoyningikketatttilfolge_33224066.pdf.

Read, P. 1982. *The Stolen Generations (Bringing them Home): The Removal of Aboriginal Children in New South Wales 1883 to 1969.* Sydney: Department of Aboriginal Affairs.

Redman, P. 2006. *Good Essay Writing: A Social Sciences Guide*, 3rd ed. London: Open University in association with Sage.

Russia Today. "'Good at Rummaging through Garbage': Italian Official Proposes Gypsies as Waste Sorters." Retrieved 13 June 2015 from http://www.rt.com/ news/229271-gypsies-roma-rome-garbage/.

Schlüter, R. 1993. *De reisende: en norsk minoritets historie og kultur* [The Travellers: A Norwegian minority's history and culture]. Oslo: Gyldendal.

Statistics Norway. 2014. *Avfallsregnskapet* 2013 [The waste accounts, 2013]. Retrieved 6 February 2016 from https://www.ssb.no/natur-og-miljo/statistikker/avfregno.

Stewart, M. ed. 2012. *The Gypsy "Menace": Populism and the New Anti-gypsy Politics.* London: Hurst and Company.

Svarstad, J. 2011. "Denne måken skulle spises" [This seagull was meant to be eaten]. *Aftenposten.* Retrieved 23 June 2015 from http://www.aftenposten.no/nyheter/iriks/ Denne-maken-skulle-spises-6633334.html.

Svendsen, C. 2011. "Griller hunder og bæsjer i buskene" [Barbecue dogs, and poop in the bushes]. *Nettavisen.* Retrieved 14 January 2015 from https://www.nettavisen. no/dittoslo/-griller-hunder-og-bsjer-i-buskene/3423078625.html.

Sundt, E. 1852. *Beretning om Fante- eller Landstrygerfolket i Norge* [Report on the *Fant* or Tramp people in Norway]. Retrieved 30 June 2016 from https://archive.org/ details/beretningomfant00sundgoog.

Thorleifsson, C. 2017. "Disposable Strangers: Far-Right Securitization of Forced Migration in Hungary." *Social Anthropology* 25(3): 318–34.

Vermeersch, P. 2006. *The Romani Movement: Minority Politics and Ethnic Mobilization in Contemporary Central Europe.* New York: Berghahn Books.

Weiss-Wendt, A. ed., 2013. *The Nazi Genocide of the Roma: Reassessment and Commemoration.* New York: Berghahn Books.

Weyrauch, W. ed., 2001. *Gypsy Law: Romani Legal Traditions and Culture.* Berkeley, CA: University of California Press.

5

Waste People/Value Producers
Ambiguity, Indeterminacy, and Postsocialist Russian-Speaking Miners

Eeva Kesküla

This chapter examines the indeterminate conditions of Russian miners who remained in Estonia and Kazakhstan after the end of the Soviet Union. Indeterminacy appears here in two main modes. The first is the ambiguous social role of miners, characterized by multiple contradictory meanings. Thus, for example, the figure of the miner has a long history, in and beyond the former Soviet space, of being both celebrated as an industrial hero and derided for a lack of cultivation. I also discuss the ambiguity of the contemporary figure of the "Russian colonizer." The second mode of indeterminacy explored in this chapter is how mine workers perceive the erosion of social distinctions that traditionally separated them from other workers and citizens. This is experienced not merely as being morally and economically unvalued, but also as being reduced to a less-than-human state. Comparison is both the subject and object of this ethnography. Mineworkers typically draw upon a relativizing/comparative discourse to articulate a sense either of their distinctiveness, or diminishment by being recategorized in a way that fails to acknowledge their uniqueness.

Both Estonia and Kazakhstan were largely industrialized during the Soviet era, with their heavy-industrial workforces mainly comprised of migrants and deportees from other parts of the Soviet Union. In both countries, "Russian" is an emic term used by miners themselves, as well by the wider population of Estonians and Kazakhs. It signifies people who are ethnically Russian, Ukrainian, Polish, German, Korean, Finnish, or Tatar migrants and deportees from other parts of the former Soviet Union, who speak Russian as their mother tongue and closely identify with Russian culture and, usually, Russian orthodox religion. Generally, Russian miners can thus be loosely classified as colonizers who settled in, or were sent to, the Soviet Union's peripheries and whose labor was used to extract natural resources that were then used in the center of the empire (Mettam and Williams 1998, 2001). During the Soviet period, they enjoyed significant prestige and wealth both as the vanguard of the working class and as Russians.[1]

After the Soviet Union's collapse, the Russian miner's position gradually changed. In many locations, large heavy-industrial enterprises became redundant. Several mines in Kohtla-Järve, Estonia, and Karaganda, Kazakhstan, were closed. In place of heavy industry, business, law, tourism, and information technologies (IT) became prestigious career areas. Parents wanted their children to study these subjects in university and work in those fields. During this period, many Kazakhstani Russians migrated back to their historic homelands in Germany, Russia, and Israel, while many Estonian Russian speakers migrated to western and northern Europe after Estonia joined the EU in 2005.

The following analysis approaches indeterminacy as a condition that a social group may find itself in when the current order changes and when that group loses its earlier place in society. I explore two cases of Russian miners who have become ambiguous characters in the eyes of society on multiple counts. They experience ambiguity through their everyday encounters at the workplace, their economic situation, and through interactions with the autochthonous population and the state. Their distinct place in Soviet society is now challenged, making them feel that they are being treated as "waste." In the new regimes, social categories of waste and value have been redefined, but Russian miners aim to challenge such new classifications through their own counterdiscourses and moralities.

The Fieldsites: A Comparative Study

In 2010, I first met Vadim, a jolly, round fifty-four-year-old man with a handsome moustache who had worked in the oil shale mine in northeast Estonia all his life. Vadim knew that miners in Estonia could retire at the age of fifty-five, but he intended to keep working as long as he could in order to provide for his three-year-old granddaughter. He proudly demonstrated how he worked at removing the roof bolts from the ceiling of the mine, showed me videos of his family, and angrily described how miners and Russians in Estonia are no longer valued and lack the social guarantees of former years. Vadim died in 2013 when he was hit by a rock falling from the mine ceiling. Work in the mine was conducted on a piece-rate basis, and his colleagues explained that older miners were therefore especially prone to recklessness.

In my second field site, in Karaganda's coal mines, in central Kazakhstan, a Russian man named Pasha maintained the lifts that took miners more than a kilometer underground. He knew how to repair the lifts, and was appreciated by his team as a man with "golden hands." After bonding with his workmates in a local café (and complaining about his low wages), he would often go home drunk, and yell at his wife and son. He would become angry when his wife Ksenia and his friends listened to Kazakh pop rather than Russian music during home parties. Yet, when Ksenia (who worked in a nearby coal washing plant) suggested leaving Kazakhstan for Russia, he feared the uncertainties that the move might involve. Ksenia longed for her sister, who had already migrated, and for better pay and a better future for her children in Russia. She was upset at how the male management treated her, and forced her to do manual work that had previously been automated. She was worried that her son would not get a job in a government agency in Kazakhstan because "his eyes did not look right."

This chapter is based on twelve months of fieldwork in an Estonian oil shale mining town in 2010, and ten months in Karaganda, a coal mining town in Kazakhstan, in 2013 and 2017. Through a comparative analysis of Estonian and Kazakhstani Russian miners, I aim to make a wider argument about the postsocialist working class, and highlight the similarities and differences in the two settings. Rather than seeing the two fieldsites as isolated units, I highlight the connections that link them through their shared history, and the similarities of the Russian diaspora. Indeed, worker discourse was astonishingly similar in these two environments, with informants such as Vadim and Pasha often expressing identical statements, word-for-word. Although the political-economic contexts of the two field sites differed, the question of shifting ethnic and class hierarchies in both places suggest similarities rather than differences, allowing broader generalizations about the postsocialist working class. This chapter shows that the experiences of indeterminacy among Russian miners emerge from constant comparisons, which appear as attempts to reorder a world that no longer complies with their moral system.

Although postsocialist Estonia and Kazakhstan differ in their political and economic context they share a history of being resource colonies of the Soviet Union. In 1997, the Kazakhstani coal mining company was privatized and bought by the international steel company ArcelorMittal, while the Estonian mines stayed in national ownership. After 1991, Estonia quickly oriented itself toward democracy, liberal economic policy, Europe and EU membership, and adopting a restrictive citizenship policy for Russian speakers who had migrated to Soviet Estonia. By contrast, Kazakhstan maintained a close political and economic relationship with Russia. In both sites, Russian speakers lost their privileged status.

During my fieldwork, both sites shared an experience of economic crisis. During 2010, my fieldwork in Estonia coincided with the start of the economic crisis and the merger of the state-owned mining company with the national power company. This shifted upper management away from the mining region, and to Estonian speakers in the capital, Tallinn. The result was the introduction of new management techniques, as well as outsourcing and redundancies for miners. In Kazakhstan, the steel and mining company ArcelorMittal posted year-after-year losses since the 2008 crisis, which resulted in stagnating wages, no recruitment, and little investment in repairs and equipment. In March 2014, the devaluation of the national currency by 20 percent meant that imported goods, real estate, and cars (the value of which was calculated in US dollars) became increasingly expensive, while incomes continued to drop. Many more miners began to migrate to Russia. The economic crisis made the future more uncertain, adding a temporal dimension to the experience of indeterminacy where not only the miners' current socioeconomic position, but also their future, was unclear.

The Russian Miner: An Indeterminate Character

In this section, I trace how experiences of indeterminacy among miners are generated by the lack of a clearly recognizable position for both Russians and miners in the former republics of the Soviet Union. Although Russians and miners are considered in both countries to be predominantly negative characters embodying a Soviet legacy by some people, they also have an irreplaceable role in extracting a mineral that is seen as a national treasure. In the Soviet period, Russian-speaking miners fit into a relatively clearly defined category. Miners, the vanguard of society, were idealized as the honest, noble proletariat who had suffered under capitalism. For the Soviets, the image of the miner signified pure masculinity, the antithesis of the fat and lazy capitalist (Ghodsee 2011). Nevertheless, this image of the worker was far from straightforward even in socialist countries, where processes of forced proletarianization fed historical antagonisms, and often led the urban intelligentsia to depict the new working class as "ignorant, backward and suspect" (Stenning 2005). The official valorization of the socialist working class resulted in extreme representations of such communities, ranging from the heroic to the ridiculous.

In postsocialist countries, when miners took political action to improve their conditions they were often seen as either violent and antiprogress (Kideckel 2008), or hopelessly passive, due to the individualized patronage system that prevented collective action (Ashwin 1999). Furthermore, they were lumped together with other groups such as rural inhabitants and other members of the working class; they were collectively seen as the Other whose morals and values did not fit a market-oriented society (Annist 2011; Buchowski 2006; Keskküla 2015; Stenning 2005).

The two sides of the miner discussed here are not only a socialist phenomenon. Alan Metcalfe shows how throughout history, the image of the miner has been ambiguous: miners are dirty, racialized and sexualized, lazy, profane and Godless, and yet also the archetypal proletarian destined to carry out a revolutionary role in history. Miners signify ambiguity; they are masculine and powerful, wild and unpredictable. They are both heroes and villains, "the vanguard or the rearguard of human progress" (Metcalfe 1990: 47). The image carries contradictory ideas of authenticity and wildness, like the Appalachian miners

who are simultaneously friendly and suspicious, talkative and taciturn, patho-
logically dependent and utterly self-sufficient, simultaneously signifying lack
and excess (Stewart 1996).

Besides being ambiguous due to their social class and profession, post-
Soviet miners are ambiguous because they are "Russian," according to the defi-
nition outlined earlier. Estonia and Kazakhstan have a significant
Russian-speaking population. In order to exploit the coal found in the
Karaganda area in the 1920s, a GULAG (KarLag) was established to which
Koreans, Volga Germans, and Chechens as well as *kulaks* (rich peasants) and
political prisoners were deported during Stalin's rule. Later, Khrushchev's
"Virgin Lands" campaign in the 1950s attracted Russians to Kazakhstan, and
many of them decided to remain in the mines; by this point a mining town had
emerged from the GULAG. Even those who were forcefully deported were
transformed into willing colonizers taking part in the modernization project to
civilize the "empty" steppe that had earlier been the home of nomadic Kazakhs
(Brown 2004). These initiatives were partly responsible for Kazakhstan becoming the only republic in the Soviet Union where the titular nation was a minority population (see Alexander this volume).

According to the 1989 census, Kazakhs constituted 39.7 percent of the population, with Russians the second largest ethnic group. By the time of my fieldwork, this balance had been reversed. In 2014, Kazakhs constituted 65.5
percent of the population and Russians 21.5 percent. The Russians in
Kazakhstan have long considered themselves to be living in a predominantly
Russian republic, culturally closer to Russia, Ukraine, and Belarus than to
Central Asia (Peyrouse 2008). All residents of Kazakhstan became Kazakhstani
citizens and although Kazakh was declared the official national language,
Russian remained the language of international communication that could also
be used in official documents. Despite still considering themselves as civilizers
of the steppe, after 1991 Russians felt less welcome as they gradually became a
minority and ethnic Kazakhs took over government structures.

When Estonia was incorporated into the Soviet Union in 1939, oil shale
mines were opened to provide heating for Leningrad. At the time, most local
men had died in the war, escaped to the West, or been forcibly deported (some
to Kazakhstan), while those that remained were working in agriculture. As a
result, thousands of migrants from European Russia, Ukraine, and Belarus were
sent to develop and work in the new oil shale mines (Vseviov 2002). In Estonia,
the Russian proportion of the population was at its highest in 1989 when it
constituted 30 percent, dropping to 24.8 percent by the 2011 census. Although
Estonians typically talk about their country's "occupation," the liquidation of
the earlier economic structure, the development of industrialization to serve
the interests of the empire, environmental pollution, and migration policies
were effectively all processes of colonization (Kukk 1991). As the Soviet occu-
pier settled in the area, the relationship of domination acquired the features of
colonialism and started to change how people in the Baltic States related to

their world with their identity increasingly shaped by the presence of Soviet power (Annus 2017). Russian miners thought of themselves as allies who had come to build up the country after the destruction of war.

The Soviet Union's collapse led to the rejection of everything Soviet by Estonia and a desire to restore the country as it was imagined to have been during the first period of Estonian independence between the two world wars (Keskula 2015). After 1991, in order to become citizens, all Estonian residents who (or whose ancestors) were not living in Estonia before the Soviet occupation in 1939 had to pass a citizenship exam that included a language test. In Estonia, the Huntingtonian "clash of civilizations" discourse was employed by the media and the elite, emphasizing that Estonia belonged culturally to the West in a way that Russia never could (Merritt 2000).

As in other post-Soviet countries, minority issues in Estonia and Kazakhstan were primarily seen as connected to questions of national security. The Estonian state constructed its identity as a territorial imaginary threatened by cultural difference with Russia (Feldman 2005). In this discourse, "Russia" signified not only the Russian state, but Russianness more generally, including the presence of Russian speakers in Estonia (Kuus 2007). Scholarly articles often focused on the potential mobilization of the Russian-speaking diaspora (see Smith and Wilson 1997) or whether Russian-speakers were loyal to the Estonian state. Similarly, in Kazakhstan, ethnic minorities were also perceived as a threat to national stability and sovereignty (Davé 2007).

In both contexts, Russian miners symbolized the violent colonial policies of industrialization and migration. They were symbolic relics of another time who were constructed as being hard to control, not quite fitting into the new society, and potentially a security theat. The media no longer paid attention to miners; the general public forgot them or associated mining regions with high crime rates and dirtiness. Nationalist and classist attitudes masked as environmental concerns allowed one journalist to tellingly refer to miners as "moles" who hollow out the land underneath ancient Estonian villages (Lepassalu 2013). Following Mary Douglas (2003), in such circumstances, miners can be seen as dirt, matter out of place, and therefore dangerous. Thus, while in both contexts Russians saw themselves as good and helpful colonizers, they sensed that after Estonia and Kazakhstan's independence, they were more often labeled as dangerous by the native population and governments and now occupied a rather indeterminate position in society.

Nevertheless, the radical changes described above do not mean that Russian miners in either contexts were rendered entirely non-valuable. The fact that miners have historically been producers of a natural resource crucial to the state reinforces their ambiguous position. In the eyes of the state, Russian miners pose a double security threat because they represent the cultural Other and control the most prized natural resources: coal and oil shale. They are irreplaceable because such energy resources are still economically central in both places. In Estonia, oil shale signifies energy self-sustainability, and, in resource-rich Kazakhstan, an economy based on natural resource export, it remains a key natural resource, guaranteeing employment for thousands of people, and an important economic safety net when oil prices fall on the global market. In 2011, Kazakhstan's total industrial production was US$113 billion, 60.8 percent of which was based on mineral extraction. Most of this was crude petroleum ($57.9 billion) while $1.3 billion was from extraction of coal and lignite (Hays 2008). Mining attracts significant fixed capital investment and foreign direct investment. Despite the slump in prices, coal mining remains one of Kazakhstan's core industries (van der Leeuw 2014). Oil shale, a brown sedimentary rock that can be used for oil production or burning in thermal power plants for electricity production, is mined in very few countries, such as China, Brazil, and Estonia. Because of oil shale production, Estonia is one of the most energy-independent countries in the EU, exporting over half of the energy it produces (Eurostat 2017). Apart from the obvious economic and geo-political benefits of the resource, oil shale has a strong symbolic meaning. Despite the oil shale industry being mostly developed during the Soviet era that many Estonians consider a period of foreign occupation, it is now seen as central to maintaining energy independence from Russia. As Kärg Kama (2013, emphasis in the original) states: "the restoration of Estonian statehood also restored the position of oil shale as a *patrimony*, the 'wealth of the nation' which is inherited with its territory and embedded in the labouring bodies and expert knowledge of the people, and which provides the key material warranty for economic growth, social security, and hence national sovereignty."

While, in general, both Estonia and Kazakhstan have operated a liberal market economy, the energy sector is controlled by the state either by attracting foreign investment in the case of Kazakhstan or subsidizing the energy sector by protecting the country from "the omnipresent Russian threat to the Estonian statehood" (Kuus 2002: 409). In sum, the ambiguity of the colonizer in the post-Soviet context emerges in two ways. First, there is a discrepancy between how Russians see their past contribution to building the Soviet nations and how the native population now evaluates it. Second, the "foreign and dangerous" Russian miners are producing a resource that is exceptionally important to the state and does not follow the same market logic as other areas of economy. Thus, their previous highly valued position is lost, but these workers are not simply regarded as excess or valueless. Nonetheless, they remain unclear about their position and their future. In the next section I explore how such indeterminacy is experienced.

Cattle and Slaves:
The Symbolic Decategorization of Russian Miners

As the Soviet glory days slipped ever further away, their labor was still needed. Russian miners expressed confusion and dissatisfaction about their unclear position in society. They argued that society no longer valued them, to the point that they were simply waste or no longer human. They expressed how in the eyes of society they were "slaves" or "nobodies," with many describing themselves using the Russian word *bydlo*. This literally translates as "cattle," but could be understood in this context as meaning "scum" or "nobody." During my second period of fieldwork, I was working in a coal processing factory of Kazakhstan where work was continuously becoming harder as there was little investment in equipment and no new workers recruited. In a lunchtime conversation with Anya and Natasha, women in their forties from the coal rocessing plant, Anya explained:

> Now we're just working scum, sorry for the expression. There is no respect, although all this money is made at the expense of the worker. What bothers me the most is the local management who should act more appropriately. When you go to them, they don't want to listen to you or help, it's as if they don't consider us humans. Earlier it was different, I am not sure why it happened like that.

Again, in Estonia, women mine workers said: "We feel as if we're slaves, like slaves of Isaura," referring to the 1980s Brazilian telenovela about enslaved plantation workers that was popular in Estonia in the 1990s.

These quotations illustrate how miners think that society and management perceives them as dirt. Instead of occupying a clear, recognized place or category in society, their self-descriptions suggest an undefined mass or liminal state occupied by people who have lost their status as both human and worker. An Estonian worker explored this idea in a discussion about the management of his workplace: "They simply lower [*snizhayut*] us, they do not consider us humans. All the newspapers are writing that it was a successful economic year, but we get nothing from the company's profit. There is profit but no bonuses or salary raise for us, they even abolished the Miners' Day."

For female Russian mine workers, the situation was more acute still. Female mine workers labored on the surface, could not claim the dangerous, savage masculinity that male miners did, and lost a gendered classification altogether. Historically, women worked on the surface in coal extracting operations. Although their salaries were less than those of underground workers, those working in coal and oil processing plants were trained as technical experts in the Soviet period and respected as such. Increasing unemployment and the changing image of women from tractor drivers to housewives and beauty pageant contestants challenged the role that women had before (Ashwin 2000; Bridger, Pinnick, and Kay 1995). This also manifested in the Estonian and Kazakhstani plants where female workers had started their career in the 1980s and were now aging, together with the equipment, not fulfilling post-Soviet standards of femininity.

As more international commissions and auditors started to come to the Kazakhstani plant, the management increasingly assigned female workers duties of cleaning and whitewashing the factory to impress the visitors. For expert female workers, this was demeaning work, suggesting domestic labor. When the commissions were visiting the factory, there were no workers in sight as they had been told to keep away from the path of important men. "Because we are already old and ugly," the women joked. Guests were usually taken to the central control room to study documentation where the switchboard operator of the shift sits. One day after a committee visit, the women told me that the management had behaved very badly with Tanya, an experienced switchboard operator:

> We do not know who came, some Englishman and Tanya was not let into the control room until he was gone. They put Alisa there instead. Because she is younger and more beautiful. But Tanya is a wonderful person, she has worked her for thirty years, survived everything, she does not wear make-up, so what? This is humiliating, she was so offended, crying the whole day. When a commission comes, they hide us because we're already dinosaurs.

In Kazakhstan, workers stated that managers called female workers *babas*, a word for an older woman who is not attractive and fit only for working. Aging equipment meant more spills from the conveyer belt that female workers had to shovel back onto it and more manual work, with managers stating "Let the *babas* clean it up!"

Managers often yelled at the women, hoping to make them work faster. Workers said that the management saw them as cheaper and more obedient

Figure 5.1. Coal-washing plant female workers cleaning the factory yard, Karaganda, photo by the author.

than technical equipment. Despite technical investment and innovation in the Estonian oil shale processing plant, the discourse of Estonian female surface workers was astonishingly similar. Tanya in Estonia explained: "The management's attitude has worsened over the last few years, they don't call us *zhenshiny*, [women] anymore, but *tyoty*." *Tyotya*, literally an auntie, is also a negative term for a slightly older, possibly less educated and less respected woman. When asking a manager to empathize with the arduous working conditions of female processing plant employees, the manager was reported to have responded: "You are not women, you are workers." Female workers felt their worthlessness in a double sense: first, they were no longer valued as specialists of complex chemical and mechanical processes; second, they were no longer valued and appreciated as women but rather categorized as a peasant- or slave-like laboring mass, deprived even of their gendered features. If male miners could at least hold on to their working-class masculinity, this was not the case for women.

Russian miners expressed their dissatisfaction at the loss of status and the uncertainty about their social place through a radical discourse of being nobody, only dirt, cattle, or slaves. Although still working, their work now lacked recognition. By claiming to be seen as dirt, they were not simply lamenting their fall from a high social position, but rather expressed their confusion about where and who they were supposed to be. They had slipped to the margins where their position and identity were unclear, merged with the rest of the working class. They did not think of themselves as scum, but experienced the changes as a decategorization to an indeterminable position. Constant comparison with how things used to be better in the Soviet period further highlighted how their place as industrial heroes of Soviet modernity had been replaced with indeterminacy.

Economic Decategorization and Dispossession

Russian miners in Karaganda often reminisced about the Soviet period when miners were better paid, and could afford long taxi rides and plane rides to Almaty to drink the local beer. An Estonian manager who grew up in a mining village remembered from his childhood: "The first person in the village to buy a TV was Uncle Kolja, a miner; the first person to buy a car was uncle Vanja, another miner." Now, miners can no longer afford everything that they desire. In Kazakhstan and Estonia, many miners had taken high-interest consumer loans to pay for holidays, flats, cars, and children's education. I conducted a survey on household economy and labor conditions with fifty mineworkers in Kazakhstan. At the time, 50 percent of the participants had a loan that they were currently paying back. "So many people are currently under the yoke of the loan. And how many suicides do we have because of that?" Pasha complained. The mortgages and loans taken by workers in the economic boom years, were now making them even more dependent upon their employer in the time of economic crisis.

Miners believe it is unfair that for labor as hard as theirs, they cannot afford a decent life with a salary that covers their needs. Although miners' salaries are in fact well above the national average, and are the highest salaries in the region, they are deemed unsatisfactory compared with when miners could (and would) buy all they wanted. Furthermore, miners are now earning less compared to some other professions, such as managers and businessmen, and this compounds their sense of injustice, causing them to doubt their position in the social hierarchy.

In Estonia, the mines are nationally owned and miners felt a stronger ownership and pride in the company. Nevertheless, they also felt a deepening divide between managers/engineers and workers. During the rearrangements related to the Estonian company's merger, the main grudge was against the management and engineers who were awarded annual bonuses (based on a new system of annual performance review) while workers received nothing. Although workers expressed their dissatisfaction in terms of losing out on money and the management profiting from miners' labor, the performance review exercise seemed to leave the workers excluded from the new rituals. Miners remembered how they used to earn more than managers did and compared it with the current unfair situation. Furthermore, not being included in the game of performance review meant that they felt they were not recognized and were thus made invisible.

Kazakhstani miners felt such inequalities even more strongly as they compared themselves with Lakshmi Mittal, the owner of ArcelorMittal, a global steel magnate based in London. This was discussed with particularly bitter discontent after Mittal paid millions of dollars for his niece's lavish wedding. This seemed especially unfair since at the time, workers were told to endure a crisis that meant staff shortages, cut bonuses, and salaries that were falling due to inflation. "How much did the wedding cost again? 58 million dollars?! Even if we worked all our lives, we could not earn that kind of money. It is not possible to earn such money working in honest way," lamented the repair and maintenance workers during their lunch break. "It is the owner [*khozyain*] versus slaves at the moment. He pays us and we are his slaves." What most annoyed the miners was that their salaries were no longer the highest, and pay differences between the owner and miners were so large it was hard to grasp. Comparisons with other social groups who seemed to have a clearer label and place in society, amplified their sense of injustice.

Indeterminacy was further embodied in uncertainty about the reproduction of a class that no longer seemed to have a place in society. In Kazakhstan, it was a dilemma whether a miner's child should become a miner. To get a job in the mine for a child meant years of waiting, hefty bribes, and special connections. Since mining was no longer prestigious, and with their social position and future unclear, many believed that it would be better if their children became lawyers or doctors. Such new middle-class aspirations were, however, often out of reach due to the cost of education in Kazakhstan and miners' lack of knowledge about which profession their children should pursue in which university.

Figure 5.2. Retired Russian miner in Shakhtinsk, Kazakhstan, displaying his Soviet-era medals, photo by the author.

Many who had paid money to complete the online courses of dubious universities in Russia, later struggled to find a job in their field. It was hard to continue as a miner and it was hard to move upward socially, so miners' children were hovering in undefined spaces, trying to find their place even more than their parents (Kesküla 2018). The 2008 economic crisis hit the industrial Russian-speaking area of Estonia the hardest, with a 20 percent unemployment rate. In Estonia, many miners' children had gone to take manual jobs in Europe, mostly in the United Kingdom, Ireland, Finland, and Norway, and had to return because there was no more work there either. Later, falling oil prices made the production of oil from oil shale unprofitable and caused lay-offs and constant fear of further lay-offs.

Thus, Russian miners' experience of economic indeterminacy was, on the one hand, symbolic, manifesting how miners' salaries had fallen compared with previous times and other professions. On the other, it was related to the inability to continue the reproduction of their life as Russian miners, as their children no longer found their place within it, and they were uncertain whether they would be better off or not by staying or leaving.

Ethnic Indeterminacy

Miners also found themselves in an indeterminate position as Russians, the representatives of the former colonial power. They had lost their special place as representatives of the heart of the empire and found it difficult to accept that

Figure 5.3. Lunchtime conversation at the Estonian mine's underground garage, photo by the author.

hierarchies had changed. Russians in Kazakhstan often found it hard to come to terms with the fact that Kazakhs now considered themselves entitled to more cultural and economic rights (see Alexander this volume).

There was a lot of resentment among Russian speakers about the privileges of the native population, especially when it came to worries about their children. Kazakhstani Russian miners noted that government and public-sector jobs were only available for Kazakhs, regardless of whether they spoke Kazakh or not. Underneath the discourse of ethnic harmony there were tensions in both countries that made Russians feel unwelcome and challenged their worth as persons. Kazakhstani miners, like Russian-speakers in Uzbekistan (Flynn 2007), were nostalgic for the Soviet period and would call the Soviet Union their homeland, cursing Gorbachev, after a few drinks, for letting the Soviet Union fall apart.

Estonian Russians expressed such nostalgia less, but also missed the social guarantees that they had before. Estonian Russian speakers felt that they were cursed because they had to work underground, calling themselves Russian Negroes (*russike negry*), referring to their slave-like position and dirty work while Estonians were working in warm offices. Mining engineers also felt that their career opportunities were limited because, while internal documentation within the mine was in Russian, anything else required knowledge of Estonian. The urgency of leaving the country or fears of ethnic conflict were significantly less in Estonia but the miners certainly felt they were second-rate citizens and discriminated against. Due to the Estonian language requirements, that many were unable to fulfill, and other opportunities in Europe, miners' children were often keen to leave Estonia. As a result, the Russian-speaking mining region had the highest statistics for emigration.

Both of the diasporic Russian groups, as with Pilkington's (1998) Russian repatriates from other Soviet republics, did not fully identify with Russians in Russia and saw themselves as somehow superior (Fein 2005; Flynn 2007). Both Estonian and Kazakhstani Russians thought of themselves as harder workers who drank less than Russians in Russia, and were more like the native population: more hospitable and home-oriented in Kazakhstan, colder, more distanced, and European in Estonia. There was a sense that no one expected them in Russia. Estonian Russians rarely considered moving back to Russia where economic opportunities were seen as lacking. In Kazakhstan, whole brigades of miners from the Karaganda region had migrated to Mezhduredzhensk, a mining town in Siberia. The reasons for this were mostly pragmatic: lower pension age, higher salaries, and easier working conditions in Russia. At the same time, messages coming back from the émigré miners in Mezhduredzhensk were contradictory, some explained that the conditions were not as good as promised, some talked about tensions with local Russians. Estonian Russian miners who mostly migrated to Western Europe, were also aware that although they considered themselves more "Western" than Russians in Russia, in the West they were considered simple manual workers who were no longer needed as soon as the economic crisis hit. Therefore, they were no longer the same as

Russian Russians but were distinct from Estonians and Kazakhs, neither emigration nor staying gave them a clearer category to place themselves in. In Estonia and Kazakhstan, they felt that their status was no longer as high as it used to be and although they felt culturally superior to the local population, this superiority was no longer recognized. The collapse of the Soviet Union removed much of the Russian colonizers' identity and it was unclear what would replace it. This echoes Laura Bear's (2007) account of Anglo-Indians who lived in the railway colonies and who, after independence, no longer had solid family or community identities to hold on to, suggesting that they now lived in a place of ghosts and ruins. After losing their economic privileges and reserved posts, the railway colony homeland ceased to exist and they could no longer claim that space. Russian miners, fearing to leave but no longer feeling welcome in the former colonies are similarly losing their place, not only in a physical sense but also as symbolic indeterminacy. Comparing themselves to the titular population further highlights their own indeterminacy of no longer belonging here or there.

Claiming the Value of Labor

Despite being refused a clear category or position by society, miners still believe in their worth through emphasizing the value of their labor. This is their way of claiming their place in a society that has cast them out as posing a security threat while taking their labor. Colonial ruins are not only abandoned places, but places where new claims for history, sites on new possibilities and political projects, new bids for entitlements are made (Stoler 2008). Rather than experiencing mining towns simply as abandoned sites of nostalgia, Russian miners claim their value and re-establish order in the world. Imperial formations that placed the Russian-speaking mining areas in the steppe and the forest, continue their own processes, but without the earlier clear direction to a bright future.

Miners further claim their worth through the ritual of complaining. The common, most empowering practice of miners was complaining vocally at the kitchen table, to the union representative, the anthropologist, their wives, about how bad conditions were, and how much better it was before. There would be anger in their eyes, spit would fly in all directions, and rage at the lack of respect would be voiced as a litany common to Russian speakers (Ries 1997) and post-Soviet miners (Kideckel 2000). Such complaining can be seen as a form of creating a religious community (Durkheim 1915) or a way of subduing and giving up real political agency away from the kitchen table. Nevertheless, confirming the importance of work to each other was the subversive, life-affirming, category-creating work that kept miners believing in their own value.

The more positive forms of complaining, where one's worth is confirmed, can take various registers. First, miners emphasize the importance of the resource mined to the national economy. Estonian miners proudly stated that every time one turns on the light in Estonia, it was down to their labor. Similarly, in Kazakhstan, workers boasted about the quality of their coal which they believed was very special and expensive and could be found only in five locations in the world. Miners knew that the nearby steel plant, which was creating value for Mittal, could work only due to the coal that they mined.

Emphasizing the value for the national economy can be done through continuing the Soviet discourse of respect for miners. Vova, a middle-ranking mining engineer in a small Kazakhstani mining town and a leader of a rock band takes great pride in his most popular song "The Coal Face":

> You do not just pick up the riches from the bowel of the earth;
> a hundred misfortunes loom upon us and
> want to shake your health.
> No, this is not a war, but again we go as if to a battle,
> to fight the Earth, for the benefit of the state,
> to the coal face, the coal face.

Drawing on some clichés from the Soviet miners' songs, such as working for the benefit of the country, Vova's lyrics nevertheless emphasize an important point: the riches of the earth only become the riches that the state benefits from through the labor of miners. This labor entails confronting accidents and health hazards, and coal only becomes valuable through the everyday risk and sacrifice of miners. In the state discourse about the usage of natural resources, labor is mostly missing, and only the impersonal natural resource that has already been taken to the surface to be sold on the national or international market becomes a commodity. Miners place labor back in the center of value creation.

Figure 5.4. Miners' rock band, Karaganda, photo by the author.

Second, their work was legitimized and value was added to the material through miners sacrificing their health. At both sites, underground workers often explained how hard and health-damaging the work was. Vadim died because it was hard for a fifty-three-year-old to compromise between his desire to earn well and maintain his health and safety. Every year such accidents happened even in the relatively safe Estonian mines. Over a hundred miners died in methane gas explosions in the Karaganda mines from 2004 to 2008. "Dangerous, dirty and risky" was the chorus of the ritual complaining.

Miners' discourses on the dangers of their work are well substantiated. Miners have a higher rate of cancer than the Estonian average; being in the damp, wet, and cold gives them joint aches and arthritis; back problems from sitting and operating machines were common. In the year 2000, the old technology that had used electric power was replaced by new technology powered by diesel in the Estonian mine. Although miners admitted that work was physically easier after the new technology was introduced, they pointed out that new diesel-fuelled machines produced many more cancer-causing fumes, which the weak ventilation system of the mine could not cope with so the miners breathed in diesel fumes (Kesküla 2016). It became easier to work but harder to breathe. The salaries were always measured against the particular hardness of work, expressed in the presence of elements like dust and gas and health-damaging conditions such as vibration. In Kazakhstani mines, which were more dangerous and prone to methane gas explosions, miners also emphasized that their high salary should be the compensation for the risk that they are taking every day when they are going to work (see Kassymzhanova and Mun 2013). Thus, coal and oil shale became meaningful and valuable for miners through the work and health that they put into it. Coal and oil shale were also seen as having central importance by the two states but this manifested itself in different terms and carried a different value register from how the miners saw it.

Furthermore, as one miner commented, they were even sacrificing their private life to bring the precious material to the surface,

> I worked in the mine for twenty-seven years, did not see the sun. I come out of the mine, tired, sit on the bus. By the time you reach home, it is already dark. Wake up at four o'clock in the morning, come back at six. Get home, have tea and fall asleep. Wake up at ten, there is no sun. I eat, the kids go to bed at ten or eleven o'clock. At four in the morning, I get up to go to work again. What do I see? I see nothing. I don't see my kids. I come home, sleep, get up, leave, come back but do not see the daylight. It is very hard.

Miners continued to ascribe central value to their labor while simultaneously feeling themselves to be devalued as persons, rhetorically calling themselves "cattle" and "Estonian Negroes." However, the context of deindustrialization and an uncertain political and economic situation does not highlight the ambiguity of their situation as valueless humans who produce value. In a situation where the hypermobility of global capital makes futures uncertain, miners' value and worth are constantly renegotiated. The understanding of the miners and the state of the value of miners' labor are contradictory, creating an indeterminacy where the image of the miner is not only ambiguous, but now in constant flux and under threat of change, in relationship to different registers of value. Reclaiming their worth through labor is an attempt to fight indeterminacy and re-establish an order in the world where the future and their place is uncertain. The discourse itself points to earlier times and imperial formations but also to the current reality where in capitalist conditions, miners continue to lose their health and lives, just for the benefit of the new nation states and the capitalist.

Conclusion: Ambiguity, Indeterminacy, Comparison

The miner in Estonia and Kazakhstan was an ambiguous character even in the Soviet period. Officially, he was a hero with the most respected profession in the mining areas. Miners' salaries, which were sometimes ten times higher than those of teachers, allowed them consumption standards that were comfortable and sometimes reached extreme luxury, allowing them to ignore the disapproval of the middle classes. While the native intelligentsia perceived the migrant population from Russia as colonizers or occupiers, their privileged status in the Soviet hierarchy and the possibility of getting by in Russian in all interactions, made the "uneducated lout" side of the image less central to miners themselves. In the postsocialist nationalizing states where local mining was more connected to global raw material markets, the ordinary frame of ambiguity that miners were familiar with began to shift. The new ambiguity appears as the ethnically suspicious representatives of a backward profession, producing what is considered the national wealth. This new situation has many unknowns that destabilize the previously ambiguous but stable characterization of the miner. Since many mines had closed and recruitment was limited due to the economic crisis, miners' children can no longer hope to have jobs as miners. Hence, the mining community as it had existed previously can no longer reproduce itself.

In such a situation, either the ethnic or the labor component of the image of the miner could potentially shift at any moment, creating unpredictability. While the former ambiguity offered an ample space of privilege for miners as a group, the current one is loaded with the threat that the ever-shifting balance of what miners are and do can be challenged on the basis of either ethnicity or the shifting register of their labor's value in mining the raw material. Miners experience the indeterminacy of future trajectories and the continuous threat that they will no longer be able to reproduce their current way of life. Without the Soviet narrative of modernity, they have no certain linear narrative of the future and only nostalgia to look back to.

Although the colonial legacy allows them to keep earning good salaries and their skills as extractors of natural resources are still needed in the new states, miners find it hard to understand their own position and meaning in the new situation. The symbolic exaggeration of referring to themselves as waste or cattle indexes the uncertainties of a position based on labor as well as a sense of challenges to their privileged ethnic position as a colonizer. Such discourses express the shifting of the old order of things where Russian miners find it hard to locate or carve out their present space as representatives of another era.

Russian miners constantly compare their current conditions to how they used to be, their current status as miners to that of other occupational groups and their managers and company owners. They compare the privileges that they had as Russians to those of Estonians and Kazakhs and they often ask about the working conditions in my other field site compared with theirs. In a situation where miners experience indeterminacy due to their ethnic and social status and can barely cling to the narrative of modernity and labor, comparisons help to create classificatory order in the world again. If miners sense that their place in the present time and place has been removed, leaving them as indeterminate dirt, matter out of place, or gently floating colonial debris, comparisons help to understand who stands where in relation to the other social groups or better times are compared to the current position of Russian miners. Exercising their moral judgment about the value of labor that is physical, dangerous, and necessary for society, indeterminacy is challenged by creating a moral order that is reaffirming the community and making the everyday more secure through morally charged comparisons.

Constructivist approaches emphasize that there is nothing natural about comparison, that comparability is a result of ethnographic inquiry, not the natural starting point, that research and writing strategies lead up to comparison. Objects are made comparable through contextualization, analytical cross-contextual framing and comparing as a strategy should be processual and exploratory (Scheffer and Niewöhner 2010). According to Marilyn Strathern (2005), anthropologists have been encouraged to think of numbers, that the alternative to one is many. This creates problems when thinking about relationships between societies, that relationships are somehow expected to exist either outside or between societies. I would argue that instead of atomized units, we have connected, messy, overlapping features of a mobile and transforming world. Working with two field sites does not mean only focusing on the similarities, differences, and reasons, but challenging the idea that two is one multiplied by two. The comparisons emerge from shared pasts, presents, and potentialities that blur the sites' boundaries and make the connections, the relationships, rather than the numbers, important. Comparative agendas are becoming legitimate again in anthropology because of increasing global connections (Fox and Gingrich 2002). If people all around the globe are increasingly reacting to comparable conditions, it becomes a more obvious challenge for scholars to compare how people react and what results culturally from their reactions.

If, as Max Gluckman (1960: 57) famously claimed, "an African townsman is a townsman, an African miner is a miner" who possibly resembles miners everywhere, then seeing whether the Estonian and Kazakhstani miners are miners who resemble miners everywhere, would certainly be better substantiated by not only looking at differences between the cases, but also paying particular attention to the similarities that allow us to make wider generalizations about miners or the global working class. This is particularly true in the increasingly connected world where mining has taken a more prominent role than ever before. For both miners and anthropologists, comparisons can function as a tool for overcoming a sense of indeterminacy and make sense of how certain hierarchies have shifted and what the moral values are that help the indeterminable dirt become a recognizable category and something of value again.

Acknowledgements

This research was supported by the Max Planck Institute of Social Anthropology postdoctoral program "Industry and Inequality in Eurasia" and the Estonian Research Council Grant PUT1263 "The Political Economy of Industrial Health and Safety: A Social Anthropology Perspective." I would like to thank the reviewers and editors for their helpful suggestions and Russian miners in Estonia and Kazakhstan for sharing their lives with me.

Eeva Kesküla is a senior researcher at Tallinn University, School of Humanities, where she is directing an Estonian Research Council project on anthropological approaches to occupational health and safety. She has done fieldwork in Estonia and Kazakhstan on labor, health and safety, and gender and class in mining communities. She has recently published in *History and Anthropology* and *Work, Employment and Society*.

Note

1. Kate Brown describes how after World War II, exiled ethnic groups in Kazakhstan started to identify themselves in the census as "Russians" and built Soviet identities fused into Soviet-Russian culture: "They began to speak Soviet-Russian in the same intonations broadcast over the radios, which began appearing in the settlements in the fifties, repeating the same phrases about the 'friendship of nations' enunciated by teachers in the classrooms which started to multiply across the steppe after the lean years of war" (2004: 191).

References

Annist, A. 2011. *Otsides kogukonda sotsialismijärgses keskuskülas* [Seeking community in postsocialist Estonian centralized villages]. Tallinn: Tallinn University Press.
Annus, E. 2017. *Soviet Postcolonial Studies: A View from the Western Borderlands.* London: Routledge.

Ashwin, S. 1999. *Russian Workers: The Anatomy of Patience*. Manchester: Manchester University Press.

———. 2000. *Gender, State, and Society in Soviet and Post-Soviet Russia*. London: Routledge.

Bear, L. 2007. "Ruins and Ghosts: The Domestic Uncanny and the Materialization of Anglo-Indian Genealogies in Kharagpur." In *Ghosts of Memory: Essays on Remembrance and Relatedness*, ed. J. Carsten, 36–57. Oxford: Blackwell Publishing Ltd.

Bridger, S., K. Pinnick, and R. Kay. 1995. *No More Heroines?: Russia, Women, and the Market*. London: Routledge.

Brown, K. 2004. *A Biography of No Place: From Ethnic Borderland to Soviet Heartland*. Cambridge, MA: Harvard University Press.

Buchowski, M. 2006. "The Specter of Orientalism in Europe: From Exotic Other to Stigmatized Brother." *Anthropological Quarterly* 79(3): 463–82.

Davé, B. 2007. *Kazakhstan-Ethnicity, Language and Power*. London: Routledge.

Douglas, M. 2003. *Purity and Danger: An Analysis of Concepts of Pollution and Taboo*. London: Routledge.

Durkheim, É. 1915. *The Elementary Forms of the Religious Life*. New York: The Macmillan Company.

Eurostat. 2017. "Energy Production and Imports". Retrieved 16 December 2017 from http://ec.europa.eu/eurostat/statistics-explained/index.php/Energy_production_and_imports.

Fein, L. 2005. "Symbolic Boundaries and National Borders: The Construction of an Estonian Russian Identity." *Nationalities Papers* 33(3): 333–44.

Feldman, G. 2005. "Estranged States: Diplomacy and the Containment of National Minorities in Europe." *Anthropological Theory* 2: 219–45.

Flynn, M. 2007. "Renegotiating Stability, Security and Identity in the Post-Soviet Borderlands: The Experience of Russian Communities in Uzbekistan." *Nationalities Papers* 35(2): 267–88.

Fox, R. G., and A. Gingrich. 2002. *Anthropology, by Comparison*. London: Routledge.

Ghodsee, K. 2011. *Muslim Lives in Eastern Europe: Gender, Ethnicity, and the Transformation of Islam in Postsocialist Bulgaria*. Princeton, NJ: Princeton University Press.

Gluckman, M. 1960. "Tribalism in Modem British Central Africa." *Cahiers d'études africaines* 1(1): 55–70.

Hays, J. 2008. "Energy in Kazakhstan." Retrieved 13 June 2016 from http://factsanddetails.com/central-asia/Kazakhstan/sub8_4e/entry-4674.html—chapter-8.

Kama, K. 2013. "Unconventional Futures: Anticipation, Materiality, and the Market in Oil Shale Development." Ph.D. dissertation. Oxford: University of Oxford.

Kassymzhanova, A., and M. Mun. 2013. "Subjective Study of Risk Assessment in Miners Work." *Procedia—Social and Behavioral Sciences: World Conference on Psychology and Sociology*, Antalya, Turkey, ed. Kobus Maree. PSYSOC 2012 82: 908–12.

Kesküla, E. 2015. "Reverse, Restore, Repeat! Dynamics of Class and Ethnicity and the Russian-Speaking Miners of Estonia." *Focaal* 72: 95–108.

———. 2016. "Temporalities, Time and the Everyday: New Technology as a Marker of Change in an Estonian Mine." *History and Anthropology* 27(5): 521–35.

———. 2018. "Miners and Their Children: The Remaking of the Soviet Working Class in Kazakhstan." In *Industrial Labor on the Margins of Capitalism: Precarity, Class and the Neoliberal Subject*, ed. Chris Hann and Jonathan Parry, 61–84. New York: Berghahn Books.

Kideckel, D. A. 2000. "The Unmaking of an Eastern European Working Class." In *Postsocialism: Ideals, Ideologies and Practices in Eurasia*, ed. Chris Hann, 114–132. London: Routledge.

_____. 2008. *Getting by in Postsocialist Romania: Labor, the Body, & Working-class Culture*. Bloomington, IN: Indiana University Press.

Kukk, K. 1991. *On Economic and Geographical Development of Estonia in 1945–1990.* Tallinn: Estonian Academy of Sciences.

Kuus, M. 2007. "Ubiquitous Identities and Elusive Subjects: Puzzles from Central Europe." *Transactions of the Institute of British Geographers* 32(1): 90–101.

Lepassalu, V. 2013. "Ida-Virumaal kodusid hävitavatel kaevandajatel jääb õigust ülegi." [Miners destroying homes in Ida-Viru County claim it is their right to do so.] In *Pealinn* 22, 4 March.

Merritt, M. 2000. "A Geopolitics of Identity: Drawing the Line between Russia and Estonia." *Nationalities Papers: The Journal of Nationalism and Ethnicity* 28(2): 243–62.

Metcalfe, A. 1990. "The Demonology of Class: The Iconography of the Coalminer and the Symbolic Construction of Political Boundaries." *Critique of Anthropology* 10(1): 39–63.

Mettam, C. W., and S. W. Williams. 1998. "Internal Colonialism and Cultural Divisions of Labour in the Soviet Republic of Estonia." *Nations and Nationalism* 4(3): 363–88.

_____. 2001. "A Colonial Perspective on Population Migration in Soviet Estonia." *Journal of Ethnic and Migration Studies* 27(1): 133–50.

Peyrouse, S. 2008. "The 'Imperial Minority': An Interpretative Framework of the Russians in Kazakhstan in the 1990s." *Nationalities Papers* 36(1): 105–23.

Pilkington, H. 1998. *Migration, Displacement, and Identity in Post-Soviet Russia.* London: Routledge.

Ries, N. 1997. *Russian Talk: Culture and Conversation during Perestroika.* Ithaca, NY: Cornell University Press.

Scheffer, T., and J. Niewöhner. 2010. *Thick Comparison: Reviving the Ethnographic Aspiration.* Leiden: Brill.

Smith, G., and A. Wilson. 1997. "Rethinking Russia's Post-Soviet Diaspora: The Potential for Political Mobilisation in Eastern Ukraine and North-East Estonia." *Europe-Asia Studies* 49(5): 845–64.

Stenning, A. 2005. "Spaces of (Post-)Socialism: Where is the Post-socialist Working Class? Working-Class Lives in the Spaces of (Post-)Socialism." *Sociology* 39: 983–99.

Stewart, K. 1996. *A Space on the Side of the Road: Cultural Poetics in an "Other" America.* Princeton, NJ: Princeton University Press.

Stoler, A. L. 2008. "Imperial Debris: Reflections on Ruins and Ruination." *Cultural Anthropology* 23(2): 191–219.

Strathern, M. 2005. *Partial Connections*, updated edition. Walnut Creek, CA: AltaMira Press.

van der Leeuw, C. 2014. "Kazakhstan Mining Sector's Challenges: Reserve Replacement and Capital Needed." In *Stratfor Worldview*. Retrieved 15 June 2016 from https://worldview.stratfor.com/the-hub/kazakhstan-mining-sector-s-challenges-reserve-replacement-and-capital-needed.

Vseviov, D. 2002. "Kirde-Eesti urbaanse anomaalia kujunemine ning struktuur pärast Teist maailmasõda" [The formation and structure of the urban anomaly in northeast Estonia after WWII]. In *Tallinn Pedagogical University Dissertations on Humanities.* Tallinn: Tallinn Pedagogical University.

6

Indeterminate Classifications
Being "More than Kin" in Kazakhstan

Catherine Alexander

Estimates diverge on how many Kazakhs were living outside Kazakhstan in 1991 when the new republic emerged from the Soviet Union. The World Association of Kazakhs (WAK) suggests 5 million, the International Organisation for Migration's (IOM) more conservative figure was 2 million. Both figures are thrown into sharp relief by Kazakhstan's 1989 census data that identified only 6.5 million Kazakhs internally, 39 percent of the overall population. These numbers and fractions matter: how they are counted and their effect on people's lives.

How we recognize or deny other people is fundamental to the formation, negotiation, and negation of social relationships. What concerns me here is, first, how such recognition operates through nation-state narratives and bureaucratic modes of knowing such as counting and classification and, second, the entailments of these representational forms. How is it that counting and statistics, so central to modern statecraft, can render people visible and calculable on the one hand, and yet inimical to containment and integration into a national or civic whole on the other? I argue that these apparently precise forms of knowing are profoundly indeterminate approximations of what they purport to know. This then builds on recent debates on what might called the biopolitics and consequences of counting (e.g., Engle Merry 2016; Nelson 2015). By juxtaposing such modes of accounting with how they are encountered, complex and varied experiences of indeterminacy appear as lives exceed or fall between the categories and narratives that seek to nail them down. Since mass migrations often foreground such demographic politics, I examine this through migrations from and to Kazakhstan over the last century, particularly since 1991.[1]

This chapter explores, partly via the politics of nation- and state-making in Kazakhstan, how proportional, multiple, and overlapping demographic categories function at different levels with different consequences. This also invites a closer examination of value ranges within a given category. Population statistics, numbers, algorithims, and the categories they enumerate seem to promise precision and thence control, but are only proxies for complex human lives and relationships. Narratives concerning the march of nations through history are similarly prone to selectivity and omission. Kazakhstan is no exception, presenting a chronicle of Soviet subjugation and subsequent Kazakh independence that has been neatly razored into a rather parsimonious, monochrome view of the recent past. But such apparent clarity hazards only a partial representation. Arguably, such incomplete accounts act as technologies of connection, weaving together imagined social wholes from constituent parts. But by looking at the gaps created, or unreflected by these approaches, multiple forms of indeterminacy appear.

Oralman[2] ("repatriate" or "returnee" in Kazakh) have been actively and formally welcomed back to Kazakhstan over the last twenty-five years as "brothers living abroad" (*shette zhurgen qandastar – qan* meaning blood in Kazakh) via a government-sponsored repatriation program. Written into both terms is the implication of a band of brothers, common ethnicity, blood kinship, but this story of return also raises questions of what belonging, relatedness, and integration mean. Oralman are often mocked by urban Kazakhs (and Russians) for a perceived lack of modern, urbane polish and have frequently found themselves in a bureaucratic void waiting, sometimes for years, for promised citizenship papers. Shocked by their acculturated, ancestral homeland, many have formed separate communities with other *oralman*, returned to their host land, or maintained complex, transboundary kin networks across and between host and homeland. In this last case, they inhabit an uncertain and indeterminate position between settler and visitor (Basch, Glick Schiller, and Blanc 1994) that challenges concepts of citizenship, nationhood, and the very notion of a territorially bounded nation-state.

Scholarly literature (e.g., Cerny 2010; Diener 2005; Laruelle 2016: 174) and media reports abound on the failures of *oralman* "integration," generally seen from politico-bureaucratic perspectives, occasionally from those of *oralman* themselves, rarely from internal migrants and continuously settled urban citizens of Kazakhstan. Jens Schneider and Maurice Crul remind us that "integration" typically emphasizes the "structural aspects of incorporation into society" (2010: 1145) aligning migrants from different backgrounds with a host country, attempting equality without uniformity.[3] Nevertheless, integration and incorporation both imply a social whole of which migrants (including returnees) are to be part. There is a shared root in the words *integer* and *integrity* after all: a whole number and the quality of being untainted. Repatriates can aggravate such assumptions, revealing holes in place of wholes where incommensurate worlds coexist and questioning similarity and difference.

Anti-*oralman* sentiment peaked in 2011 in Zhanaozen in East Kazakhstan on the 20th Anniversary of the Republic's Independence Day (see also Kesküla this volume). There were protests against poor working conditions, which ended in violent clashes with the police and citizens' deaths. Later, locals accused *oralman* of instigating the unrest. Some analyses accepted the claims, casting the protests as a consequence of marked socioeconomic inequalities between wealthy foreigners and impoverished Kazakhs in the oil regions (Satpayev and Umbetaliyeva 2015). Others suggested accusations were exaggerated (Oka 2013: 8), while Kazakh nationalists attacked "*oralman* phobia" (ibid.). Although no connection was formally made, the repatriation program was cut, the Internal Minister saying the government had "lost track" of the *oralman*: it was known that actual numbers exceeded official quotas and projections though nobody knew by how much. Two years later the program was restarted after events in the Ukraine. Fears that Russian-dominated areas of Kazakhstan might secede or welcome Russian intervention (Diener 2015) prompted a government move to place *oralman* in such regions, a numerical deterrent.

This seeming inability to descry, track, and count individuals is a common anti-representational maneuver used against immigrants. A decade earlier in Almaty, Kazakhstan's former capital, I often heard rural immigrants to the cities described as an "invisible virus" (Alexander 2008).[4] Such metaphors dehumanize people just as the common tropes deployed against immigrants describe them as a formless, liquid mass: they surge, flood, or pour into countries in waves threatening to engulf and destroy economic and social order; as such they are intractable to enumeration. Other such metaphors also evoke animals (swarm, flock, plague) thus breaking down distinctions between human and nonhuman, denying recognition of shared humanity and the possibility of social encounter. Nonetheless, as Diane Nelson (2015) so vividly shows in the context of Guatemalan state violence, the apparent objectivity of "counting" techniques can also displace or flatten social complexity and humanity.

What are we to make of these conflicting, shifting ways of understanding the *oralman's* situation, by turns welcomed, repudiated, resented, abandoned, and apparently lost track of? The *oralman* are one of many groups of people who became explicitly unwelcome in their host countries when national borders appeared or hardened after the fall of the Soviet Union. As the ethnography below shows, however, for many, the sense of that larger Soviet order continues to shape lived worlds, much as many postcolonial contexts continue to be partly formed by the regimes they nominally displaced.

Reverse diasporas, particularly in the twentieth century,[5] are relatively common and well documented as empires (including the Soviet Union) fell and new countries (re)formed often with aggressively xenophobic policies, or non-titular ethnic groups fled fearing persecution or hoping for a better life. In some instances, people have been officially welcomed back, even sought out by the "home" government as with Russia (Flynn 2003), Germany (Brown 2005; Darieva 2005), and Israel (Eisenstadt 1954). Alongside these have been returns of people who originally moved for economic reasons (e.g., Constable 1999 on ambivalent Filipina returns; Cerase 1970 on Italian repatriates). Many of these have been multigenerational diasporas, raising questions about what "return" and "homeland" mean. The experience of such returnees has been varied. As Meltem Sancak (2007) reports for Germans in Kazakhstan, some choose to remain where they are on hearing reports from repatriates about their disappointing reception. Ethnic identity formation may well be a dialectical process between smaller ethnic groups and larger social institutions (Nagel 1994), but certain moments crystallize definitions of ethnicity, especially when they unlock citizenship and its attendant rights. But some homeland states have found it hard to determine what constitutes a particular ethnicity when many conventional markers have been lost or diluted such as linguistic capacity or knowledge of tradition. In turn, multigenerational returnees can experience a sense of not quite fitting in either host or homeland.

Many of these factors resonate with the *oralman*, as discussed below. But there are also distinct features. Two other homelands appear alongside host and titular country. The Soviet Union continues to frame notions of moral community and belonging for many and, as Eva-Marie Dubuisson and Anna Genina (2012), Alexander Diener (2009), and Genina (2015) describe for Mongolian Kazakhs, homelands can also be understood in terms of mobility as well as the land itself (summarized by Yessenova 2005 as "roots and routes"), confronting head on the containment and stasis on which modern state control is premised.

What interests me here are the questions the *oralman* provoke by answering the call to return because here too, they appear excessive on a range of counts: they are out of time, they do not fit the newly imagined national community of highly-skilled professionals, they challenge the very notion of what it means to be Kazakh and that of a modern nation-state as bounded, contiguous territory. Such questions and their entailments are unsettling. One such consequence raised by returning Kazakhs is not just the metricization of the population (how many of each ethnic group) but the further qualification of ethnicity. If they exceed the criteria for being kin, as I suggest below, the question appears of what that means for those who remained.

Indeterminacy appears throughout this account in several registers. First, the state (officials, documents, legal categories, definitions, and procedures) can seem illegible, resistant to encounter for *oralman* trying to obtain papers. This is mirrored by the *oralman* being pictured in the media and by government spokesmen as intractable to representation—numberless, paperless—and hence recognition as a "full," or at any rate juridical, person. Second, the *oralman* can disturb the temporalities at play in carefully crafted national progress narratives from a fixed past to a desired future; both in and out of time, they seem uncanny. Third, their presence exposes numbers and categories as proxies, partial representations of reality, essentially indeterminate. Their situation indicates a fuzzy logic that transcends binary classification structures by enabling a perspective that is "more or less," a question of degree—and which thus challenges familiar modes of statistical statehood. It shows how counting can discount people. Last, the experience and effects of these different kinds of indeterminacy vary from threat to freedom to poverty and exclusion. For some, lacking official papers translates as constraint; but others remake and redefine social relationships outside the state, implicitly rejecting its determining authority. Some of these modalities appear as ambiguity. I am, however, restricting the use of this term to where an object, person, or event holds more than one contradictory interpretation such as apparently being "then" and "now." This does not account for all the registers listed above.

This chapter offers a critique of familiar analytic framings (e.g., Scott 1985, 1990, 2009) that are based on distinctions between state efforts at determinacy on the one hand, usually cast in a negative light (as inscribing power and marginalizing those who do not fit), and indeterminacy on the other, which appears as resistance, political or economic freedom, and is seen as "good." By tracing indeterminacy's multiple forms ethnographically, and how people conceptualize them, such analytical normativities are questioned and complicated. Seen through symbolic (e.g., Ryan 2013 following Kristeva 1982) or biopolitical (e.g., Giroux 2006 following Foucault 2003) analytical lenses, the *oralman* may be seen as "humans-as-waste" (McFann n.d.). Yet such a category fails to account for the fact that they are also valorized as insiders, may highlight the inauthenticity of the rejecting powers, or may themselves spurn the category-making state.

The ethnography below moves through several perspectives on indeterminacy shaped by my fieldwork since 2000 in Almaty's informal peri-urban settlements and central residential districts, as well as with city and district administrations. Thus, after a brief background of why the new Republic's future direction and government was initially uncertain, the chapter moves from high-level national narratives, strategies and population counts through the legal minutiae of definitional criteria for *oralman*, and the views of rural and urban citizens on their new/old neighbors to the experiences of *oralman* themselves. I conclude by drawing out the unnerving implications of making the *oralman* vital to the nationalist enterprise for Kazakhstan and the Kazakhs who stayed behind.

Population Politics: Tensions between Nationalist and Civic Statehood

Kazakhstan has a long history of being a place of political exile, labor camps, mass deportations, and pioneering settlement from the rest of the Russian/ Soviet Empire. Partly as a result, population politics are fraught. When the new republic emerged in 1991, its legitimacy and viability were uncertain. The titular nation comprised less than half the population[6] potentially questioning the right of Kazakhs to dominate government. This was further complicated by uneven geographical distribution: there are concentrations of Kazakhs in the south, but the north and west are dominated by non-Kazakhs, particularly Russians. In the end, boundaries defined during the Soviet 1920s, largely remained[7] and became naturalized into nation-state narratives of primordial links between blood and land. Kazakhstan's future as a nation-state was not a given in 1991. From many possible future trajectories, an indeterminate future, a national narrative had to be swiftly crafted that legitimized a Kazakh-led government.

There are many reasons for the comparatively small size of this titular group. As nomadic grazing lands were eroded from the seventeenth century onward with Russian colonial settlement, some Kazakh groups moved to China and Mongolia. During the Soviet period, some Kazakhs simply found themselves outside the new socialist republic's borders. Others fled political persecution. The *zhut*, a late spring freeze, in 1920–21 reduced the Kazakh population further as thousands died or escaped the ensuing famine. Forced collectivization and sedenterization in 1929–33 caused further famine and emigration to adjacent countries and then further afield (Kendirbaeva 1997; Mendikulova 1997). Conservative estimates suggest the Kazakh population decreased by a third (Pianciola 2001; Rudnytskyi et al. 2015). The ethnic imbalance was exacerbated by a continuous inflow of deportees, prisoners, settlers, and workers (Barnes 2011; Westren 2012).

The independent republic inherited, and continued to experience, the effects of these population movements as millions of non-Kazakhs returned to their own motherlands (Rahmonova-Schwarz 2010). The emigration of Slavs and Germans in particular meant that the population tumbled from 17 to 15 million, provoking concern about the depletion of the workforce in general but especially professional and technical skills, often linked to Russians.

For a Kazakh government to lay claim to Kazakhstan demanded a clear identification of people and land. At the same time, celebrations for the new nation-state were tempered so as not to alienate the substantial Russian community. Such public discourse carefully celebrates the uniqueness of Kazakhstan as the Kazakhs' homeland while stating that all ethnicities are equal. In practice, such internationalism wears a Kazakh face as it once wore a Russian one (Schatz 2004: 75–78; Kesküla this volume). Power is largely in the hands of elite Kazakhs.[8] President Nursultan Nazarbayev's declaration, prefacing the 2050 National Strategy, is deftly vague: "Kazakhstan is our land. It is a land that has belonged to our ancestors. The land that will belong to our descendants. ... We must be the true owner of our land—hospitable, friendly, generous and tolerant" (Kazakhstan Strategy 2050). He claims the country belongs to Kazakhs by ancestral right—and is multiethnic, suggesting that the much-vaunted tradition of hospitality welcomes all groups. But a guest is not the same as the legitimate co-owner of the land.

The new republic was thus ushered in on the dual claims of both civic- and nation-based statehood (Ó Beacháin 2013; Kudaibergenova 2015; Kuşçu, 2008: 8); these claims continue to tug in different directions and shape how the population and its sub-groups are counted and valued. Both the 2030 and 2050

National Strategies follow a Soviet-inflected rhetoric of progress, albeit with a different endpoint. Thus a trajectory is outlined from a traditional nomadic past, where the country is "the cradle of Kazakh civilization," to a modern democracy where a highly-educated workforce will ensure the country is a global economic player in a transnational knowledge-based economy (Kazakhstan Strategy 2050), echoing China's emphasis on developing human capital (Greenhalgh 2010). Thus, while both civic and national models stress the need for a larger workforce, the civic model foregrounds professional capacity, while nationalists lean toward increasing numbers of Kazakhs. This double narrative, which has shifted in emphasis over time, has ambiguity woven through it, paving the way for different emphases at different junctures.

In 1999, President Nazarbayev announced that the overall population was to reach 20 million by 2030, provoking many jokes that were either ribald or alluded to popular concerns: "the only way to achieve the President's goal," the jokes ran, "is to wait for a power blackout and count; open the borders to China or ask whoever counts election votes to do the census." Suspicion of counting has a long history. Nazarbayev has been cautious about explicitly calling for the proportion of Kazakhs to increase, but this was inferred by many of my informants, and presidential speeches on increasing overall numbers have been made to the WAK while discussing *oralman*.

One measure in 1992 to address the ethnic imbalance and/or low overall numbers was the call for expatriate Kazakhs to return. This would not only increase numbers, but would also foreground the afflictions of Kazakhs in the Soviet era: *oralman* were originally defined as those who had left because of Stalinist persecution. Increased numbers and redress for past suffering legitimize both the Kazakh-dominated government and preferential treatment accorded to Kazakhs. Emphasizing the need for reparation to the Kazakh people also serves to distance the present regime from the Soviet past, even though old elites often still hold power,[9] fudging sameness into apparent difference. This focus emphasizes Kazakh victims and Russian perpetrators. History is abridged into a simple tale of tyranny by outsiders out of which the contemporary land and people have resurfaced (see Grant 2001). Such is the format of Almaty's Museum of the Repression where Russian-speaking Kazakh attendants switch to Kazakh while showing visitors around exhibits, gliding past photographs suggesting some Kazakhs were also involved in identifying state enemies, pausing in front of waxworks of Kazakhs fleeing for their lives. Apparent clarity can be deceptive.

The claim of Kazakhs to the land is further emphasized through constant references to the Republic as "primordial Kazakh territory" e.g., in the constitution (Cummings 2005: 84). Public celebrations and the media have made much of Kazakh traditional dress, music, language, and festivals in the quest to cement the present to an authentic past (Davé 2007). The government has invested heavily in the local film industry, backing films such as *Nomad* (2005), which shows Ablai Khan uniting Kazakh tribes in the eighteenth century.

The film indicates the beginning of Kazakh statehood with "markers of Kazakh identity ... throughout the film: the widescreen steppe, dombras, the nomadic past, ... tribal rituals and practices" (Isaacs 2016: 147–48). Subsequent films have centered on Soviet nuclear experimentation in Kazakhstan and the traditional hospitality of Kazakh villagers to deported strangers in *A Gift for Stalin* (2008) and *Zheruiyk* (2011). A nomadic past leaves few material remains (Cummings 2005), but those on Kazakh soil have been yoked to the nationalist cause (Alexander 2004), while the new capital's architecture and interior decoration summon ersatz nomadic imagery alongside a futuristic imaginary (Laszczkowski 2016). Numerical volume would add some heft to assertions of the primordial rights of Kazakhs to Kazakhstan.

Oralman were originally pictured as erstwhile victims returning from this ruptured time of eternal stasis. Marlene Laruelle and Sebastien Peyrouse (2004) suggest that unlike other diasporas, often seen to be *lacking* genuine qualities of the home nation, *oralman* were seen as *adding* authenticity to the performance of national identity through their apparent closeness to Kazakh traditions, culture, language, history. Işık Kuşçu spells this out: "According to the nationalists, demographic preponderance of the Kazakhs, which would be made possible by the mass migration of the 'culturally and linguistically pure' Kazakhs of the diaspora, is a guarantee for sustaining the legitimacy of the ethno-national entitlement for the state and territory." (2008: 100). The terms bear attention. The question of proportional classification begins to emerge, whether one can be "more" or "less" Kazakh.

Along these lines, local scholar, Talgat Ismagambetov, criticized the tendency to cast *oralman* as increasing the proportion of "pure" Kazakh population and enforce "purely Kazakh values" (2009). Noting that some *oralman* retained links with the countries from where they had come, he said they might be seen as not working in Kazakhstan's interests at all, suggesting, rather darkly, that there were "*oralman* and *oralman*." Nonetheless, Ismagambetov highlights, albeit oddly, that "*oralman*" is an inadequate category for capturing vastly different biographies and experiences as well as indicating the possibility that the nationalist ideal of authenticity may appear as a gradient, not an absolute at the level of both the population and the person.

There is a particular local shading to the idea of acculturated Kazakhs. The National Strategies' splicing of timeless pasts to modern futures echoes Chinghiz Aitmatov's famous novel *The Day Lasts More Than a Thousand Years* (1983). Here the "simple wisdom" of local Kyrgyz earthbound tradition is juxtaposed with the Soviet space age, the implication being that such modernity is inimical to tradition. One of the novel's central themes is that of the *mankurt*, a figure purportedly taken from Kyrgyz legend. Driven mad by torture, the *mankurt* forgets who he is, to whom he belongs, and so becomes an automaton, a less-than-human slave. The term has entered everyday speech to indicate a Kazakh alienated from her own culture and people. Urbanized Kazakhs may use it ironically or somewhat mournfully about themselves, as in the case of one of my regular informants, an economist, Nurzhan, who observed sadly that while he was a *mankurt*, his daughters at least had been taught Kazakh at school and were thus "better" Kazakhs then their parents. Rural and repatriate Kazakhs use the term mockingly about acculturated, urban Russophone Kazakhs. In the early 1990s it was used to account for some successful Kazakh businessmen who were able to leap at speculative opportunities that suited neither traditional Kazakh nor Soviet values precisely because such people were *mankurt*, betwixt and between. The wife of a rural migrant to Almaty turned wealthy businessman, described her husband as *mankurt*, a "non person," saying that he had been able to seize opportunities in the 1990s precisely because he was unshackled by any rules. The term *mankurt*, in its popular usage encapsulates the doubleness of indeterminacy in the sense of gaps between categories of belonging. The entrepreneur literally seizes value from such openings but such freedom can also be a loss of self or negative freedom, where the person is formed through connections, not gaps.

Counting is clearly not straightforward. Population growth overall is required to enhance the labor force. Within that number, however, different narratives privilege educational and professional capacity, on the one hand, or ethnicity on the other, which may or may not overlap. But reverting to the level of the person being so counted and classified, a "more" or "less" understanding of authenticity begins to rear its head. *Oralman*, as the next section shows, are sometimes defined as incarnating not only a greater degree of "pure" Kazakhness than others, but also unwanted, "non-essential" features.

Defining *Oralman*

Definitions of *oralman* have added to their indeterminate condition on two counts. First the abundance of different definitions can be hard to understand or open up gaps between them (see Reno this volume). Second, each definition (whether legal, regulatory, media, or demotic) is partial. Simply put, the government's overt aim was to increase the number of Kazakhs (and the overall population) by fast-tracking repatriation. But, at this point, counting becomes difficult because there are many versions of how many ethnic Kazakhs are outside Kazakhstan, legal definitions of *oralman* have been mutable, and many have returned informally or continue to migrate back and forth. Clarity has been further muddied by constantly changing quota definitions. In practice, such proportional classification suggests that nowadays there is a wrong and a right kind of Kazakh.

The 1992 Migration Law[10] specified the right to return for all Kazakhs living abroad and all citizens whose ancestors had left because of Stalinist repressions. The 1997 amendment retained the emphasis of redressing Soviet wrongs but narrowed the definition to "a person of native ethnicity (*litso korennoi natsional'nosti*) who was expelled from the historic homeland because of political oppression."[11] This excluded those whose ancestors had simply been outside Kazakhstan's newly defined borders in the 1920s. Many of these also sought return. The 2002 amendment reflected practice by redefining *oralman* as "foreign or stateless citizens of Kazakh ethnicity, who permanently resided outside ... Kazakhstan when it obtained sovereignty."

The 2011 revision marked a significant shift requiring documentary evidence of Kazakh ethnicity and prioritizing those with higher education and skills (Oka 2013: 2–6). Recent amendments thus increasingly emphasize the ability to contribute economically suggesting acquired rather than ascribed characteristics and therefore redefining what kind of Kazakh is welcome. This was fleetingly made explicit in the president's 2012 comment that "the oralman had yet to show their worth" (Oka 2013). The various values embodied by the *oralman* thus appear as different orders of worth: rights through suffering, economic capacity, association with the land, and incarnation of the Kazakh past.

Even if definitional criteria are met, quotas were set early on limiting the number of households to be given financial and other assistance: work, housing and citizenship papers that provide access to welfare, education, good jobs, and voting rights. Partly depending on the state's economic reserves, quota numbers have varied significantly year by year since the program began (Diener 2009: 227). Mutable definitions of quota eligibility, however, introduced another raft of qualifications for who counts, again increasingly emphasizing skills.

Those not "in quota" receive no formal assistance, although they can apply to be in the next quota. Further, they frequently do not have housing or jobs, nor do they have the official papers that will allow them to work or reside in the city legally, have access to education, pensions, or healthcare. But not all "in quota" *oralman* receive promised help either. The Migration Committee has been riddled with corruption scandals about the diversion of allocated monies and housing, or *oralman* being placed in remote deserted townships. While corruption can be difficult to pin down, the official heading Almaty's Migration Committee during my fieldwork in 2000 was eventually fired after a series of complaints; her disgruntled deputy told me his boss sent her children to school in England (a sign of wealth) and further observed that she wore large diamond rings.[12]

The number of *oralman* registering their intention to settle permanently but without quota has hugely exceeded projections. By 2001, the quota of 607 families was exceeded fifteen times; in 2004 the quota of 10,000 families was exceeded by 84 percent (UNDP 2006: 10). In 2007, the government reported 7,538 persons without citizenship from CIS countries and 449 from other countries registered as stateless. The actual numbers are likely to be considerably higher. Many of these individuals have disappeared below the state radar. Marriages and births are not recorded. The number of stateless individuals lacking passports, residential papers, and the right to work legally has risen. Many also regularly move between Kazakhstan and other countries. None of the *oralman* families I met in Almaty's shanty towns in the years 2000 to 2010 were registered, although by 2016 more had acquired papers. Local NGOs, municipal officials, and the IOM suggest figures for non-quota repatriates may be double official statistics, which state that 957,772 *oralman* returned between 1991 and 2016 (The Ministry of Health Care 2014).[13] "Losing track," as the Internal Minister said after the Zhanaozen protests, begins to seem rather an understatement.

Despite scandals around lack of support, other media stories that reported *oralman* being given jobs and benefits fuelled resentment toward them, particularly during the economic crises of the 1990s and after 2008. Such stories often turned on the *oralman* for apparently manipulating the system: renting out allocated housing and claiming benefits for their vast families (see also Diener 2009).

The divide between urban and rural Kazakhs is marked. Saulesh Yessenova (2005) notes that villagers continue to be seen as hindering progress to "an advanced state of being." While, in the Kazakh-language press, the countryside is cast as the "cradle" of Kazakh culture and impoverished villagers treated with compassion, urbanites see young rural migrants in the cities (and out of place) as "morally immature ... professionally underqualified ... confused ... inhabitants of urban slums." (2005: 665). In other words, the ancient dual oppositions between town and city[14] is rehearsed again in Kazakhstan, but accentuated when *oralman* are brought into the equation. *Oralman* are often unwelcome in Almaty's peri-urban settlements where many settled alongside Kazakh migrants from rural areas, each wave of migrants frequently rejecting the next.

Rural migrants often mock *oralman*. In the 1990s and early 2000s, Almaty's informal peri-urban settlements were largely populated by young couples or single workers from villages where parents remained, looking after their grandchildren. These recent internal migrants often declared about their *oralman* neighbors that, "They're different from us; they're not like us." The discourse of difference was consistent. Young women I talked to were quick to point out what they claimed to be physical dissimilarity. Thus, giggling, two teachers in their early twenties from Narynkol in the east of Kazakhstan, told me that *oralman* from China were easily spotted as they had red cheeks, "just like Chinese people!" Later they gestured towards a neighbor, recently arrived from Uzbekistan and who, they insisted, had a "pointy face" rather than the correct Kazakh "moonface." Later, asking other migrants from Narynkol what they meant by this "difference," an outburst of examples was given: "they dress in old-fashioned clothes," said one. Another that, "they smell weird because they eat different food from us—and they speak funny Kazakh." Alibek, a young man working as a porter in Baraholka and hoping to save enough to study for a degree, observed that "[o]*ralman* are very religious, too religious." These are all familiar markers of the stranger.

Longer-standing, urban, Russophone Kazakhs often employ a similar lexicon to speak of rural migrants and repatriates alike: "They take our jobs." "They're dirty." "They're not like us." "They have too many children." A jocular exchange over dinner between a middle-class couple in Almaty is instructive.

Laughingly chastising her husband for a lack of manners as he ate with his fingers, Aigerim, the wife, said to me, "He's from Shymkent. Can you tell? They're our rednecks. TEXAN!" she shouted at him, and then again, "*mambet!*"[15] Her husband riposted, "Kholkhoznik!" before she ended the rally of insults with her final putdown: "*Oralman!*"

The language of rejection is telling. First, the markers of difference are familiar from European xenophobia, dirtiness as opposed to cleanliness (Agarin 2014; Thorfeisson and Eriksen this volume). Low employment is a continuing concern, provoking resentment of incomers with jobs. Excessive fertility is a familiar trope in racist discourse indicating a lack of discipline and control threatening to swamp local populations. Again, the distinction between edibility and non-edibility is another classic marker of structural distinction. But as I discuss in the final section, other tropes go beyond binary distinctions.

In other words, *oralman* have become shorthand for a lack of progressive modern civilization (while simultaneously strengthening claims to the "cradle of Kazakh civilization") but also evoke further incongruity. For long-standing, urban Kazakh citizens, incoming rural migrants are bad enough, but the repatriates jar all those appeals to the past by seemingly embodying the past in the present where it has no business to be. "I know we are all one people," Natalya, a Kazakh teacher mused, "and I should pity them for being backward and feel they are my people—but I don't really like them and I don't want them in my city." She was exactly the sort of person who might be described as *mankurt*: Russian-speaking, only possessed of "kitchen Kazakh," Soviet educated. Natalya's comment, recapitulating those of the migrants from Narynkol, brings

Figure 6.1. Kazakh migrants from Narynkol to Almaty in 2000, photo by the author.

abstract population politics down to earth when numbers and characteristics become unwanted neighbors. The derogatory names cast by urban and nonurban dwellers at each other suggest multiple, incommensurate imaginaries of desired national communities.

Oralman's Reasons for Return

Many *oralman* find themselves caught in multiple conditions of indeterminacy whether unable to engage effectively with state officials and processes or tolerated, but neither in nor out of the law, which, in turn, blocks access to citizenship rights. They have many reasons for returning. Some have escaped poverty, discrimination, environmental catastrophes or political repression, especially in China and Uzbekistan. In common with other return migrations of multigenerational diaspora, the homeland was usually idealized and frozen at the point at which it was left. Most thus add that they wanted to come back to their historic motherland, the land of their ancestors, to be buried in the land of their clans, to speak Kazakh, and lead the life of a Kazakh on the land by keeping animals. These reasons were highlighted more by families who left reasonable security and good jobs, especially from China.

They have had mixed fates. Some are content. One such was a forty-year-old former geography teacher from Ürümqi whose ancestors had left Kazakhstan in 1917. He sold his house and moved his family to Almaty in 2010, with no quota, renting a room on arrival. He rapidly gained a place in the quota queue, was given promised documents, and used the money from the sale of his house to set up a business as a highly successful builders' merchant in one of Almaty's new peri-urban districts, building himself a fine house in the process.

Others feel they were sold short by the government's empty promises or found themselves disorientated by a historic motherland that no longer resembles the land of their parents' or grandparents' tales, or indeed has Kazakh as a common language, particularly in the Russophone cities. The older generation is often unable to communicate, having returned with, for example, Kazakh and Chinese. Moreover, their Kazakh is often dated and, with accents that mark them as "foreign," they are ridiculed for speaking an "old" or even "pre-revolutionary" language. Even in the southern rural areas of Kazakhstan where Kazakh is more commonly spoken, it is often intermixed with Russian words and new coinages. The script is still modified Cyrillic.[16] Those whose families left Kazakhstan before the 1920s write Kazakh in an Arabic script, those coming from Turkey use the modified Latin alphabet.

Bewilderment is common, especially among some who arrived outside the quota hoping for acceptance on arrival and to be included in the next quota.[17] Many found themselves beached on a reef of unresponsive bureaucracy, waiting years to join the quota queue or for financial help and promised papers. In an interview in 2002, the local IOM representative reported many instances where passports had been removed on the promise of Kazakh replacements, which then failed to appear. Keeping animals is rarely practicable where many rural collective farms have collapsed or been abandoned to grandparents and small children. Most moved to the big cities: "at least in Almaty," a young Kazakh woman from Uzbekistan said, "you'll always find something to eat."

Many *oralman* live in the settlements that sprang up around Almaty in the late 1980s. These places have a nebulous quality. Tenure is often insecure. Deeds that were nominally granted officially have been overturned. Some inadvertently bought fake deeds, a common scam. While some areas have become formalized, others have had shacks destroyed in police raids (Alexander 2018). A property lawyer in Almaty explained to me that the status of these regions remained, "an open question." The legality of these settlements and the people who live in them appears suspended. In this sense, these lives and places echo the refugee camps described by Simon Turner (2005) where Giorgio Agamben's (2005) notion of permanent exceptionality plays out as suspended time, an unfurling present, except that many *oralman* are not physically contained in camps but made into a shadowy presence through lack of papers. The state cannot see except through documentary representation (Alexander 2007). In turn, the *sans papieres* cannot make themselves visible, or secure their dwellings and families, without documents.

Anara, now in her early nineties, returned without quota from Karapalkstan in north Uzbekistan with her daughter and grandchildren in 2005. As a child in 1921, she had gone with her village on the long march south from the *zhut*:

Figure 6.2. Shanyrak, one of Almaty's informal settlements in 2000, photo by the author.

We walked. We walked and walked. My father carried me. Most of the animals had died by then. You could see the grass beneath the ice but they couldn't get at it. Animals and people died on the way from starvation.

Sometimes we ate the dead animals but we couldn't dig through the ice to bury the people, so we threw their bodies into mountain crevasses. Some people fought the animals for grass when we found it. Sometimes we found old pumpkins and tried to eat them but they made people and animals swell up so much it killed them.

Very few of us made it to Karakalpakstan.

She sat outside their mud house on a rusty old bed frame, swinging her legs, looking down the hill to Almaty. She was in a rage of incomprehension. How was it, she said, after so much hardship, a lifetime working for the Soviet Union, and bringing up eight children, she was unwelcome in her own land? She was penniless as she was unable to claim a pension from Uzbekistan where she had worked all her life for the state. What was this state, she said, that did not look after the people who had worked for it? For all she railed against it, the overarching Soviet state still defined her sense of citizenship through labor, eclipsing changes in time and borders. Thus, refracting the state discourse of redress, Anara claimed her suffering demanded reparation from the current state as a manifestation in the present of the Soviet state. Such a take is relatively common among older citizens. The coexistent worlds

Figure 6.3. Repatriate Kazakhs from Karakalpakstan in Shanyrak in 2000, photo by the author.

suggested by Anara's account and other narratives of the Kazakh state's reemergence and progress scarcely mesh, provoking bewilderment.

Her neighbors, a Chinese Kazakh family, had returned without quota in 2006 selling everything they had, crossing the border, and buying land with a shack on it in the outskirts of Almaty in what turned out to be an illegal transaction. Three years later, neither of the sons, trained as a doctor and engineer, had been able to find work in their professions or indeed in a white collar job, despite the nominal shift to privileging such skills. They said they could not understand how to access the "powers" and ask for inclusion on the waiting list for citizenship or quota help. The sons work as porters in Almaty's huge semi-black market Baraholka. The rest of the family stay at home. "We would go back," their mother said, "but it's the shame that keeps us here. How can we go back to China saying our own motherland rejected us?"

Just as state officials say they cannot track, count, or govern this unruly, excessive population, so too what appears in many *oralman's* accounts is their difficulty in reading the state, both literally, and in terms of what and who it stands for. Bureaucratic documents have only recently been in Kazakh as well as Russian, but are still in Cyrillic. The rapidity of legal changes and requirements for quota eligibility have left many confused. The inability to read the state means families such as the Chinese family exist in limbo. They are unable to move spatially: poverty and shame keep them in place, but there is also a sense of being at a dead end. For such families, this indeterminate, paperless existence, neither in nor out of the law is experienced not as capacity for entrepreneurial freedom, as for some *mankurts*, but as spatial and temporal constraint. Anara's litany suggests nostalgia for an orderly past that seems to have vanished to be replaced by an incomprehensible system.

Such has been the disillusionment that some *oralman*, usually, but not only, Mongolian Kazakhs, have returned to their host country or continue to move between Kazakhstan and the country they moved from, keeping alive complex networks of kin and living across borders (Werner and Barcus 2015). It is worth highlighting here that many, though not all, Mongolian Kazakhs continued to be nomadic herdsmen during the Soviet and post-Soviet periods. More than most *oralman*, therefore, they seem to embody the traditional past that is celebrated in Kazakh government-sponsored films, billboards, and national strategies, and sometimes mocked by other Kazakhs and non-Kazakhs. They have also attracted most academic attention (e.g., Barcus and Werner 2017; Diener 2009; Finke 2013; Finke and Sancak 2005; Genina 2015). But the trajectories and experiences of such *oralman* can be a world away from urban secondary school teachers and engineers who have relocated from Uzbekistan, China, or further afield. Moreover, while most *oralman* (61.6 percent) have come from Uzbekistan, the second largest group (14.2 percent) come from China, and Kazakhs from Mongolia comprise 9.2 percent (The Ministry of Healthcare 2014). Nevertheless, this small group has come to stand, in national and demotic imaginaries, for all *oralman* as an undifferentiated group.[18] The category (or "whole") of *oralman*, and indeed Kazakhs as singular group in the past, has taken on the characteristics of the part. This then speaks to the tendency of categories to flatten out difference and make the infinitely variable (and thus indeterminate) limited and knowable.

In some places *oralman* from different countries have gathered together. Baibesik (meaning "cradle" in Kazakh) is one such deliberate community. In 1999, Kairat, a young Mongolian Kazakh set up an NGO, Asar ("cooperation" in Kazakh), to help *oralman*. He petitioned Almaty's Akimat (municipal administration) for land for 185 families, which was finally allocated in 2002, an hour's walk away from the city's edges. By 2005, there were 40 families, still lacking roads and utilities. Most families had no papers. Those who worked, walked to and from Baraholka, the men working as porters, women at a variety of jobs in the markets. Those with contacts worked in construction over the summer. Most children did not attend school, many of the older generation never left the settlement, unable to communicate, fearful of being caught and deported.

For some, there was a sense of having come to a point of rest. Those among the older generation from China, who had hoped to return to where their ancestors were buried in north Kazakhstan, said that now they were content to stay where they were, acknowledging they were unlikely ever to make the journey. Complex tales from younger couples of how they had decided to move either ended when they moved to Baibesik, or constructed Baibesik as a fixed point in a kin network that stretched across Kazakhstan and other countries.

Aygul, a chatty, effervescent thirty-year-old, described how her husband first traveled to Almaty from Uzbekistan for informal seasonal construction work in the 1990s. The next year she had accompanied him to see whether or not she wanted to move her young family there, her grandparents caring for the children while she was away. "To and fro we went," she laughed, "trying to decide where to go and who we should be." Eventually, as Uzbekistan shut Kazakh language schools and it became harder for non-Uzbeks to find work they decided to settle in Kazakhstan but were unable to get a quota.

Eventually, they brought their children, building their house in Baibesik, delighting in the people they found. "Here," said Aygul, "we work together and help each other. We've become a community. We have celebrations together. We have our own council. We're hyphenated Kazakhs![19] We have no need to go anywhere else, we don't need or want the Akimat here, and we don't want to live in the city. Here we're independent." She also described an intricate household economy involving remittances, gifts, and regular returns to Uzbekistan for family celebrations. The community was based on a shared experience of exclusion, as well as daily life, the rainbow element of the community as much as Kazakh ethnicity bringing them together. Her peers were similarly pragmatic, some wishing they had citizenship rights, but ambivalent about further attention from the state.

Conclusion: Excess, Indeterminacy, Recognition—and
Determining Wholes

How then do we account for these shifting nuances of this simultaneous welcome and rejection? I suggest that what emerges from these various mutating policies, plans, performances, practices, and discourses is a series of indeterminacies in different registers, some of which appear through the conflation of different levels, times, and places. Each makes clear apprehension difficult. Together they provoke an excess of meaning.

First, the plethora of legal definitions and entailments of what it is to be an *oralman*, as well as the mutable quota arrangements, let alone the velocity with which they have changed, have baffled many *oralman* and citizens. Added to this, corrupt, or at any rate obscure, practices on the part of many committees charged with implementing help offered to quota *oralman* have added to difficulties in understanding what has to be done in order to obtain official help and support. It is not only *oralman* who face such difficulties (Alexander 2018). A common phrase used by Almaty's citizens is that "the law has only been written so far," indicating with a hand gesture how laws stop short of detail. There is therefore considerable latitude for local officials to interpret or indeed misinterpret the law. This echoes Daniella Gandolfo's discussion of the constant unmaking or denial of form in a Peruvian state office as a mode of disabling encounter (2013). Indeterminacy can become an expression of power in encounters between local state officials and petitioners. For many *oralman*, the state is experienced as being unreadable and capricious to be supplicated or simply avoided. But as the ethnography suggests, the state is not uniformly illegible. Despite external definitions of *oralman*, there is no singularity in this group. They have been in different countries for different periods, some can marshal education, kin, and connections to navigate bureaucratic waters; others experience only imperturbability, unconcern, and silence.

Second, modes of identifying *oralman* as Kazakhs have troubling consequences. Dirt, as Mary Douglas puts it (1966), is matter out of place. Small daily practices from scrubbing a floor to enforcing "homeland security" represent the ongoing labor needed to keep things in order by keeping out the impure. Douglas's insight was that dirt is a relative category not an intrinsic characteristic. As the introduction to this volume observes, the interstitial anomalies on which Douglas focuses are analytically elided with questions of excess and indeed other kinds of anomalies even though they speak to different kinds of threat to order.

It is worth dissecting the tropes of rejection here as several relate to how *oralman* are treated and represented. Certainly figures are deployed that are commonly used for outsiders: dirt and bad smells evoke a sense of disgust. But other tropes are not simply shibboleths marking insiders/outsiders. The very "traditional" elements that are celebrated in state-sponsored performances and on huge billboards are simultaneously rejected as ill-suited to modern Kazakhstan.

This is the "problem" with the *oralman*. By embodying all those characteristics that are so readily and publicly performed, the *oralman* appear to *over*fulfill conventional markers for inclusion and exclusion: religion, traditional knowledge, linguistic capacity. Classification is binary. Linnean taxonomies, for example, move through binary, ranking measures to define organisms with increasing precision. Even when correspondence to a category's characteristics is along a range or to a degree, there is still a motion toward a cut-off point: all those above a certain marker are in, the others out. The logical entailment of the apparently simple notion that *oralman* have greater purity than Kazakhs who remained, brings excess via a kind of fuzzy categorization within the category of being Kazakh. This is more than the threat of something that does not fit a structural system; it destroys the system from within.

Once the *oralman* are identified as somehow more pure or authentic than acculturated Kazakhs, then the latter, by implication, become lesser Kazakhs and, on a nationalist reckoning, less entitled to the rights signified by blood and land discourses. Some Kazakh academics made this explicit, calling for positive discrimination in favor of *oralman* representation in senior political posts. The *oralman* often embody, in daily practice and appearance, characteristics that the state ritually performs in particular set-aside spaces and times, conflating quite different orders of the symbolic and the mundane. At the same time, they are caricatured as possessing extra, unwanted characteristics of boorish hicks. They are thus "more" than Kazakh in two senses: a greater degree or intensification of supposedly Kazakh qualities on the one hand, and a co-presence of those same qualities and mannerlessness on the other. Such twofold indeterminacy threatens rights on a nationalist score for those who are "less" Kazakh, but also jeopardizes the imagined community of cultured, urban, professional citizens.

This might seem simply to rehearse familiar tensions between indigenous populations versus newcomers, rural versus urban populations, and those who left and those who stayed behind. But the returnee is both more and less than the indigene. More because, as John Berger so beautifully captures in *The Seventh Man*, they have acquired a patina of elsewhere, and less because they went away. At times, this "elsewhere" seems to have altered them physically—beyond recognition.

There are further confusions. The narrative line disturbed by this revivification of the past is the continuing Soviet-flavored discourse of modernity and progress. The past and tradition are necessary for the dialectical progress of history, but they only have value in place and in time. The repatriates share the genealogy that is officially celebrated and this is what makes them so problematic, because they do not seem to share the subsequent path of development to the point where common culture overwrites shared blood, clothing Soviet idioms of modernity in a Kazakh guise. The past that has come back to haunt urban citizens disrupts stories of modernity, moving forward, and becoming a global economic player. These are uncanny citizens, simultaneously familiar and strange, out of time as much as out of place. To paraphrase Johannes Fabian

(2014), the *oralman's* value to a nationalist state are as objects in the "there and then." As simultaneous subjects in the "here and now," they disturb formal narratives of successive, forward-propelled movements. Different times bleed into each other. The past resists containment. For some *oralman*, being out of time is experienced as painful suspension, unable to change their situation as they wish.

For Julia Kristeva, in her writing on estrangement, what is most fearful in the figure of the stranger is the recognition of that same quality in ourselves, the fundamental estrangement and lack of integration of the self (1991). This gives us a way of thinking about the repudiation of many of these *oralman* who do not fit the image of a new, urban Kazakhstan. The *oralman* provoke an acute crisis of recognition, laying claim to the same rights of blood and land, but showing alternative trajectories, different—and unwanted—facets of the present collective whole. Kristeva dwells particularly on the foreigner's position between and within languages: the repatriates speak and do not speak the same language, they are—and often are visibly not—contemporary Kazakhs in the sense that prevails in the self-consciously Eurasian, "progressive" cities of Almaty and Astana, the former and current capitals. But otherwise, the *oralman* cannot be seen as strangers. For Georg Simmel (1950), the stranger has a different origin and is in a group but not of it. The *oralman* are the very opposite. They share an origin and are of but not wholly in a group. They are simultaneously in and out of place.

The final merging of distinct orders appears via the distinction between people at the level of populations, and as individuals. Or, to put it another way, the tension *oralman* incarnate is one of collapsed scale: at the level of a population, the *oralman* are welcomed and wanted to boost the number of Kazakh nationals, but in person they provoke the NIMBY argument. Nationalism, at the level of everyday living, is very different from grand politics. Abstract selected qualities are required but, as people, *oralman* become excessive. Scaled-up abstraction reduces humanity twice-over. Metaphors of less-than-human fluid mass meet partially precise demographic categories on which population counts are based.

The fragmentary logic of state classification separates the abstract quality of a number from the actual entailments of a full citizen, a person: work, housing, healthcare. These demands appear excessive, famously summed up by the Swiss playwright Max Frisch, "We asked for workers; people come instead" (Frisch 1965) Seen through Michael Herzfeld's lens of bureaucratic indifference, this is the logic that can reduce bureaucrats to "humorless automatons" (1991: 1) and also classify people as insiders and outsiders on the basis of rigidly bounded categories, rather than shared humanity, or shared alienation in Kristeva's terms. The irony is that whereas Herzfeld's account also shows how, in the Greek state, idioms of blood and kinship are objectified into bureaucratic taxonomies of pollution and exclusion in pursuit of the nation-state. In Kazakhstan, the distance between politico-legal discourse and practice is such that while the left hand extols a civic, multiethnic state, the right hand practices "Kazakification" (Sarsembayev 1999) and division between different kinds of Kazakh.

Each of these narratives of belonging evokes different social wholes or totalities, which are incommensurate and shaped by different temporalities and levels. The awkward presence of the *oralman* reveals state narratives as no more than contingent, selective patchworks, holding moments together.

Government strategic plans for the nation, together with the eclectic forms of state-sponsored media and material culture, are profoundly influenced by a teleological vision that echoes revolutionary logic, even as it rejects the previously envisaged destination. More than rejection, there is a fear of the return of repressed elements of the Soviet period, just as Ukrainian events brought the past back into the present. A similar echo plays through Anara's appeal to the powers, where Soviet and post-Soviet states merge into one unreadable aphasic authority that still arches across national borders. The mobile homeland of those who vivify the in-betweeness and multiplicity of transnationalism, as well as communities such as Baibesik, speak rather to a sociality built on praxis not telos. As such, the work of constantly remaking kin and community belongs in a time and a mode that slip unnoticed between the counting mechanisms and fixed points of origin and destiny of the state. State discourse repeatedly emphasizes that the nation-state of Kazakhstan is the cradle of Kazakh civilization. But, by naming their community "cradle" in Kazakh, Baibesik's *sans papieres* suggest their settlement, within the larger system, is the authentic embodiment of Kazakhness in practice. The effect is to cast the larger totality into indecipherable obscurity, accentuating that indeterminacy is a perspectival artifact and throwing in to doubt who is kin and who the outsider, who the host and who the guest. That final challenge then is whose recognition counts.

Acknowledgements

I am most grateful to Indira Alibayeva, Matt Candea, Matt Canfield, Michael Carrithers, Taras Fedirko, Joshua Reno, Minh Nguyen, Felix Ringel, Diana Vonnak, and Thomas Yarrow for their extremely helpful comments. This has been given as a paper in many places (including Cambridge Senior Seminar, Thomas Hylland Eriksen's ERC Oslo conference "Overflowing Landfills, Unwanted Humans, and a New Anthropology of Waste," Newcastle Geography seminar, and the Max-Planck Institute of Social Anthropology's Colloquium) and has benefitted from them all. In particular, I would like to thank Thomas Hylland Eriksen and Gunther Schlee whose thoughts have helped to shape this.

Catherine Alexander is professor of Anthropology at Durham University, previously Goldsmiths, London. Her recent publications on indeterminacy and waste include a special issue on "Moral Economies of Housing" in *Critique of Anthropology* (2018), coedited with Insa Koch and Maja Hojer Bruun, and *Economies of Recycling* (Zed Books, 2012), coedited with Joshua Reno. She coauthored the opening chapter "What is Waste" for the UK Government's Chief Scientific Adviser's 2017 report on waste, and has written widely on wastes and third sector recycling in anthropology, environmental science, and engineering journals.

Notes

1. Fieldwork contributing to this chapter was carried out 2000–2016, initially funded by St John's College, Cambridge where I held a Research Fellowship 1998–2002 and in 2002–2004 by The John and Catherine MacArthur Foundation as part of my project "Migration Patterns in Almaty and Surrounding Settlements." Pseudonyms have been used throughout except for public figures and places. The Beaufort Visiting Scholarship from St John's in 2016 allowed me to write this up.
2. *Oralman* is used here as both the singular and plural for repatriate Kazakhs.
3. "Assimilation" by contrast suggests making everyone the same (see Thorleiffson and Eriksen this volume).
4. See also Gareth Stedman Jones (2013) for similar metaphors in nineteenth-century London, Keith Cunningham-Parmeter (2011) for metaphors casting immigrants as alien, and Gerald O'Brien (2003) on a variety of metaphors used for immigrants in the United States in the nineteenth century.
5. See Russell King, Anastasia Christou, and Peggy Levitt (2015); Fran Markowitz and Anders Stefansson (2004); R.ainer Ohliger and Rainer Munz (2003); and Stephane Dufoix (2008) for a fuller discussion of twentieth-century reverse diasporas.
6. The 1989 census recorded Kazakhs as 37.8 percent of the population, barely more than the Russian fraction, but the first time since the 1939 census that Kazakhs were the largest group. In the 2014 census, the percentage of Kazakhs was 65.5 percent, a result of other groups emigrating as the number of Kazakhs increased.
7. Although note Madeleine Reeves' (2014) account of the continued mobility of many Central Asian borders, particularly between Uzbekistan, Kyrgystan, and Tajikistan during and after the Soviet Union.
8. I am not discussing clans (*zhuz*) here, another way in which the category of "Kazakh" is divided (and which are further subdivided into *ru*'s, approximately translated as tribes) and which can affect access to power and rights (Schatz 2004). Nor am I discussing other factors that throw doubt on counting methods and ethnic authenticity such as how nationality is "chosen" if one parent is Kazakh and one another nationality. The crisp delineation of nationalities and land was determined in the 1920s by Stalin's nationalities policy, which overwrote previous fluidity.
9. The current president for example, was the First Secretary of the Soviet Socialist Republic of Kazakhstan in 1991 before moving smoothly into becoming the new republic's president. He has been in power ever since. Born in 1940, he was 78 in 2018.
10. *Ob immigracii. Zakon No1437 ot 26 ijunja 1992 g. Pravovoj spravochnik "Zakonodatel'stvo".* – Almaty: Jurist, 2007.
11. It continues, "Deprived of citizenship due to the acts of mass political repressions, unlawful requisition, forced collectivization, and other inhumane acts" (Oka 2013).
12. The government's own website on Human Rights in Kazakhstan details a series of legal violations of the *oralman's* rights (Kazakhstan Human Rights).

13. My own survey in 2005 of five hundred households in one settlement revealed no formally registered people. Assessments of actual numbers are hazarded on the basis of similar surveys by NGOs, notes kept by local polyclinics, occasional police checks. The sense of vast numbers of unregistered immigrants is accentuated by the "invisible virus" discourse.

14. Where one opposition casts the country as pure, the town as degenerate, while the other contrasts urban civilization with brutish rural areas.

15. *Mambet* is a derogatory term used by urbanites for village dwellers or those from southwest Kazakhstan where often Russian linguistic capacity is poor, and people are said to be uneducated, unmannered, and often of darker skin where paler skin is valued.

16. The 2050 Strategy aims to use a modified Latin script.

17. Visas are unnecessary for short stays from most countries, although registration at a residence is necessary within five days. Many thus overstay such visas and "disappear" without formal residence or work permits.

18. But note Irina Popravko (2013) whose short report highlights differences between different *oralman* groups and differences between various "waves" of return.

19. She meant they were "Mongolian Kazakhs" or "Uzbek Kazakhs" or "Chinese Kazakhs".

References

Aitmatov, C. 1983. *The Day Lasts More Than a Thousand Years.* Bloomington, IN: Indiana University Press.

Alexander, C. 2004. "The Cultures and Properties of Decaying Buildings." *Focaal: European Journal of Anthropology* 44: 48–60.

——— . 2007. "Almaty: Rethinking the Public Sector." In *Urban Life in Post-Soviet Asia*, ed. C. Alexander, V. Buchli and C. Humphrey, 70–101. London: Routledge.

——— . 2008. "Waste under Socialism and After: A Case Study from Kazakhstan." In *Enduring Socialism: Explorations of Revolution and Tranformation*, ed. H. West and P. Raman, 148–68. Oxford: Berghahn Books.

——— . 2018. "Homeless in the Homeland: Housing Protests in Kazakhstan." *Critique of Anthropology* 32(2): 204–20.

Agamben, G. 2005. *State of Exception.* Chicago, IL: The University of Chicago Press.

Agarin, T. ed. 2014. *When Stereotype Meets Prejudice: Antiziganism in European Societies.* Stuttgart: ibidem-Verlag.

Barcus, H., and C. Werner. 2017. "Choosing to Stay: (Im)Mobility Decisions Among Mongolia's Ethnic Kazakhs." *Globalizations* 14(1): 32–50.

Barnes, S. 2011. *Death and Redemption: The Gulag and the Shaping of Soviet Society.* Princeton, NJ: Princeton University Press.

Basch, L., N. Glick Schiller, and C. Blanc. 1994. *Nations Unbound: Transnational Projects, Postcolonial Predicaments and Deterritorialised Nation-States.* New York: Gordon and Breach.

Berger, J., and J. Mohr. 1975. *The Seventh Man: Migrant Workers in Europe.* London: Verso.

Brown, A. 2005. "The Germans of Germany and the Germans of Kazakhstan: A Eurasian *Volk* in the Twilight of Diaspora." *Europe-Asia Studies* 57(4): 625–34.

Cerase, F. 1970. "Nostalgia or Disenchantment: Considerations on Return Migration." In *The Italian Experience in the United States*, ed. S. Tomasi and M. Engel, 217–39. New York: Centre for Migration Studies of New York.

Cerny, A. 2010. "Going Where the Grass is Greener: China Kazaks and the Oralman Immigration Policy in Kazakhstan." *Pastoralism* 1(2): 218–47.

Constable, N. 1999. "At Home But Not at Home: Filipina Narratives of Ambivalent Returns." *Cultural Anthropology* 14(2): 203–28.

Cummings, S. 1998. "The Kazakhs: Demographics, Diasporas and 'Return.'" In *Nations Abroad: Diaspora Politics and International Relations in the Former Soviet Union*, ed. C. King and N. Melvin, 133–52. Boulder, CO: Westview Press.

———. 2005. *Kazakhstan: Power and the Elite*. London: I. B. Tauris.

Cunningham-Parmeter, K. 2011. "Alien Language: Immigration Metaphors and the Jurisprudence of Others." *Fordham Law Review* 79(4): 1545–98.

Darieva, T. 2005. "Recruiting for the Nation: Post-Soviet Transnational Migrants in Germany and Kazakhstan." In *Rebuilding Identities: Pathways to Reform in Post Soviet Siberia*, ed. E. Kasten, 153–72. Berlin: Dietrich Reimar Verlag.

Das V., and D. Poole, eds. 2004. *Anthropology in the Margins of the State*. Santa Fe, NM: School of American Research Press.

Davé, B. 2007. *Kazakhstan: Ethnicity, Language and Power*. Abingdon: Routledge.

Diener, A. 2005. "Problematic Integration of Mongolian-Kazakh Return Migrants in Kazakhstan." *Eurasian Geography and Economics* 46(6): 465–78.

———. 2009. *One Homeland or Two? The Nationalization and Transnationalization of Mongolia's Kazakhs*. Redwood City, CA: Stanford University Press.

———. 2015. "Assessing Potential Russian Irredentism and Separatism in Kazakhstan's Northern Oblasts." *Eurasian Geography and Economics* 56: 469–92.

Dufoix, S. 2008. *Diasporas*. Oakland, CA: University of California Press.

Eisenstadt, S. 1954. *The Absorption of Immigrants: A Comparative Study Based Mainly on the Jewish Community in Palestine and the State of Israel*. London: Routledge Kegan Paul.

Engle Merry, S. 2016. *The Seductions of Quantification: Measuring Human Rights, Gender Violence, and Sex Trafficking*. Chicago, IL: Chicago University Press.

Fabian, J. 2014. *Time and the Other: How Anthropology Makes its Object*. Cambridge: Cambridge University Press.

Finke, P. 2013. "Historical Homelands and Transnational Ties: The Case of the Kazak Oralman." *Zeitschrift für Ethnologie* 138(2): 175–94.

Finke, P., and M. Sancak. 2005. "Migration and Risk-Taking: A Case Study from Kazakstan." In *Migration and Economy: Global and Local Dynamics*, ed. L. Trager, 127–61. Walnut Creek, CA: AltaMira Press.

Flynn, M. 2003. "Returning Home? Approaches to Repatriation and Migrant Resettlement in Post-Soviet Russia." In *Diasporas and Ethnic Migrants: Germany, Israel, and Post-Soviet Successor States in Comparative Perspective*. Cass Series Nationalism and Ethnicity, ed. T. Ohliger and R. Munz, 173–87. London: Frank Cass.

Foucault, M. 2003. *Society Must Be Defended: Lectures at the Collège de France, 1975–1976*. New York: Picador.

Frisch, M. 1965. "Vorwort [Foreword]." In *Siamo italiani – Die Italiener: Gespräche mit italienischen Arbeitern in der Schweiz* [We are Italian – The Italians. Conversations with Italian workers in Switzerland], by Alexander J. Seiler. Zurich: EVZ.

Gandolfo, D. 2013. "Formless: A Day at Lima's Office of Formalization." *Cultural Anthropology* 28(2): 278–98.

Genina, A. 2015. "Claiming Ancestral Homelands: Mongolian Kazakh Migration in Inner Asia." Ph.D. dissertation. Ann Arbor, MI: University of Michigan.

Giroux, H. A. 2006. "Reading Hurricane Katrina: Race, Class and the Biopolitics of Disposability." *College Literature* 33(3): 171–96.

Grant, B. 2001. "New Moscow Monuments, or, States of Innocence." *American Ethnologist* 28(2): 332–62.

Greenhalgh, S. 2010. *Cultivating Global Citizens: Population in the Rise of China.* Cambridge, MA: Harvard University Press.

Herzfeld, M. 1991. *The Social Production of Indifference: Exploring the Symbolic Roots of Western Bureaucracy.* New York: Berg.

Isaacs, R. 2016. "Cinema and Nation-Building in Kazakhstan." In *Nation-Building and Identity in the Post-Soviet Space: New Tools and Approaches*, ed. R. Isaacs and A. Polese, 138–58. Abingdon: Routledge.

Ismagambetov, T. 2009. "Oralmans or Compatriots? A New Raise of Old Question." Retrieved 26 April 2018 from http://better.kz/en/20090812/oralmans-or-compatriots-a-new-raise-of-old-question%E2%80%A6/.

Kazakhstan Human Rights. n.d. *Rights of the Oralman.* Retrieved 26 April 2018 from http://kazakhstanhumanrights.com/humanrightsanddemocracy/rights-of-the-oralman/.

Kazakhstan Strategy 2050. Retrieved 13 May 2018 from: http://kazakhstan2050.com.

Kendirbaeva, G. 1997. "Migrations in Kazakhstan Past and Present." *Nationalities Papers* 25(4): 741–51.

King, R., A. Christou, and P. Levitt, eds. 2015. *Links to the Diasporic Homeland: Second Generation and Ancestral "Return" Mobilities.* London: Routledge.

Kristeva, J. 1982. *Powers of Horror: An Essay on Abjection*, trans. L. Roudiez. New York: Columbia University Press.

———. 1991. *Strangers to Ourselves.* New York: Columbia University Press.

Kudaibergenova, D. 2015. "The Ideology of Development and Legitimation: Beyond 'Kazakhstan 2030.'" *Central Asian Survey* 34(4): 440–55.

Kuşçu, I. 2008. "Kazakhstan's Oralman Project: A Remedy for Ambiguous Identity." Ph.D. dissertation. Bloomington, IN: Indiana University Bloomington.

Laruelle, M. 2016. "Which Future for National-Patriots? The Landscape of Kazakh Nationalism." In *Kazakhstan in the Making: Legitimacy, Symbols, and Social Changes*, ed. M. Laruelle, 155–80. Boulder, CO: Lexington Books.

Laruelle, M., and Peyrouse, S. 2004. *Les Russes du Kazakhstan: Identités nationales et nouveaux États dans l'espace post-soviétique.* Paris: Maisonneuve & Larose.

Laszczkowski, M. 2016. *"City of the Future": Built Space, Modernity and Urban Change in Astana.* Oxford: Berghahn Books.

Markowitz, F., and A. Stefansson. 2004. *Homecomings: Unsettling Paths of Return.* Boulder, CO: Lexington Books.

McFann, H. n.d. "Refugees: Humans-as-Waste." *Discard Studies: Social Studies of Waste, Pollution and Externalities.* Retrieved 13 May 2018 from https://discardstudies.com/2015/09/04/refugees-humans-as-waste/.

Mendikulova, G. 1997. *Istoricheskie sud'by kazakhsko diaspory: Pro skhozhdenie i razvitie.* [Historical fortunes of Kazakh diaspora: Origin and development.] Almaty: Ghylym.

Nagel, J. 1994. "Constructing Ethnicity: Creating and Recreating Ethnic Identity and Culture." *Social Problems* 41(1): 152–76.

Nelson, D. 2015. *Who Counts? The Mathematics of Death and Life after Genocide.* Durham, NC: Duke University Press.

Ó Beacháin, D., and R. Keylihan. 2013. "Threading a Needle: Kazakhstan between Civic and Ethno-nationalist State Building." *Nations and Nationalism* 19(2): 337–56.

O'Brien, G. 2003. "Indigestible Food, Conquering Hordes, and Waste Materials: Metaphors of Immigrants and the Early Immigration Restriction Debate in the United States." *Metaphor and Symbol* 18(1): 33–47.

Ohliger, R., and R. Munz. 2003. "Diasporas and Ethnic Migrants in Twentieth-Century Europe: A Comparative Perspective." In *Diasporas and Ethnic Migrants: Germany,*

Israel and Post-Soviet Successor States in Comparative Perspective, ed. R. Ohliger and R. Munz, 3–17. London: Frank Cass.

Oka, N. 2013. *A Note on Ethnic Return Migration Policy in Kazakhstan: Changing Priorities and a Growing Dilemma*. IDE Discussion Paper 3. Chiba, Japan: Institute of Developing Economies.

Pianciola, N. 2001. "The Collectivization Famine in Kazakhstan, 1931–1933." *Harvard Ukrainian Studies* 25(3–4): 237–51.

Popravko, I. 2013. "Identity and Conflict at the Borders: Adaptation of Oralmans in East Kazakhstan." Tomsk: Laboratory for Social and Anthropological Research. Retrieved 26 April 2018 from http://lsar.tsu.ru/en/science/field-research/identity-and-conflict-at-the-borders-adaptation-of-oralmans-in-east-kazakhstan.html.

Rahmonova-Schwarz, D. 2010. "Migrations during the Soviet Period and in the Early Years of USSR's Dissolution: A Focus on Central Asia." *Revue Européenne des Migrations Internationals* 26(3): 9–30.

Reeves, M. 2014. *Border Work: Spatial Lives of the State in Rural Central Asia*. Ithaca, NY: Cornell University Press.

Rudnytskyi, O., N. Levchuk, O. Wolowyna, P. Shevchuk, and A. Kovbasiuk. 2015. "Demography of a Man-Made Human Catastrophe: The Case of Massive Famine in Ukraine 1932–1933." *Canadian Studies in Population* 42: 53–80.

Ryan, C. 2013. "Regimes of Waste: Aesthetics, Politics, and Waste from Kofi Awoonor and Ayi Kwei Armah to Chimamanda Adichie and Zeze Gamboa." *Research in African Literatures* 44(4): 51–68.

Sanders, R. 2016. *Staying at Home: Identities, Memories and Social Networks of Kazakhstani Germans*. Oxford: Berghahn Books.

Sancak, M. 2007. "Contested Identity: Encounters with Kazak Diaspora Returning to Kazakhstan." *Anthropology of East Europe Review* 25(1): 85–94.

Sarsembayev, A. 1999. "Imagined Communities: Kazak Nationalism and Kazakification in the 1990s." *Central Asian Survey* 18(3): 319–46.

Satpayev, D., and T. Umbetaliyeva. 2015. "The Protests in Zhanaozen and the Kazakh Oil Sector: Conflicting Interests in a Rentier State." *Journal of Eurasian Studies* 6(2): 122–29.

Schatz, E. 2004. *Modern Clan Politics: The Power of "Blood" in Kazakhstan and Beyond*. Seattle, WA: University of Washington Press.

Schneider, J., and M. Crul. 2010. "New Insights into Assimilation and Integration Theory: Introduction to the Special Issue." *Ethnic and Racial Studies* 33(7): 1143–48.

Scott, J. C. 1985. *Weapons of the Weak: Everyday Forms of Resistance*. New Haven, CT and London: Yale University Press.

———. 1990. *Domination and the Arts of Resistance*. New Haven, CT and London: Yale University Press.

———. *The Art of Not Being Governed: An Anarchist History of Upland Southeast Asia*. New Haven, CT and London: Yale University Press.

Simmel, G. 1950. "The Stranger." In *Georg Simmel: On Individuality and Social Forms*, ed. K. Wolff, 143–50. Chicago, IL: University of Chicago Press.

Stedman Jones, G. 2013. *Outcast London: A Study in the Relationship between Classes in Victorian Society*. London: Verso Books.

The Ministry of Health Care and Social Development of the Republic of Kazakhstan. 2016. "For 25 Years, More Than 957 Thousand Oralman Have Arrived to Kazakhstan." Retrieved 13 May 2018 from http://www.enbek.gov.kz/ru/node/334622.

Turner, S. 2005. "Suspended Spaces—Contesting Sovereignties in a Refugee Camp."
    In T. Blom Hansen and F. Steppaut, eds. *Sovereign Bodies: Citizens, Migrants, and
    States in the Postcolonial World*. Princeton, NJ: Princeton University Press.
UNDP. 2006. *Status of Oralmans in Kazakhstan*. Almaty: UNDP.
Werner, C., and H. Barcus. 2015. "The Unequal Burdens of Repatriation: A Gendered
    Analysis of the Transnational Migration of Mongolia's Kazakh Population."
    American Anthropologist 117(2): 257–71.
Westren, M. 2012. "Nations in Exile: 'The Punished Peoples' in Soviet Kazakhstan,
    1941–1961." Ph.D. dissertation. Chicago, IL: University of Chicago.
Yessenova, S. 2005. "Routes and Roots of Kazakh Identity: Urban Migration in Post-
    Socialist Kazakhstan." *The Russian Review* 64(4): 2–20.

7

The Politics of Indeterminacy
Boundary Dislocations around Waste, Value, and Work in Subic Bay (Philippines)

Elisabeth Schober

Under capitalism, the only thing worse than being exploited is not being exploited.

—Michael Denning

Of Capital and Garbage

Indignant people were assembling at a courtyard in Santos[1] in Subic Bay.[2] You could sense it in the way they gathered, everyone strolling about the yard at their own leisurely pace, eyeing us visitors[3] with a mixture of curiosity and suspicion. No quiet deference to be expected here, no submissive gestures, no one waited around for official introductions to be made; only a few handshakes were exchanged and then we were right in the middle of things. Glenda began by explaining to us how much other people's trash was worth: "Remember, it has capital. Yes, it's all garbage, but it has capital. It's not really garbage as long as it still has capital." This was a group of scavengers[4] who worked informally at a local landfill near Subic Bay, looking for valuables amid the trash. Outspoken Glenda was probably the most powerful of these seemingly powerless people: a round woman in her late fifties, with fierce eyes and a quick tongue, she is the vice president of the "Santos Scavengers and Recyclers Association," a collective that functions as a de facto trade union for its members. Francis, a quiet man sitting a few meters away from her, is the president; between them, they lead a group of some three hundred people. These scavengers, at the end of a long day's work, are all embedded within their households, among their kin; if push would ever come to shove, three to four thousand people could be easily mobilized through this particular association.

The scavengers know their potential strength, the local government recognizes it, and the police are certainly aware of it, as they occasionally come to check on this particular courtyard and its workers. During our conversation with the fifteen people assembled there, the discussion reached near boiling point, and one scavenger quietly stood up and went to the iron gate of the courtyard to close it. Too many spectators were peeking through the gate to see what was going on, and the talk was getting too political to be overheard by people randomly walking by. "We normally don't dare to have our meetings in here anymore, because we are being eyed by the police," explained Francis. Kilusan[5] activist Jenny then interjected, explaining how they had held a workshop here a year ago, during which they had not closed that iron gate and, sure enough, after a while the police had showed up to see what the group of scavengers was up to, suspiciously assembled in this courtyard. "There was this policeman who came checking on us. Because we are organizing, and trying to have our voices heard."

During our two-hour visit, the scavengers primarily discussed their weak and troubled ties to two large forces: the Philippine state (manifested in local government) and big capital (manifested by foreign direct investors). The nearby Subic Bay Freeport Zone, situated on the land that was previously home to the US Naval Base Subic Bay, has become a major vehicle for economic growth in an area that was previously only known for hosting the world's largest overseas US naval facility. "Usually, the capitalist is a foreigner," Glenda exclaimed, "[the] foreigner [is] the capitalist. I mean, look at the Philippines!" She and her associates made clear to me that among the many foreign capitalists in the Subic area, it was the Korean shipbuilder Hanjin (the largest local employer and largest foreign investor in the Philippines), that was the worst of them all. Since 2006, Hanjin has run one of the world's largest shipyards in Subic Bay, which currently employs thirty-four thousand Filipinos, a number which does not include scavengers and their relatives. While there were more than eight hundred scavenger families living in Santos, the scavengers claimed that not a single family member had found work with Hanjin during the decade they had been present in the area. "Many have ten kids," Glenda explained, "but no one was ever employed by Hanjin." In the larger Santos area, Francis added, quite a few non-scavengers did find work with the shipbuilder, but virtually all of them have since been terminated. Glenda proceeded to talk herself into a rage listing all the things the Koreans had not done for them:

Nothing was ever offered to the scavengers. [Are] there any medical missions offered by Hanjin? That's what we need, you see, medical assistance.[6] ... If they [were] looking [out for] poor people, or said, "scavengers, come here, I will give you one truckload of scrap metal." No way. You have to go to [name of local politician] first so that you can get the scrap. No good. [Reacting to laughter around her.] I'm really getting mad now ... Monopolized by politicians! Are we a part of them? Do the scavengers have a chair in the bidding [for scrap metal from the shipyard]? Or [a say] in consultations? ... You are cordially invited to attend. I will advise the president (of the association): "Go get a new haircut! Go get a dress from your neighbor, so you will be [able to] attend the meeting of Hanjin [as a] good-looking personality." If they [would] say: "I will give you ten truckloads [of waste] for your Christmas party!" Impossible. That will never happen.

The vignette above gives an indication of how some of the people involved in the Santos scavenger association seek to define their rather contested status as workers who handle materials that still "have capital," thereby also demanding recognition from powerful local actors for the productive role they play in Subic Bay. In my exploration of this remarkable self-presentation, I will contribute to understanding the larger conundrum of how a state of indeterminacy can affect workers, workplaces, and contribute to the many shapes that politics assumes in contemporary society. In the context I describe here, my use of the term *indeterminacy* refers to a condition in which workers have been stripped of older subsistence modes of production, but have not yet attained access to wage labor.[7] Foreign investors like the Korean shipbuilder above, whose presence inadvertently raises hopes for full wage labor inclusion among the urban poor of the area, typically cannot be made to employ, let alone care about, impoverished human populations living in the vicinity of their shipyard. But they are assumed to welcome the downward pressure that these sectors of society put on wage levels. However, as this chapter demonstrates, local politicians cannot afford to entirely discard these "surplus" segments of the population. It is on this latter fact that both activists and scavengers have learned to capitalize.

Hence, in a second step I also point to a mode of indeterminacy that emerges within the category of wagelessness itself, which, as a number of authors starting from Marx have argued, is by definition excluded from capital, yet often plays an unrecognized role within the workings of global capitalism. Growing "surplus populations" in the Global South, and the related issue of their inclusion and exclusion from areas of economic growth, have recently been at the center of much scholarly debate—a discussion that has, at times, veered dangerously toward turning these impoverished people into ahistorical, agencyless pawns. As Catherine Alexander and Andrew Sanchez argue in the introduction to this volume, indeterminacy "is lack of recognition." It is the lack of recognition of political agency that resides in wagelessness, which specifically interests me. Hence, the material presented here, based on a close ethnography of a group of Philippine labor activists and the working populations that they organize, raises a number of questions for existing anthropological theories of labor and political mobilization among workers.

Arguably, by asserting that the trash they handle still has value, scavengers are also making a statement about their capacity to do work under conditions of capitalism. Wage workers at the Korean shipyard nearby may find their worth somewhat reflected in the highly priced commodities that they build in Subic Bay and that then circle the globe. However, the wageless scavengers have only the unclear boundary between waste and value at their disposal. Alongside a strategy that involves appeals to earlier times in Subic when they earned wages for their work, the condition of indeterminacy occasionally allows scavengers to affirm their worth. In their attempts to influence the political, social, and economic (de-)valuation of their lives, scavengers read their current experiences of exclusion against the backdrop of memories of work that they previously held at the US base. I shall argue that such contestations over past labor forms in Subic Bay—and what these may mean for current and future modes of work—are one example of a kind of *politics of indeterminacy* that may at times emerge amid the undefined and unrecognized status that wageless workers hold vis-à-vis global capitalism.

Wageless Workers at the Landfill

Even though I had already heard of the scavengers of Santos during the first few days of my stay in the Philippines, it took me a while to make my way up to their landfill. Having come to Subic Bay to learn about the impact that the arrival of the large South Korean shipyard has had on an area previously dominated by the US military, two days after our arrival, my family and I had found ourselves confined by flood waters. Super-Typhoon Usagi had recently ploughed through the northern Philippines and, although Subic Bay was not in its direct path, the typhoon had intensified the normal monsoon, causing a number of flash floods. In the ensuing chaos, twenty people died in the Subic Bay area, mostly young children from squatter families living in remoter villages, whose makeshift houses, built closely to the mountains, were flattened by the sudden onslaught of water.

Figure 7.1. The Korean shipyard of Subic Bay, photo by Wonho Lee. Printed with permission.

Once the torrential floods had receded and the mud and rubble had been cleared away, another more insidious aftereffect of this calamity came to light: over five hundred people would subsequently be treated for leptospirosis, a potentially deadly disease transmitted by rats. National news reports on the situation in Subic Bay at that time pointed fingers at the Santos landfill, with the health risks posed to Santos's residents by rodents being repeatedly mentioned. The apparent danger represented by the thousands of people living and laboring in this infamous part of Subic Bay, however, was an issue that local residents of the area raised with me in their private conversations. NGO workers that I spoke to were particularly keen to alert me to Santos's surplus populations and the seeming squalor that they lived in. Dozens of children were said to go through the garbage every day in order to survive. Widespread consumption of "pag-pag" was a perceived health threat too, that is, people would collect and consume the meaty scraps from bones dumped in the landfill by local fast food chains, with the remainder of this food waste typically pressed together and then sold cheaply by the kilo to other poor people living in the vicinity. In the meantime, Santos's population kept growing rapidly, with more people arriving by the day, drawn by their desire to improve their prospects in an urban area located next to the Philippines' largest and most prosperous Special Economic Zone, where Korean investors nowadays dictate the conditions of life, just as the US military did a generation ago. The recent drastic expansion of Subic Bay's formal workforce, however, has, for the most part, not included these economically destitute populations seeking shelter in Santos, which has resulted in ever more people trying to make a living by heading for the local landfill instead.

My informants from Kilusan—a left-wing group that is also involved in organizing an association of workers at the Korean shipyard that I had come to investigate—insisted that I should meet their scavenger friends. "Your picture of Subic Bay won't be complete without talking to them," activist Jenny said. So, one day in February 2014, Jenny and I joined Dan, a community organizer who had previously spent two years living among the scavengers. Dan explained his work: "What they do, I do. Where they sleep, I sleep. What they eat, I eat." A few days before our meeting, one of his organizational counterparts in Manila had been murdered. Dan explained that his colleague had been gunned down after an assembly meeting, because the squatters he was helping were preventing a businessman from selling the land that the settlers were living on. Describing his comrade as someone who had been at the very center of that particular struggle among the urban poor, Dan feared that the movement his friend had organized in Manila would now quickly collapse in his absence.[8]

Stepping off the jeepney[9] in Santos, we could already smell the landfill and its neighborhood. Although I thought I had no idea what to expect, all the talk I had heard from other, more well-off Subic Bay residents of chaos reigning in the streets of Santos, rampant child labor, and massive health threats, had clearly created a certain image of life around the landfill in my head. While we slowly walked up the street that was steeply ascending the hill, I gazed into a seemingly endless number of courtyards filled with material: heaps of scrap metal, loads of old pipes, piles of wood, mountains of plastic bags, hills made out of glass and plastic bottles. Any trash item that may still be worth a peso or two could be found in large quantities here, neatly piled in the streets of Santos. Everything was organized into classes of things, divisions and subdivisions, ready to be sold to intermediaries and loaded onto their trucks for further shipment. However, nowhere during our approach to the landfill could one see any garbage in the strict sense of the word. The streets were tidy, the place much more orderly than some districts nearby. Only the stench was getting worse with every step we took. I suddenly felt rather dizzy, and it had nothing to do with the smell of rotting garbage drifting from the landfill down the hill. Instead, this was a sensation I occasionally experienced during fieldwork when I realized that everything I had held to be true about a certain situation would have to be quickly revised in my head. The landfill, which I had imagined to be an indeterminate and chaotic mass of rubbish was in fact a rather orderly place, and the "indigent" people I was to meet there clearly did not fit my preconceived notions of them, either. "This is work, no? They *are* working here?" I foolishly said, just loud enough for Jenny to give me a puzzled look.

The confusion I felt over the question of whether landfill scavenging constitutes a form of labor had to do with the main purpose of my stay in the Philippines, which was to make sense of how the powerful Korean shipbuilder Hanjin Heavy Industries-Philippines (HHIC-Phil) uses its local workforce to run its 300 hectare shipyard in Subic Bay. Currently, nearly thirty-four thousand people are employed at the shipyard, but the number of Filipinos who hope to work for Hanjin, who were briefly employed by them, or who eventually lost their faith that they would ever find work with the Koreans, is significantly larger. HHIC-Phil is only one of several employers in the area: as of 2015, the Subic Freeport Zone provides nearly a hundred thousand people with jobs, with half of these positions within the Freeport being blue-collar positions that can be found in shipbuilding, in the maritime sector, or in other manufacturing domains (Empeno 2015; see also Subic 2013; Garcia 2013). Unsurprisingly, the booming heavy industries in Subic, and the prospect of finding relatively stable, semi-formal employment in this sector, have attracted countless new people to Subic Bay. For many, the dream of a steady living did not come true, with numerous people finding themselves pushed into sprawling shantytown areas like Santos instead.

The Philippines today has only a minor, rather undeveloped formal economic sector: 77 percent of Filipinos work in the informal sector (Ofreneo 2013: 424; see also Hart 1973), eking out a living through various ways and means. The rise of informality is connected to rapid population growth on the one hand, and the decline of traditional options of creating livelihoods for the most impoverished parts of Philippine society on the other: both the fishing and the agricultural sector of the country are steadily shrinking, with the small- and large-scale dispossession of peasants and fisherfolk being the order of the day. With corporate or state-driven land- and water-grabbing, low-level warfare in the south of the country, and the ever increasing effects of climate change all impairing people's abilities to make a living (Schober forthcoming), people easily lose access to the sea, are driven off their land, or "voluntarily" leave their plots behind following a minor family catastrophe that forces them to sell their land. Ever more of these affected populations have relocated to rapidly urban- izing areas such as Subic Bay in order to improve their lot.

Foreign direct investors like HHIC-Phil thus arrive in a country heavily marked by an expanding informal sector, which depresses the formal wage sector, while the "disciplining power of high unemployment" (McKay 2006: 42) also prevents many workers from unionization. Hanjin seems to have chosen to invest in the Philippines because of this over-abundance of people who will potentially work for low wages, with the prospect of a union-free shipyard being an added incentive[10] (see Grey 2015). Be that as it may, the question of how Hanjin actually depends (or does not depend) on this "significant, rela- tively low-cost labor pool" was something that over time increasingly intrigued me. During the seven months I lived in Subic, the only conclusion I could draw from everything I would see and hear was that the Philippines very much depended on Hanjin, its most important foreign direct investor. All the while, the company itself seemed to treat its workers, and those who hoped to work for them, as disposable human material that could be hired, fired, and replaced at any moment. For instance, while the company was still employing approxi- mately twenty-two thousand people in 2012, when I came to Subic in late 2013, the number of workers had been reduced to about sixteen thousand, with the workforce then suddenly nearly doubling to its current thirty-four thousand workers by 2016.

Such fluctuations certainly require a very compressed training period of the workforce and a highly flexible labor recruitment system, which allows HHIC-Phil to bring in thousands of new workers at short notice when new shipbuild- ing orders come in; indeed, training at their skills development center usually takes only three months before the new Hanjin recruits are deemed ready for the shipyard. At the same time, Hanjin relies on an intricate network of dozens of (mostly Korean) subcontractors, with virtually all rank-and-file workers receiving six-month contracts at first. Semi-permanent contracts with the sub- contractors are handed out to these new recruits only after this testing period. This allows the company to rapidly lay off large numbers of people in case a downturn requires this action.[11]

Consequently, labor turnover rates at the shipyard are extremely high. The activists with whom I collaborated asserted that Hanjin has replaced nearly all of the original workforce that they had recruited locally in 2006/07 with a second generation of workers, who were brought in from far-flung provinces like Mindanao or Northern Luzon around 2009/10, with a third generation of workers currently being mobilized from relatively nearby locations again (for another account of the erosion of permanence in industrial work, see Sanchez 2012). Processes such as these indicate that indeterminate working conditions are by no means confined to the lives of the poorest of the poor in the Philippines today: with increasing deregulation and (sub-)contractualization, a sense of indeterminacy can easily spread to workers and workplaces that are seemingly fully anchored within the "formal" domain of the economy. However, the comparison between shipyard and landfill, together with a detour into the history of scavenging in the area, may throw up important differentiations that Subic's residents, and the scavengers themselves, make when it comes to wageless work and the (lack of) value attached to it.

A Brief History of Subic Trash: Of Value and Worthlessness in the Shadow of the Foreign Base

As anthropologists know, much like the concept of waste itself, notions of work, too, may be closely linked to societal understandings of value and worth(lessness). Sandra Wallman, in the introduction to *Social Anthropology of Work* (1980), writes that "work is 'about' the physical and psychic energy a worker puts into producing, maintaining or converting economic resources, but ... the choices, decisions and rewards of the worker are constrained by the logic of the system in which he works." The control of work, she further argues, "entails not only control over the allocation and disposition of resources, it implies also control over the *values* ascribed to them" (Wallman 1980: 300; my emphasis). Viewed in such a way, the wageless work of scavenging may allow us to shine a light on the larger value system reigning in Subic Bay, and the historical and political factors that have given rise to it: a local system of worth(lessness) that the scavengers find themselves both embedded in, and simultaneously expelled from.

Subic Bay is after all an urban region that only came into existence because of the local presence of a large US naval station; the history of scavenging in this area is intimately linked to this base. Up until the late nineteenth century (while the naval base in Subic was still held by the Spanish colonial forces), only a few small fishing villages could be found in the area. The arrival of US sailors after the Spanish-American War in 1898 would then significantly enlarge the population, with tens of thousands of Filipinos seeking to make a living out of the presence of large numbers of US soldiers in the area. With an estimated nine thousand sex workers laboring in Subic Bay in the mid-1980s, the region primarily depended on providing "rest and recreation" for the young US sailors, who left not only money behind, but also thousands of "Amerasian" children they had fathered. With no alternative local industry nearby, for many decades the primary occupation of nearly all residents in the area was the management of everything that spilled over from the base.

Unsurprisingly, this also included the management of waste, with Filipinos spending "a great deal and effort cleaning up after U.S. troops" (Belkin 2012: 163). Initially, the Aeta, a group of indigenous people who had depended on hunting and gathering in the Subic forests until the arrival of the Americans, and whose land had then been taken away in order to build the sprawling US naval base, were given privileged access to the base's landfills (see Schober 2016b). Roland G. Simbulan, in *The Bases of Our Insecurity,* points out that these rights, given in exchange for the occupation of their traditional lands, were first granted to the Aeta in 1960. However, in 1976, this agreement with the indigenous population of the area was again revoked, when a service contract system came into place that meant the Aeta became just one group among others who would now work on a rotational basis for a daily wage at the base's landfills. This waged work entailed sorting out the metal scraps, which were then sold by the base authorities in public bids (Simbulan 1985: 263–64).

Some of the older scavengers of the association in Santos like Glenda were employed through this service contract system as scavengers at the Subic dump in the 1980s. Glenda picked up her "street English" while working at the US base, and much of her self-understanding as a laborer is rooted in her memories of those days, when she was paid a wage to sort through US garbage. Much like other citizens of Subic Bay that I spoke to, Glenda missed the "good old days" when the US Navy was still a primary source of income for many people, a process I have described elsewhere as "Navy Nostalgia" (Schober 2016a). Many residents of the area tend to think of new foreign direct investors like Hanjin as second-rate replacements for the US Navy, since the Americans are still remembered as good employers, while Hanjin only pays minimum wages for high-risk work. Accordingly, Hanjin is typically thought of as an exploitative foreign agent, rather than a foreign source of wealth that locals can also capitalize on. Such expectations concerning work have been very much impacted by the memories of "easy money" to be made during those "golden days," when intoxicated sailors were rumored to leave fifty dollar tips on the table of their regular bars. "The good life," in the view of many residents of the Subic area, consequently involves partaking in foreign wealth and cultivating one's ability to successfully live off of, alongside, and, on occasion, together with wealthy outsiders. Such ideas of a successful life have impinged themselves upon people's everyday approaches to the creation of livelihoods—a phrase that, according to Susana Narotzky and Niko Besnier, entail both making a living, and making life worth living (2014).

The decline of economic opportunities came quickly once the Americans left the area. A discussion among the scavengers over the "formal" jobs that some of them have held since then proved to be particularly illuminating: a few older men had worked as security guards in the Freeport Zone when it was first established in the early 1990s, soon after the last few US sailors had departed. These jobs came about as Richard Gordon, arguably Subic Bay's most influential local politician of the twentieth century, felt that the scavengers should be rewarded for their many years of service for the Americans: work that, contrary to people's rosy recollection, seems to have claimed quite a few lives through exposure to hazardous materials.[12] However, after a few years all the waste-pickers-turned-security-guards lost their jobs, and returned to scavenging. Only one person out of those I spoke to still had a relative (a son), currently working in the Freeport. However, this son recently had his working hours drastically reduced. A few years earlier, the Freeport switched all remaining permanent contracts to temporary ones, and times have been getting tougher for people employed there, with de facto incomes on the decrease again.

While opportunities at the Freeport were drying up for the scavengers, many "old-timers" drifted toward Santos and the landfill that was established in the 1980s, where they work on their own, without a regular wage. It can be speculated that peoples' social standing in Subic Bay sank with the move from the seaside base to the hills of Santos. A fraction of the former opportunities (but perhaps not the old recognition attached to their work) were eventually restored for these scavengers when some of the waste gathered at the Subic Bay Freeport would be sent up to the Santos landfill. Work routines today are very much organized around the arrival of precious truckloads full of waste, which are mostly comprised of the household garbage of wealthy foreigners living in the Freeport (more valuable industrial waste is typically auctioned off before ever entering the landfill). Groups of up to fifteen scavengers work together, and follow a rotational schedule that gives them access to the truck loads of "outside" waste and the precious "inside" waste (from the Freeport) several times a week. Nowadays, the income of a regular scavenger rarely exceeds 150 pesos a day (roughly 2.37 euros / 2.89 dollars), less than half the minimum wage made by Hanjin workers at the nearby shipyard.

Figure 7.2. The main gate to the former US naval base, photo by Wonho Lee. Printed with permission.

The Indeterminacy of Philippine Surplus Populations

My initial disorientation over the livelihood activities of the population of scavengers in Santos also resonates with some of the recent social scientific debates on "surplus populations." Karl Marx first introduced the idea that a surplus of labor is inherently necessary for the workings of capitalism. In a key intervention titled "To Make Live or Let Die?" (2009), Tania Li argues that by delineating the notion of a surplus population, Marx was reacting to Malthusserian understandings of redundant people that were popular during his lifetime (68). Malthus, she points out, thought of surplus populations as those that would need to die in order for humanity to survive, as there would not be enough resources available to support everyone. In Marx's response to Malthus's grotesque vision of humanity's future, Marx then arguably linked his own notion of "relative surplus population" (which he also called the "reserve army of labor") closely to the idea that people who were not wage workers yet, but who had had their original means of production already stripped from them, were best understood as future laboring populations. The actual creation of a "disposable industrial reserve army" occurred through a process that Marx famously labeled "primitive accumulation." In the case of England, this entailed the creation of large surplus populations through violent land enclosures that turned peasants into a landless proletariat, who, as his narrative went, could later be exploited in the country's factories. In sum, Marx's vision of capitalism requires "a situation in which working people have been stripped of ownership or control of [the] means of production (and stripped from a community of producers as well) and must work for wages to survive" (Roseberry 1997: 31; see Polanyi [1944] 2001).

"Primitive accumulation," David Harvey has argued over recent years, was not merely the "original sin" of capitalism as Marx envisioned it (i.e., a one-time violent event that would then gradually be supplanted by more peaceful relations between the owners of capital and the recently dispossessed). Instead, Harvey claims that the violent dispossession of some populations is a process that needs to be repeated over and over again in order to allow for the expansion of capitalism into ever new territories, which is a "spatio-temporal fix" designed to ameliorate our current economic system's inherent tendency to periodically go into deep crises. Inspired by Harvey's sweeping analytical framework, the most recent wave of privatization and commodification of communal land and water, happening on a global scale and arguably occurring with ever increasing speed, has become a much commented upon phenomenon (see Hall, Hirsch, and Li 2011; Harvey 2011; Swyngedouw 2006).

The issue of surplus populations naturally relates to another important theme in the body of literature concerned with the negative developments triggered by our recent round of "overheated" globalization (Eriksen 2016); that is, is the question of people's inclusion and exclusion from domains of economic growth, and whether or not these processes are still open-ended or will necessarily lead people into permanent deprivation. There is "a growing scholarly consensus," Sharryn Kasmir and August Carbonella argue, "around the notion that these new enclosures are creating people and communities who are *permanently* constituted as 'outside' capitalism" (2014: 51; see Sassen 2014). This argument is rather similar to some of the ideas Tania Li has advanced in her work on land-grabbing (see, for instance, Li 2011). In Southeast Asia, in particular, as Derek Hall, Philip Hirsch, and Li have shown (2011), we are nowadays facing a massive wave of enclosures that seems to permanently expel larger populations from the realms of capitalist production. In this region, landlessness and dispossession have traditionally been a much less severe problem than in other localities of the world, but with population growth putting ever new pressures on the dwindling commons, and with the arrival of a particularly vicious form of capitalism, millions of people find themselves pushed into abject poverty these days, with the future perspective for an improvement of their economic situations seemingly dire.

Interestingly, Li has also argued that (post-)Marxist theoreticians, much like Marx himself, place too much emphasis on the temporal and spatial link between people's dispossession from their original means of production on the one hand, and the creation of useful "surplus labor" on the other. In "To Make Live or Let Die?" (2009), she couples a Foucauldian understanding of biopolitics with the Marxian notion of surplus population to explore a politics of "letting die," that is, the hidden structural violence that has resulted in millions of people in the Global South leading short and limited lives. "Letting die," she argues, happens in places where people no longer have direct access to natural resources that would allow them to make a livelihood on their own, while at the same time not having access to a living wage, either. And once we start to question the temporal assumptions built into a Marxian understanding of surplus populations—that their existence (and survival) are a necessity for future functioning of capital—these people's progression toward better futures begins to look rather uncertain indeed.

Provocatively, Li diagnoses an overlap between the thinking of neo-Marxists inspired by David Harvey on the one hand, and the discourses deployed by transnational economic actors such as the World Bank on the other, who, in their seemingly blind belief in some kind of notion of progress, both argue that surplus populations at the end of the day somehow have to matter to capital. Li, however, ascertains that the "perilous condition [of surplus populations is] a sign of their very limited relevance to capital at any scale" (2009: 67). To put it starkly, when viewed from Li's perspective, one may only come to the conclusion that the lives of scavengers like Glenda and Francis will never matter to a large conglomerate like Hanjin, and leaving their fate up to the markets to decide will not lead to strategies of "make live" of such people, but rather, to one of "let die."

Li's stance, that we need to put our faith in a biopolitics of state-driven "make live" when it comes to what were called "marginal" populations half a generation ago, is an argument that in some ways resembles interventions made by prominent philosophers such as Achille Mbembe (2004), Giorgio Agamben (1998), or

Zygmunt Bauman (2003). In a wholesale critique against such approaches published in the *New Left Review*, historian Michael Denning warns us of the slippery slope between repeatedly speaking of bare and superfluous life and drawing the conclusion that "there really are disposable people, not simply that they are disposable in the eyes of state and market" (2008: 80). Denning argues (in a similar vein to a number of anthropologists, who have frequently thrown the widespread conflation of wage labor with work into doubt[13]) that the problem in how surplus populations are discussed these days is rooted in erroneous understandings of what the term "work" potentially encompasses. "Capitalism," Denning argues, "begins not with the offer of work, but with the imperative to earn a living" (2008: 80). Simultaneously, he encourages readers to be wary of a false sense of emergency so prevalent in the analysis of suffering these days, where upon closer examination one may often only encounter a state of "poverty-as-usual" (Denning 2008: 80).

Today's discussions around surplus populations are a prime example of "analytical approaches to indeterminacy that counsel only either hope or despair," (Alexander and Sanchez this volume). It is indeed striking how the surplus populations of our day and age, in the way they have recently been theorized, seem to yet again have so little control over the course that their lives take. In the way they make their case for renewed state engagement with surplus populations, Bauman, Mbembe, Li, and others seem to have fallen into the same trap that Marx and his followers have rightly been taken to task for: their actors run the risk of becoming ahistorical, agencyless pawns that are either willfully cast away or need to be purposefully retained by the state. A slightly more nuanced picture may emerge, however, if we insist on prioritizing "situated encounters" (Alexander and Sanchez this volume) of the kind that ethnography brings about, which may reveal many "critical junctions" (Kalb and Tak 2005) between history writ large and the daily struggles of our interlocutors over how to maintain meaningful lives, at the interstices of which new forms of politics can also emerge. For instance, amid the growing political, economic, and social anxieties that would subsequently crystallize into the violent singularity that is President Rodrigo Duterte's Philippines today, my interlocutors creatively employed the indeterminate suspension of waste between worthlessness and value,[14] and sought to put a particular history of labor under a previous temporal regime to use that, in their view, meant they were workers in the here and now, too.

Conclusion: Navigating the Loaded Space between "Discardable People" and "Dangerous Underclass"

The government is saying the economy is getting better and better, but it never reaches us...

—Francis

Many of the concerns raised by scavengers involved in the association revolve around their frustrations over making their working lives matter to both capital and state, which are forces that are understood as jointly undermining their ability to make a livelihood. Kathleen Millar has written that "the aims and methods of mobilization in a situation of informal employment shift significantly from those of formal unions. The use of strike or demands for higher wages and benefits ... do not make sense in situations of self-employment and unregulated work" (2008: 32). What leverage do scavengers then have that would allow them to improve their lot? It turns out that toward transnational conglomerates like Hanjin, their few bargaining chips seem indeed rather worthless. Representatives of the state, however, can be pressured through various ways and means.

Much time was spent during fieldwork discussing various former and present governors, *barangay* (village) captains, and city mayors, and how much or how little they did for the scavengers. A recently elected politician, for instance, had fallen into disregard among my informants, when he had invited the scavengers for a meeting with him and then showed up several hours late. The meeting, Glenda explained, was scheduled for eleven o'clock in the morning, so they had made sure to be there half an hour early:

> One truck [full] of people, six jeeps from Santos. With our eagerness to hear the voice of [the local politician], we go to the convention center. We arrived there at ten o'clock, our appointment is at eleven. But the convention center is already prepared for us. He arrived at two o'clock in the afternoon! No lunch! Some were dancing already, some singing already. I requested the group leader to speak on [our] behalf, to pass the time, waiting for [him]. [He] talked to us for no more than an hour.

An option that the scavengers sometimes use in their attempts to improve their lives involves taking advantage of the fact that, seemingly in the eyes of these local politicians, they represent an underclass that has been infiltrated by left-wing elements. After decades of low-scale warfare between the Philippine military and the Maoists, the threat of a significant communist uprising in the Philippines is steadily on the decline, and guerrilla fighters in this part of the archipelago have been reduced to a few handfuls of fighters in nearby mountain ranges. However, social mobilization through leftist groups is still a force to be reckoned with, and the pushback against such collectives continues to be violent indeed. Glenda gets to the heart of the matter when she says that "if (the politicians) will not take care of us scavengers, (if) they will not grant our requests: Rally!" Fear of a more widespread disruption through the actions of such impoverished groups, which could disturb the exceptionally peaceful and orderly image of Subic Bay, and which has been an essential component in attracting foreign direct investors to the area, is clearly a factor in the kind of patron-client politics that I witnessed in this Philippine urban area. Ultimately, at times a lack of respect was accorded to the scavengers, but to discard them was a hazardous business for any local politician who wanted to maintain order and stability in their economically vital region.[15]

Is this a kind of politics of "let live" in the sense that Li proposes? Not quite. To be sure, the scavengers and their work have "very limited relevance to capital at any scale" (2009: 67), and it is only the state that at first glance seems to be somewhat open to negotiations at all. However, this does not mean that the politics that people like the Santos scavengers engage in is necessarily about their relationship with the state.[16] As I have shown in this chapter, their politics is imbued with the indeterminacy that surrounds their labor status, suspended between waged and wageless work, and their actual targets, more often than not, are foreign actors who in Subic are usually understood as the main addressees of claims for recognition to be made. The surplus populations of Santos hence need to be reckoned with by local actors of the state, not out of a sense of humanitarian conscience along the lines of Li's argument but rather because the scavengers are an active social force in this economically rather important community that at times needs to be placated in order to keep peace in the region. By extension, also keeps important foreign direct investors in place.

What is more, Li is right in her critique of all-too-neat Marxist imaginations of future usefulness of surplus labor, but such a perspective could arguably be augmented with a focus on other temporal aspects related to wagelessness, such as deliberate attempts to utilize past experiences for potential future gains. Suspended between the initial casting off from their land (or other natural resources) and full incorporation into capitalist wage labor, surplus populations often stand outside of the usual binaries that narratives of progress are based on. Such indeterminacy, in the case presented here, is countered by some of the scavengers involved in the Santos association by invoking past experiences of waged labor during US Navy times in order to ask for a wider appreciation of their activities as productive in the sense that they, too, once were, and still are, part of the bigger picture. This is, in essence, what I mean by a *politics of indeterminacy*: a form of mobilization of labor that can at times emerge due to the exceptionally ambiguous status that wageless workers hold vis-à-vis global capitalist actors. Specifically, by harking back to Subic's recent past under the auspices of the US Navy, which actually did involve work contracts handed out to scavengers, these actors made claims that things could be better again for them, too, because in fact they had been in the past.

Acknowledgements

I am grateful for comments and suggestions I received from Andrew Sanchez, Catherine Alexander, the anonymous reviewers, Keir Martin, Thomas Hylland Eriksen, and the participants of the "Waste and the Superfluous: Precarious Living amidst Worlds of Waste" workshop that took place at University of Oslo on 14–15 September 2015.

Elisabeth Schober is an associate professor in Social Anthropology at the University of Oslo. Previously, she has investigated responses to US bases in South Korea. Recently, she has focused on the challenges emerging from the relocation of manufacturing from South Korea to the Philippines. She is the author of *Base Encounters* (Pluto Press 2016) and has coedited (with Thomas Hylland Eriksen) a special issue of *Ethnos* titled "Economies of Growth or Ecologies of Survival?"

Notes

1. This is a pseudonym for a poor urban district close to Subic Bay, a coastal region of the Philippines that is rapidly urbanizing these days. Pseudonyms have also been given to all individuals mentioned in order protect their anonymity.
2. Fieldwork in Subic Bay was conducted between September 2013 and April 2014 as part of Thomas Hylland Eriksen's ERC Advanced Grant-funded project ("Overheating: The Three Crises of Globalization").
3. My husband (who is a Korean national and often joined me during fieldwork in Subic) and I accompanied two activists associated with Kilusan to the yard that day (see also endnote 5) to hold a group discussion with workers on issues relevant to them and their lives. As had been the case before when we had held similar group discussions with Kilusan allies, the unusual pairing that my husband and I made (a Korean man in the company of a white woman) had first to be explained to our Filipino hosts. That is to say, our Kilusan friends had to clarify that my husband was not working for the unpopular Korean shipbuilders in town.
4. The English word "scavenger" is the term that the landfill workers use to describe themselves (also in political contexts such as in the name of their association). Given this emic usage, I have opted to keep the name in my writings as well, despite the obvious negative connotations of the word that alternative terms such as "waste picker" may not have.
5. Kilusan para sa Pambansang Demokrasya (KPD; Movement for National Democracy) is an affiliate of the broader Bayan coalition that was forged in the 1980s as a socialist alternative to the armed Maoist movement led by Jose Maria Sison. KPD organizers are particularly active in the Zambales region where Subic is located The group's activists focus on shaping multi-sectoral revolutionary alliances among the most impoverished segments of Philippine society (i.e., among poor urban communities, fisher folks, indigenous people, and informal laborers).
6. Health problems among the scavengers are grave. There are many medical issues to be addressed without health insurance from smaller issues such as athlete's foot, which they suffer from regularly because they cannot afford boots that would also protect them from sharp objects sticking out of the trash, to frequent diarrhea and infections, to the prevalence of tuberculosis in the area.
7. A popular term for related processes is of course that of precarity, which I have engaged with at length elsewhere (see Schober 2018b). For this chapter, I have stayed clear of this notion as I believe it does not add much to the analysis of the material presented here. Labeling the working lives of the scavengers "precarious" is the most self-evident point that could be made about them. Here, however, I am much more interested in exploring how their indefinite status, which comes with wageless work, translates into an everyday politics that operates around inclusion and exclusion, hence, indeterminacy is the more useful concept here.
8. Well before Rodrigo Duterte's "War on drugs" officially began in mid-2016 (and has in the meantime resulted in thousands of state-sponsored casualties), journalists, lawyers,

activists, and indigenous leaders had frequently fallen victim to extrajudicial killings linked to government forces. Under the presidency of Gloria Macapagal-Arroyo (2001–10), for instance, about eight hundred people were murdered in this way. Under the presidency of Benigno S. Aquino III (2010–16), during which my fieldwork took place, hundreds of civil society actors also lost their lives. At the time of my stay in the country, the realm of "private" contract killings was also rapidly expanding, with the "going rate" for a murder in Subic Bay, for instance, having been 10,000 pesos (190 euros) per person in 2013/14, when new reports of people losing their lives over disputes over money, property, or drug-related issues reached me nearly every week.

9. Repurposed jeeps that are the most common means of public transportation in the Philippines.

10. Hanjin Heavy Industries has been marred by prolonged labor struggles at their original, much smaller shipyard in Pusan, South Korea (see Baca 2011; Robinson 2011), while an informal "no-unions" policy seems to be in place at the Freeport Zone in Subic Bay. Labor scholars Fong Yin Chan and Philip F. Kelly have noted on this policy that "many investors and early tenants cited the unofficial banning of unions in (the Subic Bay Freeport Zone) as one of the main incentives for locating here" (2004: 150).

11. HHIC's large network of subcontractors has also been blamed for the fact that health and safety standards at the yard have proven to be very lax at times, leading to the deaths of thirty-eight people who perished due to work-related accidents and to the non-lethal injuries of thousands of workers over the years (see Schober 2018a).

12. See, for instance, Tritten 2010.

13. For a recent rendition, see the work of Kathleen Millar (e.g., 2014). Based on her work on scavengers in a landfill in Brazil, she argues that scavenging is a form of informal work that can open a particular window into our current economic system: "While not part of the inner logics of capitalism, informal employment is nonetheless tied to its rises and falls, its growth and expansions, its adjustments and transformations. We cannot comprehend the informal economy without an understanding of the political economy of capital accumulation. But neither, for that matter, can we comprehend capitalism without attention to the lives of the millions of unemployed in our world" (2008:32).

14. More could be made out of the comparison between shipyard and landfill workers, too, which I cannot fully engage in here due to spatial constraints. For instance, the social standing of these two different sets of workers in the wider community of Subic Bay would seem to be tightly linked to the perceived value of the things they work with (i.e., trash versus ships). Wageless labor of the kind that the landfill affords, one could argue, has the effect, but not quite the appearance of wage labor. Even though a messy landfill may look completely different from an orderly, modern workplace like the shipyard, scavenging certainly allows economic survival as shipbuilding does. But the difference in appearance between wageless workers vis-à-vis the shipyard workers in their uniforms was indeed an issue that led to frequent contestations over differences in value. The shared ground of uncertainty that affects both waged and wageless workers in Subic, it seemed, was too unacknowledged by the laborers themselves, which made the work of activists such as the ones affiliated to Kilusan very hard on a day-to-day basis.

15. The local specificities of engaging with politics are connected to similar developments around scavengers organizing in other regions of the Philippines. The three thousand scavengers laboring at the Payatas landfill site in Manila (which was the site of a landslide disaster claiming three hundred lives in the year 2000), for instance, have recently gained some appreciation as an "organized and recognized force" keeping the growing waste problem in urban areas of the Philippines at bay (van Kotte 2013), while scavengers in Pampanga are hailed as "environment heroes of the province" by local politicians (Mapiles 2015) who have begun to recognize them as a force that needs to be considered.

16. A number of scholars have in the late 1990s/early 2000s focused on the ability of different groups that are part of the informal economy to engage in disruptive street politics, which

in turn has forced state authorities to respond to them (e.g., Bayat 1997; Cross 1998; Goldstein 2004). The difference between "informal politics" (Cross 1998) and a "politics of indeterminacy," however, is not marginal or driven by an attempt to address the same old problem from a slightly different angle. But it stands for a diverging perspective that engages with a particularly precarious moment in time—both when it comes to Philippine history and from the longue durée perspective of global capitalism.

References

Agamben, G. 1998. *Homo Sacer: Sovereignty and Bare Life.* Stanford, CA: Stanford University Press.

Asis, D. 2011. *Seeking Fairness and Justice: Toxic Wastes Left Behind at the Former U.S. Military Installations in Clark and Subic, Philippines* [Literature Review]. Retrieved 10 February 2018 from https://globaldale.files.wordpress.com/2011/11/toxic-wastes-left-behind-clark-subic-literature-review-final-revised-nov-12-2011-pdf.pdf.

Baca, G. 2011. "Resentment of Neoliberals in South Korea: Kim Jin-Sook and the Bus of Hope Movement." *The Journal of Eurasian Studies* 8(4): 125–40.

Bauman, Z. 2004. *Wasted Lives: Modernity and Its Outcasts.* London: Polity Press.

Bayat, A. 1997. *Street Politics: Poor Peoples Movements in Iran.* New York: Columbia University Press.

Belkin, A. 2012. *Bring Me Men: Military Masculinity and the Benign Façade of American Empire.* London: Hurst & Company.

Chan, F. Y., and P. F. Kelly. 2004. "Local Politics and Labor Relations in the Philippines: The Case of Subic Bay." In *Labour in Southeast Asia: Local Processes in a Globalized World*, ed. R. Elmhirst and R. Saptari, 129–57. London: Routledge.

Cross, J. C. 1998. *Informal Politics: Street Vendors and the State in Mexico City.* Stanford, CA: Stanford University Press.

Denning, M. 2008. "Wageless Life." *New Left Review* 66: 79–97.

Empeno, H. 2015. "Subic Work Force to Breach 100,000-mark by Year-end." 20 August. *Business Mirror.* Retrieved 10 February 2018 from http://www.businessmirror.com.ph/subic-work-force-to-breach-100000-mark-by-year-end/.

Eriksen, T. H. 2016. *Overheating: An Anthropology of Accelerated Change.* London: Pluto Press.

Garcia, R. V. 2013. *State of the Freeport Address* [Speech Delivered on 18 March]. Retrieved 10 February 2018 from http://subicbaynews.net/wp-content/uploads/2013/03/2013-SOFA-03182013- FINAL.pdf.

Giroux, H. A. 2012. *Twilight of the Social: Resurgent Publics in the Age of Disposability.* Boulder, CO: Paradigm.

Goldstein, D. 2004. *Spectacular City: Violence and Performance in Urban Bolivia.* Durham, NC: Duke University Press.

Grey, E. 2015. "Southeast Asia's Shipbuilding Evolution." *Ship-techology.com.* Retrieved 10 February 2018 from http://www.ship-technology.com/features/featuresoutheast-asias- shipbuilding-evolution-4572766/.

Hall, D., Philip Hirsch, and T. Li, eds. 2011. *Powers of Exclusion: Land Dilemmas in Southeast Asia.* Honolulu: University of Hawaii Press/National University of Singapore Press.

Hart, K. 1973. "Informal Income Opportunities and Urban Employment in Ghana." *Journal of Modern African Studies* 11(1): 61–89.

Harvey, D. 2011. *The Enigma of Capital: And the Crises of Capitalism*. Oxford: Oxford University Press.

Kalb, D., and H. Tak, eds. 2005. *Critical Junctions*. Oxford: Berghahn Books.

———, eds. 2014. *Blood and Fire: Toward a Global Anthropology of Labor*. Oxford: Berghahn Books.

Kasmir, S., and A. Carbonella. 2015. "Dispossession, Disorganization and the Anthropology of Labor." In *Anthropologies of Class: Power, Practice and Inequality*, ed. J. G. Carrier and D. Kalb, 41–52. Cambridge: Cambridge University Press.

Li, T. M. 2009. "To Make Live or Let Die? Rural Dispossession and the Protection of Surplus Populations." *Antipode* 14(6): 1208–35.

———. 2011. "Centering Labor in the Land Grab Debate." *The Journal of Peasant Studies* 38(2): 281–98.

McKay, S. C. 2006. "The Squeaky Wheel's Dilemma: New Forms of Labor Organizing in the Philippines." *Labor Studies Journal* 30(4): 41–63.

Mapiles, J. 2015. "Governor Wants HELP Packages for Scavengers." *Business Mirror*, 20 February. Retrieved 10 February 2018 from http://businessmirror.com.ph/governor-wants-help-package-for-scavengers/.

Mbembe, A. 2004. "Aesthetics of Superfluity." *Public Culture* 16(3): 373–405.

Millar, K. 2008. "Making Trash into Treasure: Struggles for Autonomy on a Brazilian Garbage Dump." *Anthropology of Work Review* 29(2): 25–34.

Narotzky, S., and N. Besnier. 2014. "Crisis, Value, and Hope: Rethinking the Economy." *Current Anthropology* 55(S9): S4–S16.

Ofreneo, R. E. 2013. "Precarious Philippines: Expanding Informal Sector, 'Flexibilizing' Labor Market." *American Behavioral Scientist* 57(4): 420–43.

Polanyi, K. [1944] 2001. *The Great Transformation: The Political and Economic Origins of Our Time*. Boston, MA: Beacon Press.

Robinson, T. K. 2011. "South Korea's 300 Day Aerial Sit-in Strike Highlights Plight of Precarious Workers in Korea and the Philippines." *Asia-Pacific Journal*. Retrieved 10 February 2018 from http://apjjf.org/2011/9/45/tammy-ko-Robinson/3644/article.html.

Roseberry, W. 1997. "Marx and Anthropology." *Annual Review of Anthropology* 26: 25–46.

Sanchez, A. 2012. "Deadwood and Paternalism: Rationalising Casual Labour in an Indian Company Town." *Journal of the Royal Anthropological Institute* 18(4): 808–827.

Sassen, S. 2014. *Expulsions: Brutality and Complexity in the Global Economy*. Cambridge, MA: The Belknap Press of Harvard University Press.

Schober, E. 2018. "Between a Rock and a Stormy Place: From Overheating to Expulsion in Subic Bay (Philippines)." *Ethnos* 83(3): 473–488.

———. 2016a. "Building a City: Korean Capitalists and Navy Nostalgia in the Subic Bay Area." *History and Anthropology* 27(5): 488–503.

———. 2016b. "Indigenous Endurance amidst Accelerated Change? The U.S. Navy, South Korean Shipbuilders and the Aeta of Subic Bay (Philippines)." In *Identity Destabilised: Living in an Overheated World*, ed. T. H. Hylland Eriksen and E. Schober, 135–152. London: Pluto.

———. 2018a. "The (Un-)Making of Labour: Capitalist Accelerations and their Human Toll at a South Korean Shipyard in the Philippines." In *Regular and Precarious Labour in Modern Industrial Settings*, ed. C. Hann and J. Parry, 197–217. Oxford: Berghahn Books.

_____. 2018b. "Working(wo)man's suicide: Transnational Relocations of Capital; Repercussions for Labour in South Korea and the Philippines." *The Journal of the Royal Anthropological Institute* 24(S1): 134–47.

Simbulan, R. G. 1985. *The Bases of Our Insecurity.* Manila: Balai Fellowship.

"Subic Workforce Breach 90,000 Mark." 2013. *Sun Star (Pampanga edition),* 3 January. Retrieved 10 February 2018 from http://www.sunstar.com.ph/pampanga/business/2013/01/04/subic-workforce-breach-90000-mark-261257).

Swyngedouw, E. 2006. "Dispossessing H2O: The Contested Terrain of Water Privatization." *Capitalism Nature Socialism* 16(1): 81–98.

Tritten, T. J. 2010. "Decades Later, U.S. Military Pollution in Philippines linked to Deaths." *Stars and Stripes,* 2 February 2. Retrieved 10 February 2018 from http://www.stripes.com/news/decades-later-u-s-military-pollution-in-philippines-linked-to-deaths-1.98570.

Van Kotte, G. 2013. "Manila's Waste Scavengers Are Integrated into the Recycling Chain." *The Guardian,* 29 January. Retrieved 10 February 2018 from https://www.theguardian.com/world/2013/jan/29/manila-philippines-recycling-payatas.

Wallman, S. 1980. "Social Anthropology of Work (Book Review)." *Current Anthropology* 21(3): 299–314.

Epilogue

Indeterminacy
Between Worth and Worthlessness

Niko Besnier and Susana Narotzky

On Valuation

In the early days of a discipline whose origins were inspired by the taxonomic impulse of the natural sciences, anthropology attempted to understand different human societies in relation to Western civilization within an evolutionary framework. Anthropologists thus described and organized their empirical observations in categorical bundles. Nevertheless, the data always exceeded the categories that anthropologists devised, which prompted the researchers to come up with new categories or, alternatively, disregard, silence, or miscategorize what did not fit.

Anthropologists' attempts to develop theories of kinship offer a good example of the problems they faced: to explain inconsistencies, they multiplied taxonomies, or attributed them to process, to the fuzziness of categories, or to change over time. An early example of just how messy the taxonomic problems of kinship were is E. E. Evans-Pritchard's (1940) classic monograph on the Nuer, which he described as a fiercely egalitarian society fixed on patrilineal descent. After painstakingly drawing out the lineage categories, their spatial organization, and their structural dynamics of fusion and fission, Evans-Pritchard concedes that in actual practice, bilateral descent was as important as patrilineal descent, alliance was as important as descent with frequent adoptions, and that there were deep structural inequalities under the public veneer of egalitarianism, all of which he labeled "transient." However, if one begins with these exceptions to reanalyze Nuer social structure, the resulting picture one obtains of Nuer society at the time turns out completely different (McKinnon 2000). What Evans-Pritchard considered transient and out of place now emerges as part and parcel of the system and provides a very different perspective on the system as a whole. Likewise, John Comaroff (1980) analyzes marriage payments among the Tshidi of South Africa as an ambiguous, time-bound, and flexible relationship that entangles multiple generations (alive, dead, and yet-to-be-born) in a maze that can always be reconfigured and rein-terpreted as something else, and he then goes on to deconstruct the category of marriage in African bridewealth societies.

Anthropology offers a long genealogy of concern with that which does not fit in established classification systems, or at least do not fit easily. Yet, for a long time, anthropologists were primarily concerned with "solving" the puzzle of matter that does not fit. For example, the theory of liminality developed by Arnold van Gennep and Victor Turner constructed liminality as a valuable yet temporary state, a perilous transition between stable states that would eventu-ally reaffirm stability. For Mary Douglas, society needs matter out of place to reaffirm its coherence and order, but also to harness its potential power. While "dirt is essentially disorder" and "disorder spoils pattern" (1991: 2),

> it also provides the materials for pattern. Order implies restriction; from all possible materials, a limited selection has been made and from all possible relations a limited set has been used. So disorder by implication is unlimited, no pattern has been realised in it, but its potential for patterning is indefinite. This is why, though we seek to create order, we do not simply condemn disorder. We recognize that it is destructive to existing patterns; also that it has potentiality. (1991: 94)

And society, which she defines as form in contrast to nonform, does so by ritu-ally taming, reconfiguring and finding a place for nonform.

It is only relatively recently that anthropologists have questioned these assumptions. Having abandoned the organic structural idea of a unique and complete social order, with its categories and oppositional structure (e.g., line-ages, myths), the discipline has taken a pioneering role among the social sci-ences in showcasing the fact that different understandings of society coexist, but are locked in a struggle for domination, and that categories are fundamen-tally unstable and fuzzy. For example, the theory of perspectivism, based on Amerindian mythology and shamanistic practices, introduced a fluid categori-cal framework that superseded the nature-culture dichotomy. It suggested that humans and nonhumans shared a common primordial humanity, a "culture," but differed in their physical representation, their "nature." This view inverted Western understandings of the nature-culture categorization where culture was the variable attached to humanity, and nature was what humans shared with other species. This "multinaturalist" process supported practices of meta-morphosis between species that underlined the ambivalent subjective positions of humanity in different world orders (Descola 2013; Viveiros de Castro 2012). Drawing on ethnographies of Melanesian societies, anthropologists like Marilyn Strathern (1988) have exposed the relational, mutable, and partible character of personhood and identity, while others have demonstrated that sex-gender categories are predicated on the exchange of matter like blood and food among people, nature, and cosmology (e.g., Herdt 1984; Meigs 1984). Rather than being in transition to greater legibility, persons, objects, and categories that fail to conform to stable states can remain in protracted or permanent suspension. Matter out of place, the abject, the marginal, and the exceptional can, in fact, provide a very different perspective on the system that marginalizes them. They thus need to be taken seriously.

This collection of ethnographic essays does just that by proposing a novel angle on the question through the lens of indeterminacy. In their introduction, Catherine Alexander and Andrew Sanchez explain that indeterminacy has three fundamental features: it is not recognized by extant systems of classification; its course in the future is unknown; and it resists and questions classificatory systems. Indeterminacy differs from other analytic tools that have been mobilized in the past. For example, in contrast to Mary Douglas, who considers purity and impurity (and its variants) as structured in reference to one another and to a world conceived as a whole, Alexander and Sanchez see indeterminacy as constituting a third, in-between modality that does not lend itself to binary classification, while both value (purity) and waste (impurity) are aspects of form. They consider "classification, as a way of apprehending reality, [as] itself essentially indeterminate."

Indeterminacy is constitutive of classification systems based on the opposition between value and waste in that it plays a mediating role in their production, a point to which we will return presently. But the opposition is the result of a process of selection (what has value and what does not), which raises the question of the criteria upon which this selection is predicated.

"To classify is human" (Bowker and Star 1999: 1), but inherent to classification is a semantic vagueness about categories that do not fall neatly in a system of inclusion and exclusion. The category "other" is often mobilized as a loophole for such categories. Although many classification systems consist of competing or overlapping categories that exert control and moral legitimacy (Boltanski and Thévenot 1991), much of what goes on in everyday life is at best vaguely ascribed to a category because its semantic vagueness is "good enough" to get on with ordinary matters. Thinking of the binary contrast between value and waste as resulting from choices that free agents make in a process of adjudicating value is what produces indeterminacy. For example, despite its anxiety to produce order, state bureaucracy in fact often works through vagueness, as in the case of how state agents interpret the law (a system of classification par excellence) in a discretionary and flexible fashion (Dubois 2010). Classifications often make space for arbitrary application, while at the same time creating anxieties that preclude agency.

Valuation is a complex process. For example, one can distinguish three distinct principles of classificatory judgments for comparing things and people (Fourcade 2016). Nominal judgments are conceptual acts predicated on essence that generate categories and interpretive acts that fit objects into these categories. Cardinal judgments, predicated on quantities, measure difference and assess its significance. While ordinal judgments, predicated on relative positions and designed to rank objects, create inequalities. In social life, nominal judgments of kind intersect with ordinal judgments of worth and, in ideologically democratic and egalitarian societies, ordinal judgments that rank nominal difference are measured through the quantification of individual "choices" (Fourcade 2016: 182–84). Statistical ranking makes difference commensurable. Tools that measure equivalence, such as money, assess value, but they also produce hierarchies. What Jane Guyer (2004) calls "performances of valuation" involve intersecting ordinal and cardinal judgments in which negotiations over different scalar values measure hierarchically ordered qualities and enable commensuration, a process that allows for disjunctures between numerical scales that may become sources of gain. The different scales of valuation constitute a "repertoire" that is performed and enacted in different occasions (2004: 51–67). In practice, then, binary classificatory systems and indeterminacy as a "third" concept result from the failure of classificatory practices that are at best an ideal type. Indeed, many of the cases analyzed in this volume can be understood as struggles over different, incomplete, and often vague categorical schemes.

For example, in her analysis of Russian-speaking miners in Estonia and Kazakhstan, Eeva Keskülä invokes indeterminacy to explain how this group lost its former place in society when the Soviet Union collapsed. The miners lost their social privileges as Russians, miners, highly remunerated workers, and gendered laborers in the new political and economic order. They are disrespected as anachronisms, their work is devalued, and they feel that others see them as slaves, scum, or nobodies. But they claim a different grid of valuation, which showcases hard work, sacrifice, skill, the health hazards they endured, and their contribution to the national wealth. Their social position is thus riddled with ambiguities and overlaps. The miners claim social worth within shifting regimes of value. Loss of status increases uncertainty and devalues social expectations, yet the miners are aware of their relational value position in the present order and contest it. Similarly, the transgender activists among whom Elena Gonzalez-Polledo conducted fieldwork use their experimental art to disrupt identity politics and resist institutional contexts that universalize the category transgender.

Liminality, Ambiguity, Uncertainty, and Indeterminacy

According to Alexander and Sanchez, indeterminacy differs from a number of cognate analytic categories, such as liminality, ambiguity, and uncertainty. In its original theorization, liminality always implied a transition from one stable state (e.g., childhood) to another stable state (e.g., adulthood). In contrast, indeterminacy does not imply that an entity that is taken out of a stable state will eventually be reintegrated into another. The detached fragment becomes a particle whose future configuration may be indeterminate. Here an analogy to Heisenberg's theory of indeterminacy in quantum physics and its philosophical extension in metaphysical indeterminacy is useful (Barnes 2010; Skow 2010; Torza 2017; Williams 2008). Metaphysical indeterminacy shares commonalities with semantic vagueness but it extends its purchase to actual worlds and is therefore analogically closer to quantum physics. Hence the classical anthropological concept of liminality gives way to a position where all future outcomes are not only possible but may in reality all coexist. Contingency is the anthropological version of this multiple actuality. However, in its quantum physics version, indeterminacy is not absolute but statistically relative. In an analogous manner, contingency is not the equivalent of indeterminacy; the latter is statistically weighted (i.e., using cardinal value registers) according to past measures of actualization (i.e., empirical social facts).

One example of the indeterminacy of fragments is the debate that Joshua O. Reno explores with respect to the future determination of waste in landfills. The question is whether the radical indeterminacy of future outcomes advances the anthropological task of explaining social practices. The waste fragment eschews relations, but relations linger, and as Reno concedes, waste management regulations (and, we would add, the entire social world of formal and informal interactions and devices in which it is entangled) make certain outcomes more possible than others.

Indeterminacy also differs from ambiguity if one defines ambiguity as the possibility that an entity has several simultaneous and potentially contradictory meanings. In language, ambiguity defines a situation in which an utterance's truth value can be interpreted in different ways, although generally disambiguation is possible by clarifying context. Ambiguity also calls to mind Peircean indexicality, signs that have no meaning in and of themselves but acquire value when placed in a particular context. Yet indexes are always potentially multivalent. Semantic vagueness addresses a similar problem, namely that of utterances that are not semantically precise, and therefore whose truth value is uncertain. In some cases, vagueness can be resolved by reference to context, but in other cases it is impossible to determine the truth value of the utterance (Kennedy 2011). These problems in the philosophy of language are relevant because they address questions of "mapping" or positioning within a semantic grid. Likewise, they discuss truth value judgments and point to cases where it is impossible to adjudicate meaning between adjacent categories, revealing the unknowable aspect of certain vague propositions. A pressing issue that emerges, then, is to determine the relevance of vagueness in classificatory systems, focusing on cases where truth value cannot be determined. The present volume addresses this through a particular construction of indeterminacy.

Lastly, indeterminacy is not uncertainty, if uncertainty is what people experience, for instance, when they face the risk of stock market speculation or when they engage in extreme sports that challenge norms of safety. Uncertainty is also embedded in the potential misfirings and misalignments of face-to-face communication, in the firm cultural belief in the opacity of other people's minds (Rumsey and Robbins 2008), or in the collapse of political regimes that formerly provided clear answers to existential questions. Ironically, the neoliberal faith in optimal market allocation expresses the will to minimize uncertainty by focusing attention on the individual's actual behavior, thus eliciting the tacit (often unconscious) knowledge hidden in natural communication systems (Hayek 1948; Polanyi 1967). The market makes hidden tacit knowledge transparent and allegedly minimizes uncertainty in the allocation of resources through the competitive process and the pricing mechanism. Behavioral economics and big-data analysis have compounded this theory: measuring actions supersedes the need to understand actions, and the uncertainty of the future is statistically minimized. Hence high risk (and potential gain) accrues from countering predictable outcomes and hedging against predictable loss. For the editors, uncertainty is relevant to indeterminacy "only insofar as it reflects conditions of dissolution or category loss produced by economic and political exclusion; the material infrastructure of previous times that has yet to find its place; and, finally, a sense that future pathways are rarely as determined as grand narratives suggest but emerge as a dialogue between people's attempts to plan and shape futures and contingent events beyond their control" (Alexander and Sanchez this volume). The value of indeterminacy as a concept, then, hinges on a critique of totalizing categorization and on causal determination of future outcomes.

If indeterminacy differs from the more widely theorized categories of liminality, ambiguity, and uncertainty, one can also ask what it shares with them. For example, while early theorists of liminality did indeed see liminal states as transitions from one well-defined category to another, one can ask whether this was not an artifice of their own anxieties about structure, and whether, in actuality, liminal entities always emanate from a stable category and are eventually transformed into another stable category. Rather, they may well be suspended in a state that is too vague and heterogeneous to be domesticated by extant systems of classification, from which they challenge these classificatory systems. This is the case, for example, of transgender categories in Polynesia and elsewhere, which do not conform to locally recognizable gender categories but instead index a nebulous outsiderness and generic cosmopolitanism (which themselves are the object of constant negotiation and anxiety) that confront the moral codes in which local gender categories are anchored (Besnier 2011). This is also the case of people in extreme exclusionary spaces devoid of future expectation such as Nazi concentration camps, where moral categories that used to frame their past social life were suspended beyond classificatory orders, a situation that does not preclude social interaction regulated both externally and internally, albeit beyond classification (Narotzky and Moreno 2002). Thus "permanent" liminality may not be as oxymoronic as it may appear at first glance and, viewed in this light, liminality may share more with indeterminacy than it differs from it. In these examples, indeterminacy is an active situation with which people engage creatively, as the editors point out, but often strive to create some sort of predictable outcome.

Excess, Residue, Exclusion, and Hidden Connections

A particularly thought-provoking aspect of indeterminacy as an analytic category is its capacity to help us understand how some entities remain outside extant systems of classification. Thus, in Joshua Reno's analysis of garbage landfills in the United States, the fragment of paper that escapes the rubbish collectors or the potential toxic leak from the landfill are indeterminate because they potentially undermine the boundary between the filth and danger of the landfill and the wholesomeness and safety of lived space. They are also indeterminate because the manner of their incorporation with other fragments in the landfill (or outside of it) is unknown, and the possibility that they will remain outside any category systems is open.

However, whether entities can be entirely disconnected from systems of classification is an empirical question. Thus the fragment of paper or the leak continues to be embedded in structures of social relations and in economic systems. Fragments of paper on the side of the road enable the people employed to pick them up to make a living and the leak ensures that the expertise of the people in charge of analyzing it continues to be useful. So both the piece of paper and the leaking substance are still connected to a context that provides various possible meanings. Even a totalizing classificatory system, such as the law, is in fact full of loopholes, which is the reason why the practice of the law gives so much attention to interpretation and precedent. In Norway, as Thomas Hylland Eriksen and Cathrine Moe Thorleifsson document in this volume, the state has exerted considerable efforts to absorb the minority group of Travellers into its modernist project based on settled existence, wage work, and education, but some Travellers have contested these efforts by asserting difference in a national context anxiously predicated on homogeneity. The newcomer Roma, in contrast, have not been so successful in that the state has no interest in integrating them and many want them to "go back where they came from," precluding any kind of mobilization in a political arena in which they have no say.

The contributions to this volume provide precisely the kind of ethnographic materials that provoke a debate about under what conditions and from what perspective an entity falls outside of a system of classification. They suggest that the terms "debate," "struggle", and "contention" should be wedded to any discussion of determinacy: what we are witnessing in the various case studies are anxieties and conflicts over what can be determined and what cannot, about who defines the grids of classification and how, what devices and technical infrastructures support categorization and standardization, and what power can be brought to bear in the making and unmaking of particular webs of (in)determination. Indeterminacy is always in dialogue with determinacy, from which it derives its very meaning.

The comparison of the various ethnographic contexts represented in this collection conjures a question that we consider important: what is the entity that lacks determinacy? Different indeterminate entities pose different questions. For example, the figure of the "repatriate" or *oralman* in Kazakhstan (Alexander), people of Kazakh origin whom the state invites to migrate "back" to the country, is indeterminate in several ways. The *oralman* does not find a place in the state's dominant discourse of progress "from a fixed past to a desired future," both because the *oralman* is a backward country bumpkin and emerges from a larger world that the state strives to be part of. The figure also falls between the cracks of census categories, as the *oralman* is at once neither Kazakh nor immigrant, but both. In addition, repatriates often lack state-issued identification, a lack that can be as empowering and liberating as it can be restrictive and precarious. Seen as a property of an entity (a person or a figure), indeterminacy is a matter of ontology. But all these modes of indeterminacy can be also understood as characteristics of relationships, between the *oralman* and the state in particular, but also between the *oralman* and an "ordinary" Kazakh, in which case indeterminacy is no longer a matter of ontology, but of shifting social relations, which in our view calls for different questions.

Thus people who do not belong and objects that stand outside recognized classification regimes are invariably embedded in webs of relationships of their own. Such webs can connect the person or object to the system that expelled them in the first place, as in the case of refugees from the Middle East and elsewhere in the contemporary moment, who are suspended in indeterminacy in Western Europe (unwanted by Eastern and Southern Europe, yet forced by the Dublin Convention to remain there); yet they are still connected to the national contexts whose wars they are escaping, they become connected to NGOs and solidarity networks that provide support, and they create structures of their own. The indeterminate can produce their own system of classification and their own expulsion, as is the case of Polynesian transgender who lay claim to a larger world of morality that exceeds the provincialism of the local. Indeterminacy as a feature of relationships provides a different perspective and raises different questions from indeterminacy as an ontological category.

Indeterminacy showcases the future in primordial fashion. If something is determined, then what is going to happen in the future is known or at least knowable; in contrast, indeterminacy is the negation of a clear path toward the future. This is where the contrast between indeterminacy and uncertainty becomes productive: uncertainty is contained by the management of risk, whereas indeterminacy does not assume that the future can be controlled, because the risk is unknown. However, thinking in terms of risk implies an a priory binary contrast between gain and loss that generates either good or bad results of action (by an individual rational agent) within a moralized framework. An alternative is to abide by the assumption in physics that indeterminacy, devoid of its moral orientation, does not lead to risk but instead to outcomes that are unknowable but can be circumscribed through empirical calculation, thereby minimizing the unknown.

This is the essence of the debate about the future of waste between sociologists Myra Hird (2013) and Zsusza Gille (2013) that Reno animates: for the former, what will happen to a landfill is ultimately unknowable because its contents are indeterminate and its future is completely open, which presents a paradox for political activism focused on making waste determinate; for the latter, we know enough about what may happen when waste leaks and poses a danger to the environment to swing into action. Knowledge about anything comes in many forms and is always partial and situated (Haraway 1988), and knowledge about the future of waste is no exception; we may not know what the chemical reactions are going to be from waste leakage, but we know at least that there is going to be a reaction, upon which we can base an activist politics. The fact that the future is unknowable does not to imply that our actions, particularly political ones, are not projected toward certain goals. Likewise, it does not imply that evidence about past social facts is irrelevant in the attempt to know the future outcomes of present actions.

At the same time, human actions generate material results, be they in the form of infrastructures, objects, regulations, and so on, which are embedded in historical processes that are themselves complex and multi-faceted. Thus in the same fashion that indeterminacy is about the future, it is also about the past. Our projects are always embedded in and informed by pre-existing structures, webs of relations, and selective memories of moralized outcomes of human actions. Indeed, what is particularly thought-provoking is the power of our actions to articulate a knowable past with an indeterminate future, yet this power is bounded by the fact that the result of our actions (and their interpretation) can differ significantly from the intentions that underpinned them and for differently situated actors.

The gigantic industrial infrastructures erected in Bremerhaven, Germany, in the late nineteenth century and over the course of the twentieth century, are a particularly telling example (Ringel this volume). Some of the structures in question, such as the Emperor's Lock, were considered utter folly when they were originally built because of their unnecessarily grandiose proportions, yet they ended up having a new life when megaships emerged that were in need of large berthing facilities. Postindustrial downturns made other structures obsolete and they were abandoned, until they were made economically productive again for urban renewal and tourism. In contrast, the city's "scrap houses" are today deemed too derelict to do much with, and they just stand there—but who knows what novel use may be found for them in future, in the same way that the outsized shipping facilities are ridiculous at one moment and a godsend at another? As Marxist theorists of urban gentrification (e.g., Harvey 1973; Smith 1996) have demonstrated, capital accumulation takes place when the build environment is devalued, tenants are dispossessed, and urban space is revalorized. In order to produce value from inner-city centers, they first have to be depleted of value and alienated from their original purpose. These examples illustrate the constant transformation over time of the meaning of categories, objects, and practices and the temporal fragility of the boundary between the knowable and the unknowable, the determined and the undetermined.

Worthlessness, Waste, Value, and Worth

As matter and metaphor, waste is provocative. If we understand waste as removed from dominant systems of value, it also appears as a space of creativity that may produce other values, a position of hope that may challenge dominant classification systems with other forms of recognition. Indeterminacy thus emerges as a Janus-faced category, signaling both the displacement to an outside realm and the opening of domains of possible worlds. But how does it relate to value if valuation is understood as a multiple and overlapping grid of classificatory systems involving nominal, ordinal, and cardinal judgments, with their vagueness and loopholes? Is waste opposed to value? How is the production of value predicated on the production of waste?

In Elisabeth Schober's account of scavengers in Subic Bay, Philippines, unwaged workers order and classify the waste that they sell to intermediaries, a task that their leader Glenda defines as having value in market terms: "Remember, it has capital. Yes, it's all garbage, but it has capital." These are people who have been dispossessed of their former means of livelihood (fishing, agriculture) because of land and water grabbing and later of the possibility of wage work. As a result, they have gravitated to the landfill near a Special Economic Zone to make a living by scavenging. Their lives are devalued as they are excluded from other means of making a living and they are defined by others as a surplus population. But they define their work as "work," a category that commands recognition and respect and is validated by the anthropologist and the left-wing activists who guide her. Moreover, they are aware of the value work commands both economically, as it reenters the chain of value through intermediaries, and politically, as they leverage their power to disrupt peace and drive away investments. One could argue that the agency, power, and hope of their politics is not so much one of indeterminacy as one that rests on the tension between worth and worthlessness, value and waste. As they become worthless according to a regime of value focused on waste and squalor, they reconfigure other forms of self-worth and produce other kinds of economic and political value, through struggle and negotiation, which are partially linked to capital.

Tensions between worthlessness and worth-making are central to understanding how capitalist accumulation works (Alexander and Reno 2012). Marxism captured some of these tensions with the concept of surplus population, but even more so with the concept of primitive accumulation, which David Harvey (2003) further expanded as accumulation by dispossession. Enclosures produced people who had become worthless unless they entered into a particular relation with the owners of the means of production. This situation benefitted people at the upper end of a scale of social worth now measured in cardinal terms of aggregate wealth. Simultaneously, other scales of social and moral worth emerged based on respect for work and solidarity, which competed with scales of valuation based on wealth. This is but one possible story of world actualization, and we are not advocating for a teleological modern grand narrative. But it is about relationships that are formed and transformed through shifting connections, overlapping grids of meaning and vagueness, rather than about ordered totalities from which fragments (physical, semantic) are detached, suspended in an indeterminate position, eventually to be recognized by other imagined ordered worlds. As Alexander and Sanchez suggest in their introduction, "the will to control through fixity, numbering, containment, and classifications, is typically manifested through the modern state, which expels, [or] forcibly assimilates ... those who do not fit" (Alexander and Sanchez this volume) makes the exclusion and displacement of indeterminacy a potential space of opportunity, creativity, and hope. The will and the struggle to control, we argue, is also based on multiple grids of value and systems of valuation overlapping, conflicting, and connecting, claiming transient power through ambiguity and vagueness, eschewing fixity to assert control.

Niko Besnier is Professor of Cultural Anthropology at the University of Amsterdam and Research Professor, Department of Social Inquiry, La Trobe University. In 2012–17, he directed a project entitled "Globalisation, Sport, and the Precarity of Masculinity," funded by a European Research Council Advanced Grant. He has conducted research on gender and sexuality, the body, economic precarity, and language and interaction. His last (co-authored) book is titled *The Anthropology of Sport: Bodies, Borders, Biopolitics* (University of California Press, 2017), which also appeared in French and Spanish translations in 2018.

Susana Narotzky is Professor of Social Anthropology, University of Barcelona, Spain. She has been awarded a European Research Council Advanced Grant to study the effects of austerity on Southern European livelihoods (*Grassroots Economics* [GRECO]). Her work is inspired by theories of critical political economy, moral economies, and feminist economics. Recent writing addresses the themes of making a living in futures without employment, political mobilization, and class. "Rethinking the Concept of Labour," *JRAI*, 2018, is her last publication.

Note

Susana Narotzky acknowledges funding from the European Research Council Advanced Grant "Grassroots Economics: Meaning, Project and Practice in the Pursuit of Livelihood" (GRECO), IDEAS-ERC FP7, Project Number: 323743, and from the Generalitat de Catalunya Fellowship Program ICREA-Acadèmia (2016–21).

References

Alexander, C., and J. Reno, eds. 2012. *Economies of Recycling: The Global Transformation of Materials, Values and Social Relations*. London: Zed Books.

Barnes, E. 2010. "Arguments against Metaphysical Indeterminacy and Vagueness." *Philosophy Compass* 5(11): 953–64.

Besnier, N. 2011. *On the Edge of the Global: Modern Anxieties in a Pacific Island Nation*. Stanford, CA: Stanford University Press.

Boltanski, L., and L. Thévenot. 1991. *De la justification: Les économies de la grandeur*. Paris: Gallimard.

Bowker, G. C., and S. L. Star. 1999. *Sorting Things Out: Classification and Its Consequences*. Cambridge, MA: MIT Press.

Comaroff, J. L. 1980. "Bridewealth and the Control of Ambiguity in a Tswana Chiefdom." In *The Meaning of Marriage Payments*, ed. J. L. Comaroff, 29–49. London: Academic Press.

Descola, P. 2013. *Beyond Nature and Culture*, trans. Janet Lloyd. Chicago, IL: University of Chicago Press.

Douglas, M. [1966] 1991. *Purity and Danger: An Analysis of the Concepts of Pollution and Taboo*. London: Routledge.

Dubois, V. 2010. *The Bureaucrat and the Poor: Encounters in French Welfare Offices*. Farnham, UK: Ashgate.

Evans-Pritchard, E. E. 1940. *The Nuer: A Description of the Modes of Livelihood and Political Institutions of a Nilotic People*. Oxford: Clarendon Press.

Fourcade, M. 2016. "Ordinalization: Lewis A. Coser Memorial Award for Theoretical Agenda Setting 2014." *Sociological Theory* 34(3): 175–95.

Gille, S. 2013. "Is There an Amancipatory Ontology of Matter? A Response to Myra Hird." *Social Epistemology Review and Reply Collective* 2(4): 1–6.

Guyer, J. I. 2004. *Marginal Gains: Monetary Transactions in Atlantic Africa*. Chicago, IL: University of Chicago Press.

Haraway, D. 1988. "Situated Knowledges: The Science Question in Feminism and the Privilege of Partial Perspective." *Feminist Studies* 14(3): 575–99.

Harvey, D. 1973. *Social Justice and the City*. Baltimore, MD: Johns Hopkins University Press.

———. 2003. *The New Imperialism*. Oxford: Oxford University Press.

Hayek F. A. 1948. *Individualism and Economic Order*. Chicago, IL: University of Chicago Press

Herdt, G. H. 1984. "Semen Transactions in Sambia Culture." In *Ritualized Homosexuality in Melanesia*, ed. G. H. Herdt, 167–210. Berkeley, CA: University of California Press.

Hird, M. 2013. "Is Waste Indeterminacy Useful? A Response to Szusza Gille." *Social Epistemology Review and Reply Collective* 2(6): 28–33.

Kennedy, C. 2011. "Ambiguity and Vagueness." In *Handbook of Semantics*, vol. 1, ed. C. Maienborn, P. Portner, and K. von Heusinger, 507–35. The Hague: Mouton de Gruyter.

McKinnon, S. 2000. "Domestic Exceptions: Evans-Pritchard and the Creation of Nuer Patrilineality and Equality." *Cultural Anthropology* 15(1): 35–83.

Meigs, A. 1984. *Food, Sex, and Pollution: A New Guinea Religion.* New Brunswick, NJ: Rutgers University Press.

Narotzky, S., and P. Moreno. 2002. "Reciprocity's Dark Side: Negative Reciprocity, Morality and Social Reproduction." *Anthropological Theory* 2(3): 281–305.

Polanyi, M. 1967. *The Tacit Dimension.* London: Routledge and Kegan Paul.

Rumsey, A., and J. Robbins. 2008. "Introduction: Cultural and Linguistic Anthropology and the Opacity of Other Minds." *Anthropological Quarterly* 81(2): 407–20.

Skow, B. 2010. "Deep Metaphysical Indeterminacy." *Philosophical Quarterly* 60(241): 851–58.

Smith, N. 1996. *The New Urban Frontier: Gentrification and the Revanchist City.* London: Routledge.

Strathern, M. 1988. *The Gender of the Gift: Problems with Women and Problems with Society in Melanesia.* Berkeley, CA: University of California Press.

Torza, A. 2017. "Quantum Metaphysical Indeterminacy and Worldly Incompleteness." *Synthese.*

Viveiros de Castro, E. 2012. *Cosmological Perspectivism in Amazonia and Elsewhere.* Manchester: HAU Network of Ethnographic Theory.

Williams, R. G. 2008. "Ontic Vagueness and Metaphysical Indeterminacy." *Philosophy Compass* 3/4: 763–88.

Index